CW01649572

Richard Cashman has long had a passionate interest in cricket. He has played and watched the game in a number of countries including England, India, Sri Lanka, Canada and the United States, and is a regular contributor to *Cricketer.*

'AVE A GO, YER MUG! is his second book on cricket. His first, PATRONS, PLAYERS AND THE CROWD was published in 1980.

Richard Cashman holds an M.A. from Monash University and a Ph.D. from Duke University (USA) and is presently a Senior Lecturer in History at the University of New South Wales.

EX LIBRIS
Keith Bain

'Ave a Go, Yer Mug!

Australian Cricket Crowds from Larrikin to Ocker

RICHARD CASHMAN

COLLINS
Sydney

© Richard Cashman, 1984

First published in 1984 by William Collins Pty Ltd, Sydney
Typeset by Post Typesetters, Brisbane
Printed and bound by The Globe Press, Melbourne

The National Library of Australia
Cataloguing-in-Publication data:

Cashman, Richard, 1940-.
'Ave a go yer mug.

ISBN 0 00 217287 9.

1. Cricket — Social aspects — Australia.
2. Spectator control — Australia — History.
3. Crowds — Australia — History. I. Title.

306'.483

CONDITIONS OF SALE: This book is sold subject to the condition that it shall not, by way of trade or otherwise, be lent, resold, hired out or otherwise circulated without the publisher's prior consent, in any form of binding or cover other than that in which it is published and without a similar condition including this condition being imposed on the subsequent purchaser.

Acknowledgments

Even though I first joined the crowd at major cricket matches in the early 1950s I've attended comparatively few of the many first-class matches played in Australia. So this book draws on the perceptions and comments of many observers whose eyes have become crinkled from the glare while following the progress of a small piece of leather in the distance. I am greatly indebted to many former and current players, umpires, media persons, members of the police force and spectators themselves. Space does not permit me to thank each person individually but many are mentioned in the text and I hope they will find this sufficient.

Many officials at the various associations and cricket libraries of the country have provided statistics and answered numerous queries. These include: Grantley Evans, Robert Spence and Ian Sturgess of the QCA; Bob Radford and John Wood of the NSWCA, and Cliff Winning at the Library there; John Wood and John Ahern at the Sydney Cricket and Sports Ground Trust; Ken Jacobs of the VCA; Rex Harcourt at the MCC Library; Richard Watson and Rob Lewis of SACA; John Rogers and Kingsley Preston at the WACA; Kevin Connor, Peter Hadlow, Cedric Knight and John McKenzie of the various Tasmanian associations. Special thanks are due to Pat Mullins who provided me with full access and generous assistance to the best cricket collection in the country.

Others have helped by commenting on drafts of this book. They include: Lois Bryson, George Franki, David Frith, Michael McKernan, Pat Mullins, Roger Page, Bob Radford, Keith Sandiford, Martin Sharp, Wray Vamplew and Cliff Winning. I am also indebted to Braham Dabscheck, Ric Finlay, Chris Harte, Kersi Meher-Homji, Bill Reynolds and Kenneth Wolfe who have followed up queries and helped my research. Ross Kingsley helped dig up some material on barracking.

I wish to thank photographers John Boase, Lawrence Dunne, Ric Finlay, Lionel Keen, and Kersi Meher-Homji and thanks are also due to Ronald Cardwell and Pat Mullins for permission to publish from their collections. The same acknowledgment is extended to the proprietors of the *Advertiser*, the *Age*, the *Courier Mail*, the *Sydney Morning Herald*, the *Mercury* and the

West Australian. Thanks are also due to the Cinesound Library, Sydney; the John Oxley Library, Brisbane; the Melbourne Cricket Club; the Queensland Cricket Association and Telecom Australia for illustrations. The book is enhanced by three cartoons drawn by Phil Schofield and the other cartoons are reproduced courtesy of *Australian Cricket*, Jeff Hook, Bill Mitchell, PBL Marketing and Mac Vines and the *Brisbane Herald*. McNair Anderson Associates agreed to permit reference to the results of a poll.

I cannot end without a brief mention of the many unsung and anonymous spectators — from ladies and gentlemen to larrikins and ockers — who have made up the rich tapestry of Australian cricket crowds. Without them there would have been no manuscript. I hope this book does them justice.

Contents

Preface		
CHAPTER ONE:	Colonial Crowds: Larrikins, Ladies and Long Lunches	11
CHAPTER TWO:	The Patron on the Hill: Evil Barracker or Shrewd Shilling Spectator?	38
CHAPTER THREE:	Bumper Well-Behaved Crowds Between the Wars	69
CHAPTER FOUR:	Television, Tin Cans and Transistors: The Impact of Technology on Crowds	104
CHAPTER FIVE:	'Ugly' Ockers and Full Eskies	130
CHAPTER SIX:	World Series Cricket and Beyond	153
Notes		

Preface

Crowds are mentioned in almost all cricket books but they are usually part of the background, and are relegated to the fringe of the subject. It is time that crowds were recognized as a vital element of the game. Cricket takes place, as all cricket works attest, both within and beyond the boundary. Every book refers not just to good shots, unplayable balls, dropped catches and match incidents, but also to selections, the politics of boycott, gossip, the employment of cricketers, sponsorship, team talks and psychologists, pre-game tactics, mateship, cricket ideology and, of course, crowds.

Of all the off-the-field elements crowds are probably the most significant. Crowds can both inspire and humiliate players. They have been blamed for taking wickets and even losing matches. The constant cry for brighter and better cricket, whether it relates to scoring runs or bowling overs more quickly, is related to getting crowds through the turnstiles and giving them value for money; presumably so they will come back. That, at least, was the object of the exercise up to the 1930s when the listening crowd and later the home-watching crowd became even more important than the crowd at the game. Crowds can alleviate tension with humour, help batsmen to concentrate (batsmen focus on the crowd in between balls), they can enliven a dull passage of play and add to the drama of a situation. It is no exaggeration to say that crowds make much of cricket.

A study of the crowd will reveal much about the game and its context: the changing and complex relationship between the paying customer and the performer; the official definition of acceptable crowd behaviour and its enforcement by the police. Then, too, the way in which the crowd sees and perceives the game will be shaped partly by the stands and facilities provided. A history of the crowd will also reveal things about society at large: about humour and violence; about attitudes towards agencies of social control and changing conventions of public behaviour.

Many players believe that there are significant differences in crowds from one Australian city to another: Perth is supposed to be the most partisan, while Adelaide is described as the most conservative — a Lord's-type crowd — and Brisbane the most coarse and vulgar. Up to the 1970s Sydney and Melbourne were considered the most knowledgeable. There is also a widespread belief in the existence of national cricket-watching traditions. In the popular mind each country has developed its own traditions: in England crowds are supposedly more reserved and polite; Pakistan's are the most riot-prone; India's the most noisy, numerous and volatile; and the West Indies are enthusiastic, produce rum-inspired barrackers and lately have become riotous.

What are the main ingredients of the Australian tradition? Is the Australian crowd unique? And is the history of Australian crowds one more of continuity or more of change? How valid is a 1912 observation, quoted in the *Referee*: 'An English cricket crowd rather gives one the impression that it has come to see a spectacle and be entertained. An Australian has come to play.'

The rise and fall of cricket crowds and of crowds at all forms of popular culture (sport, films, pop music) is another question worth pursuing. We have yet to understand why all forms of popular entertainment enjoy peaks and suffer declines in public support.

This book does not pretend to be an extensive and complete history of cricket crowds and ground facilities. More attention is paid to major rather than minor crowds, and there is a greater focus on the larger rather than the smaller centres. It is not possible to write a complete history of the subject because very little research has yet been undertaken. Rather a number of themes relating to crowds such as barracking, crowd control, humour, the differences among the States and country and city spectators, and the impact of the media and technology on cricket-watching traditions are explored to ascertain whether today's crowds are really much worse or much better behaved, whether they are less humorous and less original, how much they add to or detract from the game than crowds of the earlier years of Australian cricket.

CHAPTER ONE

Colonial Crowds: Ladies, Larrikins and Long Lunches

Patricians

When Test cricket was first played in Australia there were two distinct tendencies evident among crowds. One was patrician, and drew more on English example; it was found more in the Members' Reserves. The other, the plebeian tradition, more visible in the Outer, was much less imitative and more indigenous in inspiration.

Judging from match advertisements and reports of the 1860s, 1870s and 1880s patricians were more prominent because those who ran cricket then believed that colonial cricket should be run along English lines. They also promoted cricket as a fashionable and even exclusive game; while the masses were welcomed as paying spectators, they were subsidiary to the patricians.

The cost of gate entry bears eloquent testimony to this. It cost 2/- to gain admittance to the Outer and 4/- for grandstand entry at the First Test played at the Melbourne Cricket Ground (MCG) in March 1877. This ground charge represented about one-third of the minimum daily wage. Cricket prices at international matches have never been so high. By the 1930s, for instance, it still cost 2/- to sit in the MCG Outer even though the basic wage had increased considerably so that 2/- now represented from one-sixth to one-seventh of a minimum daily wage.[1] Adelaide followed Melbourne's stand gate entry lead, when it staged its First Test from 12–16 December 1884, and there were complaints in the local press about the steep charges. Entry costs were more reasonable for Sydney's first Test in January 1882 (1/- to the ground and 2/6 to the stand area), but prices had been prohibitively high for the ordinary person at international fixtures in the 1870s. When the team captained by W. G. Grace met the XVIII of New South Wales at the Albert Ground, then Sydney's premier ground, in January 1874, admission was half-a-crown (2/6) and it cost a crown (5/-) to sit in the stand area. Charges at club cricket, 6d in the 1880s, were much more reasonable.

Some people thought that charges at international matches were far too high. 'Employer' wrote in the *Argus* on 20 December 1873 recommending that charges should be reduced by half for *bona fide* workmen for the international match, All-

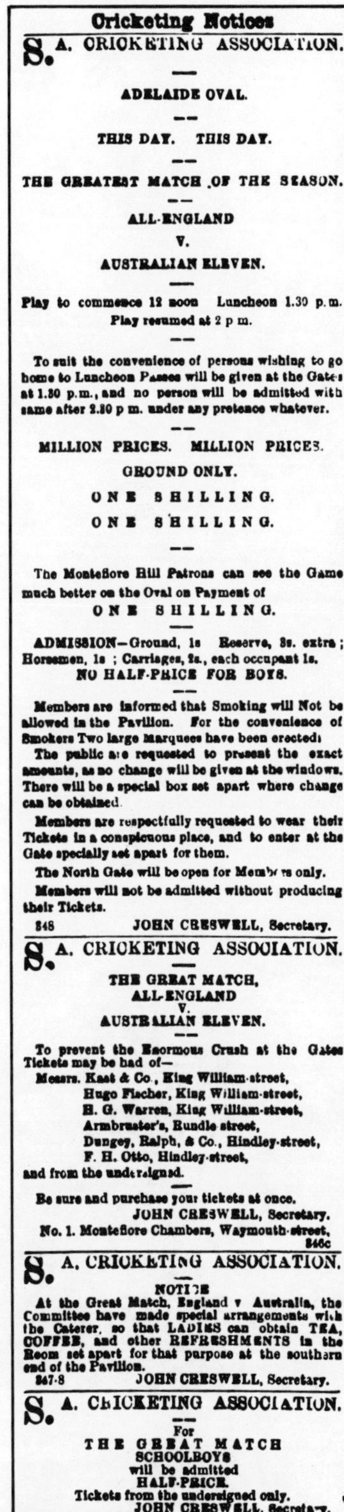

Cricketing Notices

S. A. CRICKETING ASSOCIATION.

ADELAIDE OVAL.

THIS DAY. THIS DAY.

THE GREATEST MATCH OF THE SEASON.

ALL-ENGLAND
V.
AUSTRALIAN ELEVEN.

Play to commence 12 noon Luncheon 1.30 p.m.
Play resumed at 2 p m.

To suit the convenience of persons wishing to go home to Luncheon Passes will be given at the Gates at 1.30 p.m., and no person will be admitted with same after 2.30 p m. under any pretence whatever.

MILLION PRICES. MILLION PRICES.
GROUND ONLY.
ONE SHILLING.
ONE SHILLING.

The Montefiore Hill Patrons can see the Game much better on the Oval on Payment of
ONE SHILLING.

ADMISSION—Ground, 1s Reserve, 3s. extra; Horsemen, 1s; Carriages, 2s., each occupant 1s.
NO HALF-PRICE FOR BOYS.

Members are informed that Smoking will Not be allowed in the Pavilion. For the convenience of Smokers Two large Marquees have been erected.

The public are requested to present the exact amounts, as no change will be given at the windows. There will be a special box set apart where change can be obtained.

Members are respectfully requested to wear their Tickets in a conspicuous place, and to enter at the Gate specially set apart for them.

The North Gate will be open for Members only.

Members will not be admitted without producing their Tickets.

348 JOHN CRESWELL, Secretary.

S. A. CRICKETING ASSOCIATION.

THE GREAT MATCH,
ALL-ENGLAND
V.
AUSTRALIAN ELEVEN.

To prevent the Enormous Crush at the Gates Tickets may be had of—
Messrs. Kast & Co., King William-street,
Hugo Fischer, King William-street,
H. G. Warren, King William-street,
Armbruster's, Rundle street,
Dungey, Ralph, & Co., Hindley-street,
F. H. Otto, Hindley-street,
and from the undersigned.

Be sure and purchase your tickets at once.
JOHN CRESWELL, Secretary.
No. 1. Montefiore Chambers, Waymouth-street,
346c

S. A. CRICKETING ASSOCIATION.

NOTICE

At the Great Match, England v Australia, the Committee have made special arrangements with the Caterer, so that LADIES can obtain TEA, COFFEE, and other REFRESHMENTS in the Room set apart for that purpose at the southern end of the Pavilion.

347-8 JOHN CRESWELL, Secretary.

S. A. CRICKETING ASSOCIATION.

For
THE GREAT MATCH
SCHOOLBOYS
will be admitted
HALF-PRICE.
Tickets from the undersigned only.
JOHN CRESWELL, Secretary.
No. 1, Montefiore Chambers, Waymouth-street.

Match advertisements for the 1884 Adelaide Test included special prices for horsemen and carriages and arrangements for Ladies and Smokers.

England XI vs Victorian XVIII. Otherwise his employees would be forced to watch the game from the vantage point of the trees or from outside the ground:

> Sir, I am a large employer of labour, and am accustomed to give my hands a Christmas box. As a lover of cricket I would like to give them tickets for the match. As far as I can learn, the majority will go on Friday and Saturday next, but they will be up in the trees and outside the fence. If the financial committee will issue factory tickets in packets of not less than 20, either for the first two or the whole four days, requiring an undertaking from the employer that the tickets will not be misapplied, I think that the move would be successful. In many cases the recipients would take their wives and acquaintances, who would pay full price, so that the reduction in the factory tickets would be amply repaid. I would suggest a reduction of 50 per cent, to employers of *bona fide* workmen.
>
> Yours &c.
> 'Employer'

There is no record that any such concessions were introduced. Keith Sandiford, who has investigated English cricket crowds in the Victorian era, has found a similar pattern there. When one of the most popular attractions, the two-day Eton vs Harrow fixture, drew over 40,000 in 1873, steps were taken to reduce the size of the crowd: entry cost for those on foot was raised from 1/- to 2/6. The problem with large crowds was that they not only stretched facilities but also were inclined to become unruly.[2]

A chain was all that separated Outer patrons from the play at the Melbourne Cricket Ground in 1877.

Gate entry charges in Australia became possible with the enclosure of cricket grounds from the mid-nineteeth century. Melbourne was the first ground to be enclosed, or partly enclosed; and the initial intercolonial match between Victoria and New South Wales in January 1856 was the first occasion when spectators had to pay at the gate: admission was 1/-, with ladies free. It is not known when Sydney spectators were first charged to watch the game but by 1863, at least, temporary fencing around the Domain enabled officials to levy a ground and stand entry fee. The Albert Ground, located 'in the heart of Redfern, on the east side of Elizabeth Street, about opposite the present Redfern Oval', was opened in 1864 and became Sydney's first permanently enclosed ground.[3] It was the focus for major cricket until the Sydney Cricket Ground (SCG) replaced it in 1878.

Match arrangements further underline the social side of early Australian cricket. The City Catering Co. of 315 George Street placed the following advertisement in the *Sydney Morning Herald* on 18 February 1882 to inform grandstand patrons of facilities provided for the First Test played in Sydney:

THE CITY CATERING CO.
will provide
REFRESHMENTS and LUNCHEON
in
NEW GRAND STAND

A Special Room set aside as LADIES' REFRESHMENT ROOM for Ladies, or for Gentlemen when accompanied by Ladies only, where Refreshments of all kinds may be had.

The LADIES' LAVATORY will be found near the LADIES' REFRESHMENT ROOM.

GENTLEMEN may depend on the quality of the DRINK supplied at GRAND STAND BAR underneath the Stand.

LUNCHEON. 2s 6d, for Ladies and Gentlemen of the Grand Stand and Lawn.

The same paper informed its patrons, on 19 February 1892, that for the England vs New South Wales match Abel and Co. would serve luncheon in the Members' Pavilion and that 'tea provided in the Ladies' Pavilion' was by Fresh Food and Ice Company. No mention was ever made of catering facilities for spectators in the Outer. Special arrangements for ladies were also advertised in the *Argus* of 25 December 1873 for the All-England XI vs Victorian XVIII match at the MCG: patrons were advised that 'a substantial Grand Stand, to hold 1,500 people has been erected', that 'a commodious cloak room will be provided for the use of the ladies' and 'unlimited seat accommodation has been provided round the ground'.

Lunch itself could be an extended and formal occasion lasting up to an hour and even an hour-and-a-half by the time toasts were drunk and the speeches finished. Champagne lunches — a taste for champagne being, as Alan Gibson noted in his book *The Cricket Captains of England*, a mark of the amateur — were regular features of intercolonial matches in Melbourne until the mid-1870s when the more plebian beer replaced champagne. Mr O'Brien of Tattersall's Hotel, for instance, provided an 'excellent luncheon' for a 'large company' at the New South Wales vs Victoria match at the Albert Park ground in 1871. After the sumptuous meal, speeches were made by Mr Driver, President of the Association; the Earl of Belmore, the Governor; and by Tom Wills, the Victorian Captain. Since the match had started half an hour late, Outer patrons must not have had much cricket to watch until mid-afternoon. Back in 1862 the Melbourne paper, *Yeoman*, had complained on 13 September about the 'sad want of punctuality' in starting cricket matches stating that it was quite common for the public to have to wait from one to two hours. Things had not improved a great deal by the First Test at the MCG 15–19 March 1877, when some spectators had turned up early after they had been informed, mistakenly, by the *Argus* that the game was to begin at 10 a.m. The *Argus* had stated that the match would start at 10 a.m. and finish at 5 p.m. because of poor light late in the afternoon. There would 'only be a half-an-hour' lunch break at 2 p.m. In actual fact play began at 1.05 p.m. on the first day, 12.45 p.m. on the second, and 12.20 p.m. on each of the succeeding days.

The lack of punctuality reflected the fact that cricket then was a less formal and organized game. The *Yeoman* also complained about the 'habit of smoking on the field'. 'How many a good catch has been missed,' it asked, 'by the smoke of a cigar getting in the eyes of a fielder, or by the hurried attempts to stow away a pipe!' However, it is also true that the adjustable starting times and intervals reflected the fact that the interests of the ordinary spectator were a matter of low priority.

A major cricket match was an occasion to be seen on the lawn or in the grandstand. Games were always under the patronage, and usually in the presence, of the Governor of the day, with his family also in attendance. The first intercolonial game played at the Domain, in 1857, was also watched by 'nearly all of our representatives in the Legislative Assembly' along with the 'grave legislators of the Upper House, graver judges, and reverend dignitaries of the church'. With all that political weight in attendance it was not surprising that a public holiday or a half-holiday was decreed for the first day of a major match. Then there were the ladies, 'staid matrons and blooming girls' as the *Sydney Morning Herald* pointed out on 15 January 1857, who came to promenade, to enjoy social intercourse and, just possibly, to watch cricket too. The *Argus* of 19 March 1877 opted for a cynical explanation of the presence of ladies at the First Test at Melbourne and damned them with feint praise: 'The reserve was gay with the bright dresses of hundreds of ladies. Such self-denial as induced fair onlookers to sit there for hours, in order to "rain influence" on a game which few of them understood the simplest rules, was worthy of public admiration.' Even the *Australasian* of 17 March 1877 could not hide its surprise at feminine interest in the game: it noted that 'the lawn was occupied by a numerous company of the youth and beauty of Melbourne, many of whom, seemed to take more than a passing interest in the game'.

Cricket in Australia, as in England, had a fashionable and social side which it has never quite lost. It later became quite common for some papers to identify prominent women at the Tests and to describe their outfits. One report in the Adelaide *Advertiser* of 2 November 1936 included the ensembles chosen by hundreds of women. Among the first mentioned were: Mrs Dunstan, the Lady Mayoress, who wore a 'full musquash coat over a black gown and a small brimmed velour hat trimmed with cire ribbon'; Lady Parsons chose a 'pointed fox fur with a three-quarter coated black cloth ensemble and a black velvet hat'. While it became a common practice for the press to sneer at the 'fair sex' at cricket, for their limited knowledge of the game and their social aspirations, it should be noted that many of the gentlemen must have come not just to watch the game but also to exchange political and social gossip, to establish business contacts, to attend luncheons and to drink. The SCG has a revealing crowd figure which indicates that some hundreds of spectators and members attended the ground on a Test match day entirely washed out. One wonders whether such members visit the ground (and stay, presumably, in many cases) in the slim hope of seeing some play or whether the cricket itself is a convenient backdrop or excuse for a day of conviviality.

To add to the atmosphere on the lawn and in the stand a band was always in attendance. In earlier times it was always a German band, but at the First Test at the MCG, Allan's Premier Band performed an assortment of waltzes, quadrilles and galops together with an overture and a grand march. The published programme of light classical music to be performed at the 1892 Melbourne Test, under the baton of Mr Julius Herz, provided the right tone for the occasion:

1st January
M.C.C. MILITARY BAND

March, *'The Empire'*	Godfrey
Overture, *'The Barber of Seville'*	Rossini
Waltz, *'Eldorado'*	Royle
Selection, *'Ruy Blas'*	Lutz
Cornet Solo, *'The Snowflake Polka'*	Sibbolt
Gavotte, *'Queen Christina'*	Schmid
Waltz, *'Immortellen'*	Gungl
Selection, *'The Gondoliers'*	Sullivan
Lancers, *'The Pelican'*	Williams
Waltz, *'Sweetest and Dearest'*	Fau
Selection, *'Ind Melodies'*	Hartmann
Galop, *'The Outpost'*	Godfrey

Anyone who attended cricket grounds in Australia and England from the 1850s to the 1870s would not have noticed a great deal of difference in the ground arrangements. The Domain, the setting for the first intercolonial match in Sydney in 1857, became, according to the *Sydney Morning Herald* of 15 January 1857, a 'cleared enclosure, with its face of smooth turf' which was surrounded by 'a large number of tents and marquees of all shapes' and beyond that 'by a belt of trees'. *Bell's Life* of 16 January 1857 described the Melbourne arrangements for the next New South Wales vs Victoria match in more detail:

The fashionable world of late nineteenth century cricket: Ladies and Gentlemen at the Sydney Cricket Ground.

> When we arrived... we found this beautiful spot looking gay as a racecourse, handsome booths occupying one-half of the circle, and gay flags fluttering in the pleasant breeze. On the right of the permanent pavilion of the MCC were a commodious refreshment tent for lunch and other creature comforts, under the control of the well-known Terry; and the Sydney booth, a roomy and tastefully decorated erection, under the able management of Mr Joseph Huff. On the left were two confectionery and fruit stalls, a printing press, and the booth of Mr How; whilst, about the centre of the extreme wing, were the pavilion for His Excellency, and a reserved promenade for ladies. The Victorian eleven had a private marquee at the far end of the same side and the New South Wales had a retiring place adjoining Mr Huff's booth.

The printing press, located in a marquee, produced score cards at the fall of each wicket. There were no scoreboards at the ground then. Most of the facilities were temporary and were dismantled at the end of each match.[4]

There was also a distinct rustic atmosphere about early colonial cricket matches. The *Australasian* of 28 December 1867 recounted that the MCG was surrounded by a 'low iron fence' in 1856 which was not enough to stop the cattle, from the nearby paddock, coming on to the ground for a good feed of clover and then quietly composing themselves 'to rest on the best wicket-ground'. The same source added that 'erratic goats used to camp in the pavilion, and a flock of sheep was no unusual sight from the verandah'. There was also a carnival-like atmosphere at early games at the MCG: when Stephenson's team played there in 1861 'outside the ground there were fruit and sweet stalls, Aunt Sallies, shooting galleries, hurdy-gurdies and small boys sold cards which had pictures of players on one side and the scores on the other'.[5]

Major cricket in Sydney was played at the Domain until 1871; the wicket was at the bottom of a hollow. One Victorian player believed that the Victorian loss in 1857 was due to the slope of the ground on one side of the wicket and the long grass away from the wicket. The New South Wales bowler, Captain Ward, noted *Bell's Life* of 24 January 1857, bowled left-handed from the southern wicket and 'every ball that was touched went up the hill'. The boundary at the Domain was marked by a rope which was a common practice at many grounds; others, such as the MCG in 1877, had a single chain suspended on posts. Adelaide Oval did not have a fence until 1885 while the SCG was initially surrounded by a 'three-rail fence nearly 2 metres high' which was later replaced by a picket fence.[6] When it was replaced by a wire fence in 1982, hundreds of pickets, once struck and occasionally removed by the blows of Trumper and Bradman, were consigned to the scrapheap. One wonders why the Sydney Cricket and Sports Ground Trust failed to capitalize on the ever-expanding 'cricketana' industry: there is no question that autographed SCG pickets would have sold handsomely.

Many of the first grandstands built were temporary and

sometimes unsafe. The stand constructed for the sixth intercolonial match at the Domain pointed out the *Sydney Morning Herald* on 26 January 1861 was not completed in time for the start of play. When it was finished it was pronounced 'entirely safe' by the architect, Mr Hilly. However, the public had other ideas; there was a general impression that it was unsafe and few availed themselves of a good view and a comfortable position. More permanent grandstands were established during the 1860s. Melbourne had a new grandstand in 1862 which could accommodate 6,000 and was then described as the best in the world. Sydney's Albert Ground had a 'big grandstand and a pavilion with a verandah running three sides of it' when it was opened. By the time major cricket was played at the SCG, in 1878, a grandstand had been constructed, and a few years later, in 1881, the MCG could boast of a two-storey Members' Pavilion which included a refreshment bar complete with 'liquor and oyster counters', a billiard room, reading rooms and visitors' dressing rooms. The first modern stands built at Adelaide date from 1882.

It is significant that facilities for Outer patrons developed a little more slowly. It was not until 1885 that mounds were graded at Adelaide Oval and a Hill emerged. Work began on Sydney's now-defunct Paddington (north-eastern) Hill in 1883. Sydney's main Hill dates from the 1870s when a prototype of the Hill existed: there was 'some kind of hill on the eastern side of the ground' capable of accommodating 1,790 persons; 'the slope and row of seats at the bottom of it were known for many years as "the terrace"'. But the Hill, as we know it, was not established until the 1890s when the mound was raised to its present level; by the late 1890s it had become 'known popularly as the Hill with a capital H'. The Hill Stand, popularly known as the Bob Stand because ground entrance was a shilling (a bob), was built in 1895. The advantage of a hill was that it both improved the view of the ordinary spectator and expanded the ground's capacity.[7]

Ground improvements — mounds, hills, fences, terrace seating, scoreboards and outer stands — partly represented a growing interest in facilities for the ordinary spectator but they were also introduced as methods of crowd control. There had always been two sections of the Outer crowd: those who paid and obtained legitimate entrance, and those who peeped through fences, or watched through cracks or who climbed on to overhanging trees to obtain a free view of the game. Ground improvements therefore restricted the access of the non-paying public to cricket. Susan Millbank, in her study of the early history of the South Australian Cricket Association (SACA), has shown that the right to restrict the poorer sections of society from watching top cricket caused considerable debate in the South Australian legislature. In 1897 a Mr Price accused the Association of following tactics 'which would prevent the people seeing through the fence'. Then a Mr Brooker suggested an amendment to the lease agreement to allow free admission to a section of the Oval so that people could 'witness sport', while a Mr Poynton declared that the SACA 'were not at all considerate of those who could not afford to pay admission'.[8]

Segregated crowds was another feature of Australian cricket inherited from the English. There were further divisions in the members' enclosures. Apart from the special areas, such as the Governor's box, there were ladies' reserves (later stands) and even special areas for smokers; there was a Smokers' Marquee at Adelaide in 1884 and Sydney had a Smokers' Stand which was removed to the No. 2 ground in 1909 to make way for the Sheridan Stand. It was considered bad form for patrons not to observe the niceties of social demarcations. In fact the *Sydney Morning Herald* of 23 February 1892 reported an incident at the SCG when the smokers, who were not permitted on the lawn, invaded it and caused 'clouds of smoke' (from pipes and cigars presumably) to 'invade' the Ladies' Stand.

Within the reserves behaviour was governed by the rules of polite society and presumably was limited to restrained applause in the English tradition. The one exception to this was the male-only smokers' area: the occupants there were sometimes very jocose and were not backward at yelling at spectators who occasionally blocked their views; they even indulged in a little barracking when play became tame. The Adelaide *Advertiser* of 20 January 1902 reported some of the 'inane conundrums' which were called out by smokers at the Adelaide Test:

A segregate crowd at The Gabba in 1899: the Smokers' Stand (left); main grandstand (right); and standing Outer patrons (foreground). The Outer mound was ungraded.

SOME
PEOPLE
THAT NEVER
PAY.

Query: Why did the wombat?
Answer: Because the cricket made him.
(Other conundrums were based on the names of players: Howell, Jessop, Maclaren, Darling and Hill).
Query: When did Bill Howell?
Answer: When he saw Jess'op out.
Query: Why was Maclaren Blythe?
Answer: Because Darling was Hill (at ease).

Such barracking was quite different from the more basic and earthy barracking which developed in the Outer.

Some traditions die hard in cricket and Adelaide retained a men-only section of the Members' Stand until the 1981–82 season. The area was directly below the dressing-rooms and the policy was justified on the grounds of player bad language and the possibility that cricket groupies might distract some of the cricketers. Pressure was brought to bear on the Association and the restriction was altered to members only. It was not until July 1983 that women acquired the right to membership of the Melbourne Cricket Club. However, because the club has a waiting list of over 50,000 it was likely that females would not be admitted for 26 years. It is anticipated that the club will introduce a form of provisional membership in 1984 which would allow women so elected to enter the Long Room. The Long Room has been open to women only twice since the MCC was instituted in 1838 — during the 1956 Olympics and for the Queen during the Centenary Test in 1977.

Press reporting of cricket also underlined its class character at this time. Written in florid and ornate language, match reports were clearly intended for the well educated. One written by 'Our own correspondent' of *Bell's Life* in 24 January 1857 established this:

> Hilliard having found a fresh partner in McKone, continued to hit away boldly but judiciously, the latter doing his best to follow the good example, and eleven more had been added to the score before an insinuator from Wills dismissed the latter gentleman to the *otium cum dignitate* of the tents — fifty-one runs and four wickets down. Mr Still was the next in rotation to shoulder his 'Clapshaw' and face Hilliard, and from his well-known ability as a batsman a treat was looked for — *l'homme propose* etc., however, for after contributing a single to the general fund, Still was run out.

Plebeians

The cricket establishment may well have wished to monopolize the game, or at least to define and to some extent restrict popular participation, but from very early times in the colonies cricket had an immense following. Side by side with the patrician involvement was a vigorous plebeian tradition: more boisterous, sometimes even violent, less imitative and more indigenous, and more in tune with working-class rather than elite values. From time to time the plebeians threatened to overwhelm the patricians, and to appropriate cricket for the people.

Cricket, along with horse racing, was one of the earliest recreations in New South Wales and by the 1820s a number of clubs had been established. Teams were brought together from all sections of society. Some, such as the military, played in tall black hats, while others were composed of private gentlemen. Others, notably the Australian Cricket Club, was formed initially by a few mechanics. E. W. Gregory, father of two Test players, was a member of this club.

Cricket was appreciated right across the social spectrum. One Sydney paper, the *Monitor*, complained in 1827 that 'a parcel of ill-dressed vagabond-looking native boys, are continually playing at cricket in the environs of the town' (Hyde Park) on the Sabbath 'besides playing at fives in the Market-house' on the same day. Cricket by the 1830s was a popular spectator sport. Club games were usually watched by hundreds of people and an 1832 match between the 17th and the 39th regiments drew a 'large throng' (possibly 2,000) spectators including 'several well-dressed females'. Two years later a game, which involved a number of lawyers, led to the adjournment of the Supreme Court.

Cricket, even then, was not free from controversy. When a team of native-born youth, the Australian Cricket Club, met eleven Englishmen, the Mary-le-bone Cricket Club, in 1832, a dispute arose concerning a catch in front of the wicket and 'a challenge to a fight led to a disturbance' which nearly finished the match prematurely. While there is no record of the details of this disturbance, we do know that three years later 'Tom, the Native' took up a cudgel and pounded a player, undoubtedly an Englishman. This incident occurred during a series of matches between an Australian-born team and a side of Immigrants. Tension built up after a player had written to the press declaring that the batting of the opposition was 'atrocious', their bowling 'melancholy', and added that 'there is not one decent Native player to be found'.[9]

By the 1830s a devotion to sport, and cricket in particular, had gripped all sections of society. With the further expansion of cricket clubs, together with the beginning of intercolonial competition in the 1850s and international games in the 1860s, the country, as one source put it in the 1850s, had become 'cricket mad'. When New South Wales met Victoria in Sydney for the first time in January 1857 the *Sydney Morning Herald* of 15 January 1857 exclaimed, 'We have never seen more excitement amongst all classes of citizens as prevailed on this occasion.' One observer, who attended the match over the three days of play, estimated that nearly a quarter of the population attended for some part of the time and 'that the business of the town ... was quite interrupted'. He did not put this down to laziness but to the fact that 'the people are so well to do as to be able to spare more holidays and really enjoy themselves more than people of other countries'.[10] To ensure against a business loss one enterprising auctioneer, John G. Cohen, advised the public that 'in consequence of the Intercolonial Match' (the 1863 encounter), 'the Sale will commence at half-past 10 o'clock', which was an hour-and-a-half before the scheduled match commencement. Some businessmen, such as the publican Cunningham, were more fortunate in that he could move his enterprise to the Domain. He advertised: in the *Sydney Morning Herald* of 6 February 1863, that:

> CUNNINGHAM'S Hotel removed to north-east corner of the ground opposite Grand Stand. Wines and spirits &c., of first quality, and the best attendance.
>
> CUNNINGHAM and MARTIN will be happy to see friends at the Domain ground, opposite Grand Stand. Every article guaranteed the best quality.
>
> SANDWICHES and Pork Pies, at CUNNINGHAM'S Booth.

Cricket took another leap forward with the arrival in Melbourne of the first English team in 1861 led by the Surrey captain, H. H.

Arrival of the All England XI at the Cafe de Paris, Bourke Street, Melbourne, 24 December 1861, demonstrates the immense following of the game then.

Stephenson. No fewer than 3,000 enthusiasts turned up at the wharf to greet the cricketers and they were cheered all the way into the city. For the match against the Melbourne XVIII the biggest crowd on record assembled: a local paper estimated it to be 25,000 but admitted that the figure could have been as high as 30,000 or even 40,000. Whatever the total it was an impressive gathering because the city population at this time was only 125,000. A painting of the crowd indicates that while some watched the match from the stands put up for the game, or from the tents, others stood, and yet others were on horseback or in carriages, and some others even climbed the tall trees which ringed the ground.

For the team's Sydney match there was also a bumper crowd, estimated at 30,000, which, if correct, represented about one-third of the city population (then 96,000). The visitors drew good crowds in the country as well: some 5,000 bearded miners turned up at the diggings settlement of Castlemaine to see their local XXII inflict one of the few defeats on the Englishmen. It was not surprising that the tour proved immensely profitable for the organizers, Messrs Spiers and Pond, with a clear profit of £11,000. Major cricket, with its immense crowd-drawing capacity, was clearly big business.

Cricket continued to attract big gates until the early 1880s as the crowds for the first four-Test series show:

1876–77 2 Tests (8 days)	1 MCG	17,500–25,000
	2 MCG	14–19,000
	Total	38,000
1878–79 1 Test (3 days)	1 MCG	11,500–15,000
1881–82 4 Tests (15 days)	1 MCG	45–52,500
	2 SCG	32,775
	3 SCG	15,018
	4 MCG	11,500–13,000
	Total	109,293
1882–83 4 Tests (14 days)	1 MCG	49–54,000
	2 MCG	20–22,000
	3 SCG	53,523
	4 SCG	43,706
	Total	169,729

(Melbourne's figures are estimates based on newspaper reports; the MCG has no official crowd records prior to 1909. Sydney's records date back to 1882, hence the precise figures. Such figures also reveal a growing official interest in crowd numbers.)

Sydney's 1883 two-Test total of 97,229 over eight days was an impressive figure which represented 45% of the 1881 city population of 225,000. Sydney crowds were much larger than Melbourne's at this time where 72,500 attended six days, or just one-quarter of the city total of 268,000.

The large amount of newspaper space devoted to match reports and arrangements — ground regulations, catering facilities, transport details, ticket outlets, match times and entertainments — suggest further that a major match loomed very large in the calendar of city life. Typical of the lengthy match advertisements was the wordy and somewhat repetitive screed put out by the Directors of the Albert Ground and published in the *Sydney Morning Herald* of 23 January 1874 for the match between the XVIII of New South Wales and the W. G. Grace's English team. It left little to the imagination: among other things it informed patrons that 'no horses would be admitted', that 'pass cheques' would be issued from 1 p.m. to 2 p.m. only, that ticket-holders were to exhibit their tickets on all occasions, that 'children under 12 (in charge of adults)' would be admitted to the stand at a cost of 1/-. It detailed many of the ground regulations and the dire consequences which would result from any non-compliance.

When English social commentator, Richard Twopeny, visited Australia in the 1880s he put cricket at the top of his list of Australian sports 'because all ages and all classes are interested in it, and not to be interested in it amounts to a social crime'. Professor Ken Inglis has suggested that it is hard to compare the popularity of one sport with another in colonial times. The Melbourne Cup of 1880 attracted 100,000, which was more than one-third of Melbourne's 1881 population of 268,000. Sculling, too, drew crowds as large as 60,000 in the 1880s and it is estimated that some 170,000 attended the funeral of champion sculler Henry Searle in 1889. However, there is no doubt that cricket crowds at this time were among the larger sporting assemblies.[11]

Why was cricket so popular in the nineteenth century? Historians Cumes, Inglis and Mandle, have explored some of the reasons for cricket's popularity. There was, first of all, a great dearth of leisure facilities in the early days of the colonies and, at the same time, there was a great thirst for leisure because of the harshness of existence and the rigours of work. For the ordinary citizen, drinking, gaming and, to some extent, sex were the only available outlets. The elite were a little more fortunate in that they could consume fine dinners and attend balls among other diversions. So when a horse racing carnival was organized in 1810 and cricket matches were played soon after, they came as a welcome relief for a society starved for public entertainment.

Cricket also had an advantage over football in that the major codes were not organized until later in the century and it was not until the 1880s and 1890s that the public imagination was captured and crowds of up to 12,000 were recorded at football games. However, the real expansion in football crowds did not take place until after 1900.

Cricket had, and still has, an even more important asset in that it was a national game, played in all States and appreciated by all sections of society; it was closely associated with and played a role in the emergence of Australian nationalism. Cricket derived great strength from its international contests and particularly by 'an unfilial yearning on the part of young Australia to triumphantly thrash the mother country'. This spirit arose in part from an inferiority complex which sprang from two sources: a concern that the convict strain might have had a detrimental effect on the local population and a fear that Anglo-Saxon qualities might have deteriorated under the hot sun of the southern continent. The achievements of colonial cricketers in besting the Englishmen in Australia in the First Test and in defeating them in England in 1882 were considered a reassuring sign of the vitality of Australian manhood. Successful cricketers became national heroes and were lionized.

Inglis has suggested another reason for the popularity of cricket and outdoor recreation in general. With its open spaces, many parks and favourable climate, Australia provided an environment conducive to sport. Inglis considers that the number of public holidays and the Saturday half-holiday and the Australian school system may have augmented this tendency so that 'there may well have been as many boys and young men playing cricket among Australia's four millions in 1900 as among Great Britain's nearly forty millions'.[12]

Crowd Violence

Huge attendances, plebeian spectators and a limited crowd control techniques created law and order problems right from the start of major cricket. The *Sydney Morning Herald* of 13 January 1857 recognized the problem when it commented on arrangements for the first intercolonial match in Sydney in 1857: 'An area of 200 yards is marked out for the players, into which it is to be hoped that the public will not attempt to intrude.' Match advertisements of the 1860s and 1870s indicate that cricket authorities continued to be concerned with the problem of public order at cricket. Domain patrons were advised in the *Sydney Morning Herald* of 6 February 1863: 'For the preservation of order the ground will be protected by the committee, assisted by the police. Any person drunk, disorderly, or otherwise breaking through any of the above regulations will be removed from the ground.'

Even more specific were the notices placed in the Press for matches at the Albert Ground in 1871 and 1874:

> The ground will be under the surveillance of the police. The ordinary rules of the Albert Ground will be strictly enforced, and anyone infringing the same will be liable to be removed from the ground.
>
> Notice — All persons found Gambling, or with Gambling instruments in their possession, will be removed from the ground, the Police having received instructions to that effect.[13]
>
> Any person found trespassing, injuring the fences or trees, &c., or otherwise damaging, will be prosecuted. The Regulations of the ground will be strictly enforced.
>
> THE GROUND WILL BE UNDER THE SURVEILLANCE OF THE

> POLICE. Any person encroaching within the Playing Ground will be expelled at the gates.[14]

Such notices reflected the times: incidents, and even violence, were regular features of intercolonial games, particularly at Sydney. One of the worst outbreaks occurred on the second day of the 1863 New South Wales vs Victoria match at the Domain. On the first day the home side had worked itself into a good position scoring 108 and taking eight Victorian wickets for 51. However, Victoria staged a recovery on the next day adding another 25 runs for the last two wickets and then dismissing four New South Wales batsmen for just 11 runs. The incident occurred three runs later when the Victorian keeper, Marshall, stumped the batsman, Jones, who had wandered from his crease believing that the over was completed and the ball was dead: the New South Wales umpire, Driver, had called over and already four or five fieldsmen had begun to change places. The Victorian umpire, Smith, who was at square leg and later claimed that he had not heard the call of over, had other ideas and gave Jones out on the appeal from Marshall. Jones 'was about to leave the field when he was told to retain his place at the wicket' which he then did as it was the opinion of the home side that he was not out. For the next 20 minutes an 'angry dispute' took place during which time spectators rushed on to the field. Play was then called off for the day, but as the Victorian captain, Wills, headed for his tent, he was struck on the face by a stone.

The match was resumed the next morning after considerable wrangling. Jones was allowed to resume his innings but the Victorian umpire refused to continue even though the New South Wales umpire resigned in the interests of continuing the game. Not all the Victorian players accepted a majority team decision and Marshall and Greaves headed back to Melbourne leaving the visitors two short for the second innings. With such a handicap Victoria totalled only 45 in the second innings and lost the game by a wide margin, 84 runs.[15]

Marshall was an unpopular figure in Sydney because he was involved in another incident which had occurred in the previous Sydney match in 1861 when play was suspended for half an hour. It was the opinion of the Sydney crowd that when Marshall 'put the wicket down' he was 'attempting smart practice'. He was 'hooted lustily' and some of the crowd 'rushed the ground'. This incident again centred on the question of precisely when a ball became dead. It occurred on the second day of the game during a partnership between two New South Wales batsmen, Kettle and Gilbert. Being 'lame' Kettle secured the services of a runner, Newcombe. It was after Gilbert and Newcombe had successfully negotiated a run that Kettle wandered out of his crease (perhaps in the same way as Rodney Hogg did in a 1979 Test to pat down the wicket) whereupon Marshall 'put down the stumps'. Kettle was given out by the Victorian umpire who subsequently

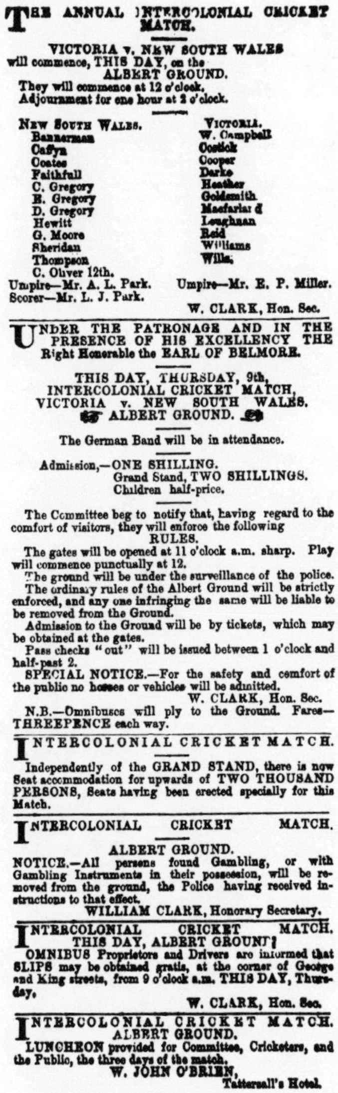

THE ANNUAL INTERCOLONIAL CRICKET MATCH.

VICTORIA v. NEW SOUTH WALES
will commence, THIS DAY, on the
ALBERT GROUND.
They will commence at 12 o'clock.
Adjournment for one hour at 2 o'clock.

NEW SOUTH WALES.	VICTORIA.
Bannerman	W. Campbell
Caffyn	Costick
Coates	Cooper
Faithfull	Darke
C. Gregory	Heather
E. Gregory	Goldsmith
D. Gregory	Macfarland
Hewitt	Loughnan
G. Moore	Reid
Sheridan	Williams
Thompson	Wills.
C. Oliver 12th.	
Umpire—Mr. A. L. Park.	Umpire—Mr. E. P. Miller.
Scorer—Mr. L. J. Park.	

W. CLARK, Hon. Sec.

UNDER THE PATRONAGE AND IN THE PRESENCE OF HIS EXCELLENCY THE Right Honorable the EARL OF BELMORE.

THIS DAY, THURSDAY, 9th,
INTERCOLONIAL CRICKET MATCH,
VICTORIA v. NEW SOUTH WALES.
ALBERT GROUND.

The German Band will be in attendance.

Admission,—ONE SHILLING.
Grand Stand, TWO SHILLINGS.
Children half-price.

The Committee beg to notify that, having regard to the comfort of visitors, they will enforce the following

RULES.

The gates will be opened at 11 o'clock a.m. sharp. Play will commence punctually at 12.

The ground will be under the surveillance of the police.

The ordinary rules of the Albert Ground will be strictly enforced, and any one infringing the same will be liable to be removed from the Ground.

Admission to the Ground will be by tickets, which may be obtained at the gates.

Pass checks "out" will be issued between 1 o'clock and half-past 2.

SPECIAL NOTICE.—For the safety and comfort of the public no hosses [sic] or vehicles will be admitted.

W. CLARK, Hon. Sec.

N.B.—Omnibuses will ply to the Ground. Fares—THREEPENCE each way.

INTERCOLONIAL CRICKET MATCH.

Independently of the GRAND STAND, there is now Seat accommodation for upwards of TWO THOUSAND PERSONS, Seats having been erected specially for this Match.

INTERCOLONIAL CRICKET MATCH.

ALBERT GROUND.

NOTICE.—All persons found Gambling, or with Gambling Instruments in their possession, will be removed from the ground, the Police having received instructions to that effect.

WILLIAM CLARK, Honorary Secretary.

INTERCOLONIAL CRICKET MATCH.
THIS DAY, ALBERT GROUND.

OMNIBUS Proprietors and Drivers are informed that SLIPS may be obtained gratis, at the corner of George and King streets, from 9 o'clock a.m. THIS DAY, Thursday.

W. CLARK, Hon. Sec.

INTERCOLONIAL CRICKET MATCH.
ALBERT GROUND.

LUNCHEON provided for Committee, Cricketers, and the Public, the three days of the match.

W. JOHN O'BRIEN,
Tattersall's Hotel.

Advertisements for the 1871 intercolonial match demonstrated official concern over gambling in particular, and law and order in general.

admitted that he had mistaken Kettle for Newcombe, or perhaps had forgotten that a runner was involved and was within his crease. (Theoretically all three should have remained within the crease until the ball was clearly dead.) The match only resumed after the visitors agreed to allow Kettle to resume his innings. According to one source an incident had occurred, in the very first intercolonial match in Sydney in 1857, over a run out. A disturbance was 'very nearly occurring' but was prevented when the visiting captain capitulated and decided to allow a home batsman to resume his innings.[16]

There were a number of ingredients to cricket unrest at this time. Intercolonial rivalry was a critical factor. The Sydney crowd, the *Argus* of 7 February 1863 commented 'always display the most lively sympathy with their champions'. In fact it was considered positively dangerous, some players recalled a few decades later, for any Victorian player to 'walk the streets after they had won the match'; he might be confronted by the comment made to one player: 'There's a Victorian cricketer, 'eave arf a brick at him.'[17] The Melbourne Press echoed some of these sentiments, in a more subdued form, suggesting that the Sydney crowd was the more partisan and volatile, for up to this time Melbourne had yet to witness a major crowd disturbance. It is also quite clear that incidents in the 1860s focussed on the umpires and that their respective identification with each team compounded inter-city rivalry. The system of appointing umpires remained a critical problem for the next two decades.

Finally there was an uncertainty about rules and a willingness of players to both question and openly defy the decisions of the umpires. This was the spark, and 20 minutes of animated discussion was a very considerable spark, which could ignite a crowd. There are some interesting parallels between the 1860s and the late 1970s in that Marshall's stumpings of 1861 and 1863 are not dissimilar to Miandad's controversial dismissal of Hogg in 1979. On both occasions the challenge of a past convention led to debates on the spirit in which the game should be played.

The 1870s introduced a new dimension to cricket disorder, gambling, and witnessed the worst outbreaks of crowd disorder in Australian cricket history. Melbourne, which up to this time had prided itself on its well-conducted crowds, was rudely awakened in 1873. The incident in the Challenge Cup Final happened just after the W. G. Grace-led English side had arrived at the South Melbourne ground to watch the final of the Challenge Cup, South Melbourne vs Melbourne, before a crowd of 6–7,000. When Grace arrived one of the local players boasted about their crowds: 'You can see we manage our crowds better than you do in England. Our spectators are impartial and good-tempered. We never experience any unpleasantness in our cricket grounds.' Within 15 minutes his remark was refuted. The game was then evenly poised as the home side moved to 8–133 in quest of a winning (second innings) total of 150. Then there was another 'dead ball' incident which was also linked with spectator gambling. After the South Melbourne batsman, Major, had narrowly avoided being run out, the Melbourne keeper, Gibson, threw down the ball in disgust. Gibson then turned round to speak to some of his team members. Major, meanwhile under the impression that the ball was 'dead' left his crease to talk to his partner only to discover that Gibson stumped him. The umpire upheld the appeal. 'A great excitement was raised, and the crowd rushed the ground' in part because of bets made on the result for, as the *Australasian* put it, 'the game was close and interesting, there was some money on in small sums, and party feeling ran very high'. South Melbourne refused to continue unless Major was reinstated. When Melbourne rejected this the match was abandoned — the first instance recorded in Australian cricket history. Several of the Melbourne team were hooted as they left the ground and Gibson, whom the English cricketers believed had indulged in 'sharp practice' — and Grace must have known this because he was an expert in the art — was even 'pelted with stones by a number of disorderly larrikins'. Next day produced a unique score card in the Press: it listed Major as 'stumped (disputed) . . . 3'.

The Challenge Cup was not decided for six weeks after a series of unusual events which resulted in East Melbourne, rather than Melbourne or South Melbourne, being named the champions. Several weeks after the dispute the Committee had declared Melbourne the winner since South Melbourne had not sent in another man after Major was adjudged out by the umpire. The MCC, dissatisfied with winning the Cup in 'such an unsatisfactory manner', then handed back the Cup for competition again. They may well have been surprised by the result of such a sporting action because they were then ignored by the Committee who decided that the Cup should now be contested between an East Melbourne XI and a Richmond XV, even though the latter team had been soundly beaten by South Melbourne.[18]

Sydney almost had a riot in the same season. In the All England vs Combined XV of Victoria and New South Wales, 'It seemed,' Grace later wrote, in his *Reminiscences*, 'as if we were to be robbed of a hard-earned win by an ugly incident.' After the home captain and some of the spectators had objected to an umpiring dismissal, the dismissed batsman was advised to return to the crease and claim the right to resume his innings. At one point there was the unusual sight of three able-bodied batsmen at the wickets. Grace then took his team off, which apparently resolved the stalemate and defused the situation. Later the visitors were able to carry on and win the match.

Four years later a minor incident was reported by the *Argus* of 2 April 1877 in the Second Test played at the MCG. Going for a fourth run the Australian batsman, Murdoch, was adjudged run out. The finish was an extremely close one but the umpire, Terry, 'gave his decision with a peremptoriness which allowed he had no doubt whatever about it'. His actions brought immediate cries around the ground of 'Not out' and 'Find another umpire', shouts which came not only from the Outer but also from the members.

Australian crowds have never accepted the English conventions of restrained behaviour and polite applause; there has always been a significant exuberant and vocal number of spectators who believe that they have a right to criticize umpires and players and even tell them how to conduct the game. When W. G. Grace was dismissed for a second time against New South Wales in 1874, caught by the same fieldsman from the same bowler there was a 'tremendous shout of jubilation' and 'hats, caps, umbrellas, walking-sticks' went up in the air;[19] there was similar rejoicing when Boyle dismissed Grace at the MCG in 1873 for among the crowd were 'about 1,500 Bendigo men, who had come because Boyle was their champion' and 'they went fairly mad and cooeed with true Australian fervour.'[20]

The 1879 Riot

By far the most celebrated and infamous incident of this era, a cricket riot, occurred on 8 February 1879 on the second day of the England vs New South Wales match at the SCG with the Governor and his wife as 'pained witnesses'. After England had totalled 267 the home side managed only 177, despite an excellent innings of 82 not out by the popular idol, Murdoch, and was forced to follow on. In front of a Saturday crowd of around 10,000 Murdoch and Bannerman took the score to 18 before Murdoch was given run out by the Victorian professional, Coulthard, who had been engaged as an umpire by the English team on the recommendation of the Melbourne Cricket Club. Such an unpopular decision brought an immediate chorus of 'groaning and hooting' and cries of 'Not out', 'Go back, Murdoch!' and 'Another umpire' by a batch of 'adult larrikins'. They were led, according to the *Australasian* of 15 February 1879 by a 'well-known and ill-favoured bookmaker' who had backed the local side to the extent of nearly £1,000.

Gregory, the home captain, instead of sending in another man, hesitated, and Lord Harris, the English captain, possibly headed towards the pavilion to discuss the situation with Gregory at about the same time. Then a large number of 'larrikins', sitting at the bottom of the terrace and within the boundary fence, 'made a rush for the centre of the ground' noted the *Sydney Morning Herald* of 10 February 1879 and were quickly followed by 'hundreds of roughs who took possession of the wickets'. Subsequent disclosures in the Press and at court make it clear that the protests emanated both from the pavilion and the Outer. In fact Mr Driver stated that it was the 'inmates of the pavilion', spurred on by a bookmaker, who had 'initiated the disturbance' though it is not entirely clear whether the juvenile element which rushed the ground included members.[21] Presumably it did because not only was the bookmaker ejected but a number of members had their fees returned and were banned.

The English team soon found itself in the centre of a 'surging, gesticulating, and shouting mob' continued the *Sydney Morning Herald* in its account of the riot; it was later estimated that some 2,000 spectators poured on to the ground. One person tried to strike Coulthard but was floored. Harris was struck across the body with a whip or a stick, by a 'rough'. Another English player, Hornby, promptly tackled his captain's assailant and with the assistance of some gentlemen and members dragged the person to the pavilion. This was no easy task as some of the 'roughs' made unsuccessful attempts to snatch their cohort from the clutches of Hornby. No serious injuries resulted from the fracas. Hornby had his clothes torn, and was struck on the face, and a few others had scratches. Harris had even landed a few blows himself, in self defence, or so the *Australasian* thought. The mêlée lasted 30 minutes and throughout it the pavilion bell was rung, rather optimistically it seems, with 'the vigour of a fire alarm' to encourage spectators to clear the ground.

Meanwhile Gregory seemed to be doing his best to aggravate the situation. He had come to the conclusion, possibly based on Murdoch's version of the run out, that Coulthard was incompetent and should be replaced. Harris refused whereupon Gregory told him that the game was over. (Harris had kept his team on the field throughout the riot fearing that Gregory might claim the match through forfeit.) Gregory later relented and decided to let the match continue, with Coulthard officiating, but the crowd would not accept this and twice more invaded the pitch so that the match was called off for the day. It was completed on Monday without further incident.[22]

It is worth exploring some of the ingredients of this riot to establish its links with previous unrest. One continuing factor was the strong crowd identification with the home team which represented a form of nationalism or perhaps chauvinism. It was possibly fuelled by the reported comments of two English professionals, Emmett and Ulyett, who referred to the crowd as 'sons of convicts' and supposedly about the time Harris was struck. Emmett and Ulyett later denied making the remarks and were supported in their stand by the other umpire, a future Prime Minister, Edmund Barton. In the face of these denials the *Sydney Morning Herald* reporter stuck to his guns and published a letter on 13 February from a 'well-known citizen' who wrote, 'I can only tell you that I heard the remark, and that it spread like wild fire round the ground.'

The controversy over an umpire represented another link with the past and it was the opinion of the *Australasian* of 15 February 1879 that it would be a happy day when the 'present loose system of appointing umpires is done way with'. The problem with this system was that a particular umpire was identified with a team and was regarded as something less than an impartial arbiter of the law. The system also encouraged captains to question the authority of umpires from time to time and assume some of the decision-making powers themselves.

Regarding the 1879 incident, Harris later admitted that he may have made a mistake selecting a professional umpire on the recommendation of the Melbourne Cricket Club, as he had no idea of the depth of inter-city rivalry.

The Causes of Disturbances

Gambling constituted a new problem for cricket authorities in the 1870s. The pastime had had a long association with Australian cricket, as it had with the English game, and was originally part of cricket's fashionable past. No one complained of gentlemen playing for £20 stakes in the 1830s, and the Press reported the betting for a match in 1832; it was between 2 and 3/1 for the Australian Cricket Club. Bets were not only laid in money but also in 'boots, snakeskin shoes, sawn timber, fat pigs, drip-stones, fish, butter and maize'. Gambling was, from the very earliest times, an Australian passion, and there is a record of a £300 bet, a very large sum, in 1832. Gambling was still respectable in the 1850s and indeed the first intercolonial match originated from a Victorian challenge to New South Wales cricketers for a 'side bet of £500'.[23] Match odds were published regularly in the papers, for example the books gave 2/1 on Victoria in 1856 but New South Wales won.

Gambling in cricket took a variety of forms: there were bets on the outcome of the game, for example, in the match between New South Wales and Victoria in 1858 *Bell's Life* reported on 16 January that the betting was 'slightly in favour of Victoria' but New South Wales had 'plenty of friends'. In the same game there was also a wager of £100 as to whether New South Wales batsman, Gilbert, would pass the score of the Victorian batsman, Bryant. The *Australian Cricketer's Guide* even published a list of Rules for Cricket Betting in 1859.

By the 1870s gambling had lost its respectability and was looked upon as an evil and authorities at the Albert Ground promised to remove gamblers from the ground in 1871. With the larger crowds and expanded plebeian involvement, it is likely that gambling took on wider proportions and became better organized by the bookmaking fraternity. Gambling also went out of vogue because it conflicted with the fast-emerging amateur ideal which stressed the purity of sport free from the taint of money. Lord Harris, a great apostle of the amateur ideal, regarded gambling as a great blot on colonial cricket. He believed that the 1879 disturbance was 'started and fomented by professional men' of the bookmaking fraternity and considered it disgraceful that some members of the New South Wales Cricket Association (NSWCA) had 'aided and abetted the bookmakers' in raising the shout of defiance against the umpire's ruling.

The reply of the Secretary at the NSWCA contained one very revealing comment on the extent of gambling and the apparent inability of the Association to stamp it out. He pointed out that 'betting on cricket matches is strictly prohibited by the trustees of the ground' but confessed that this operated 'so far as it can be prohibited' in spite of 'large placards [which] have always been kept posted throughout the pavilion and its inclosures'.[24]

Gambling remained a 'problem' in the 1880s. An 18 February 1882 Test match notice published in the *Sydney Morning Herald* reminded patrons that betting was 'strictly prohibited'; however it was still around in the 1890s. There was an 'undoubtedly exaggerated' but probably partly true report in *Blackwood's Magazine* in 1892 that 'in Australia the game is entirely in the hands of speculators and bookmakers, who regard it simply as a vehicle for heavy betting, just as the "ring" regards horse racing in England'.[25] Thereafter gambling faded as a problem for cricket administrators only to surface in 1981 when Lillee and Marsh placed a bet against the Australian side and secured a handsome return.

The deployment of police in 1879 suggests that the local Association had only the haziest idea of crowd control techniques and if Melbourne arrangements were similar, as they probably were, it makes the 1873 boast to Grace a very hollow one. After the riot the Association was criticized for having only 'a small body of police present' and of failing to take decisive measures when the riot began by sending in a 'strong body of police and having the ground cleared'. According to the *Sydney Morning Herald* of 10 February 1879 those police at the ground were 'too late to get to the centre of the ground when the rush occurred, and subsequently found it difficult to make their way through the crowd'. The *Australasian* of 15 February 1879 even stated that three policemen were noticed 'waiting on the safe side of the fence until the disturbance was almost over'.

Crowd control was a very real problem in the colonial era because of the limited distance, and barriers, between players and spectators. On the occasion of the riot, 'larrikins' were permitted to sit inside the fence and there was no physical barrier, and presumably no policemen, between them and the players. It was also common for spectators and even animals to wander over the oval prior to play and during the intervals. An 1883 notice advised that 'all dogs found on the ground are liable to be destroyed'. Authorities, relying on the co-operation of patrons, rang a bell for the ground to be cleared at the beginning of the day and after each interval.

'Larrikins' and 'roughs' emerged as another problem for cricket administrators in the 1870s. Larrikins were defined as a youthful anti-social element, prone to 'turbulence and drunkenness' and gambling. They were discovered by the media and respectable opinion in emerging cities of the 1870s, even though they or their prototypes must have been around well before then. Larrikins, the *Sydney Morning Herald* pointed out on 11 February 1879, could be found not only at cricket matches but could also descend and disturb a picnic at Chowder Bay or cause trouble in the Chinese quarter. A cricket crowd has always been a microcosm of society at large so that it is hardly surprising that some larrikins should have found their way into the SCG and made their presence felt there.

Drink may have been a factor in colonial cricket unrest but it appears to have been a relatively minor cause of disorder in the nineteenth century which is surprising given its major role in the twentieth century. There seems little doubt that liquor was readily available at all colonial matches and the long-established link between the publican and cricket was maintained in the colony as indicated by Cunningham's advertisements in 1857. This tradition was still in evidence at the turn of the century when spectators were invited by an advertisement placed in the *Sydney Morning Herald* of 26 January 1899 to:

WET THE CRICKET MATCH
With
SYDNEY LAGER
Drawn through ice

Sydney Lager is on Draught
in the Members' Pavilion

Liquor was available in the Outer also.

Liquor, for reasons which are not entirely clear, did not loom large in the official mind as a cause of crowd violence. In fact it is scarcely mentioned. Drink was only mentioned as a problem in relation to player performance. Champagne lunches and hospitality in general, for instance, were blamed for some up-country losses and form reversals by touring sides. The *Yeoman* of 13 September 1862 also complained of the evil of 'nobblerising'. No one would object if the players left the field for refreshments from time to time: however the extent to which the practice was carried was judged as 'perfectly ridiculous'. This source suggested that the practice of leaving the field for a nobbler was nothing less than a 'dodge' to get rid of a 'sticker', or a batsman with a large score, because there was a distinct possibility that after this interval, the batsman might well have lost his sight of the ball.

The 1879 riot had drastic consequences for Australian cricket. The Murdoch-led Australian team was boycotted for much of the 1880 tour and found it hard to discover opponents. It was only towards the end of the season that Harris, an important figure in English cricket, relented and one Test was arranged. The Harris criticisms of Australian crowds also established a tradition which has continued to this day. English objection to Australian crowd behaviour has surfaced in almost every tour and has been one of the enduring characteristics in the history of Australian crowds.

By concentrating at such length on violence in colonial cricket there is a danger of overlooking, and distorting, the more exemplary behaviour of the majority of ordinary spectators which went unreported. It is likely that most of the reported incidents, with the possibile exception of the 1879 riot, involved very few Outer patrons. We know very little about the behaviour of a typical spectator of the Outer at this time but judging from the descriptions of the 'shrewd shilling spectators' in the 1900s, it is likely that the great majority were an appreciative audience who knew and loved the game.

Cricket In The Doldrums?

After the successful 1882–83 tour of Australia, cricket in this country underwent a period in the doldrums, or as Tommy Horan put it, a 'period of decadence', which lasted nine seasons. Crowd attendances at tests plummeted. Given that cricket had established such a broad popular base prior to this the reasons for the decline puzzled contemporary observers as they have intrigued cricket historians since.

The drop in Test crowds was spectacular. Following the success of Shaw's 1882–83 team which attracted 169,729 spectators in four Tests, with an average of 42,432 per match, there were only 94,134 patrons at five Tests in 1884–85; 17,528 at two Tests in 1886–87; and just 1,971 spectators at the one Test played in the 1887–88 season. The February 1888 Test, planned to celebrate Sydney's and Australia's centenary, has the odious distinction of being by far the worst-attended Test in Australian cricket history. It is worth exploring the reasons for this.

The daily crowd figures show that this Test was affected badly by rain:

Date	*Crowd*
Friday, February 10	1,173
Saturday, February 11	No play
Monday, February 13	No play
Tuesday February 14	700
Wednesday, February 15	98
Total	1,971

Sydney had a downpour two nights before the game and it rained solidly during the next day so that the first-day uncovered wicket was very much in favour of the bowlers. On the first day England was bundled out for just 113 by Turner (5–44) and Ferris (4–60) but by stumps the innings of the home side had been reduced to disaster, 8–35. Australia's fate was sealed when the match resumed four days later: Australia was all out for 42, then England scored 137, which left 209 for the home side to win: by stumps they were 5–47. There was little public interest in the last day's play, which took just over an hour, despite a good innings of 25 not out by Blackham, scored when the pitch was at its worst.

However, there were deeper reasons — money and the administration of the game — which account for the decline of public interest in major cricket. When Shaw's team visited Australia in 1884–85 they found it difficult to arrange contests with full-strength local sides. The problem arose because the home players demanded half the proposed Test gate. The English professionals, 'who had travelled thousands of miles in pursuit of their profession', were outraged by the demands of the so-called amateurs playing in their home country. After much haggling a series of matches was organized eventually but the series victory for the visitors had a hollow ring because a number of leading colonial players refused to play against them. Some gave domestic and other personal reasons for staying out but they were not believed because, 'The real cause of this disturbance was money,' wrote Lillywhite, 'nothing but money!'

The next tour, the 1886–87 professional team of Shaw and Shrewsbury, also suffered because of a depleted home side. They won both Tests against an Australian side which lacked Scott and Bonnor, who had remained in England after the 1886 season, and Giffen, who had declined to play. The following season was a disastrous one because the cricket rivalries of Sydney and Melbourne resulted in two English teams touring at the same time; it was a 'prominent case of folly' as Lord Hawke put it. The fiasco arose because of a total lack of communication between the NSWCA and the MCC. The two tours resulted, wrote Tommy Horan, in a 'satiety in the public appetite for cricket'. There was also the problem, as Inglis has suggested, of 'too little mystique associated with the matches against England when the mother country was represented twice over'. Both tours lost money. The two visiting teams did join forces, on one occasion at least, for the lone Test at Sydney. Unfortunately Sydney–Melbourne differences manifested themselves even then: the home side lacked the Victorians Horan, Bruce and J. W. Trumble and South Australian Giffen.[26]

The crowd decline of the late 1880s provided a salutary lesson for administrators, they could not assume public support even for the most popular game in the country. The public demonstrated that it would desert cricket if there was too much cricket, or the formula was not right, and if the sides were unevenly matched. There are some interesting parallels between 1887–88 and 1978–79, the second season of World Series Cricket, when there were virtually five teams of international cricketers in the country at the same time and a surfeit of cricket. Many people believed then that international cricket, Tests in particular, were in danger from public over-exposure. Decline in the 1880s demonstrated that cricket, like any other form of popular culture, could have its troughs along with its peaks.

Tommy Horan believed that public disillusionment with Test cricket in the 1880s also affected crowds at other levels. While this is true, to some extent, it is also clear that intercolonial cricket was much less affected; the public retained some faith in the annual New South Wales vs Victoria clash still believing it to be a good contest. The January 1888 contest at the SCG handsomely outdrew the Test which was played two weeks later: there were 16,690 spectators at five days of the intercolonial game.

SCG crowd figures for the nine seasons from 1882–90 substantiate this trend: there was no significant decline in the New South Wales vs Victoria contest:

February 1882	22,252	(5 days)
February 1883	9,718	(2 days)
February 1884	13,752	(4 days)
February 1885	10,333	(4 days)
February 1886	23,580	(5 days)
February 1887	2,483	(2 days)
January 1888	16,690	(5 days)
January 1889	4,118	(4 days)
January 1890	17,167	(4 days)

Average per match:	13,344
Average per day:	3,431

However, there is no question that success at the top level of cricket rubs off on to the lower tiers of the game. When Lord Sheffield's team brought a revival of interest in international cricket, there was a comparable rise in intercolonial, or Sheffield Shield as it became, crowds. Ten seasons of New South Wales vs Victoria games at the SCG, from 1890–91 to 1900–01, attracted 263,393: an average of 26,340 per match and 5,853 per day.

CHAPTER TWO

The Patron on the Hill: Evil Barracker or Shrewd Shilling Spectator?

Expansion From The 1890s

The 1890s witnessed a resurgence of interest at all levels of cricket. The public imagination was captured by three successful tours, with teams led by Lord Sheffield in 1891–92 and A. E. Stoddart in 1894–95 and 1897–98, and with the introduction of the Sheffield Shield competition in 1892–93. Club cricket in Sydney, Melbourne and Adelaide was reorganized along electorate lines which enhanced its appeal. By linking a club with

A special enclosure for VIPS, including Lord Hopetoun and the Chief Commissioner of Railways, at the 1901 Sydney Test.

The crowd outside the *Age* office, 1896, waiting for scores to be posted from the Second Test, Manchester.

a suburb, cricket capitalized on the growth of suburbs: cricket and football clubs were an important means of establishing the identity of newly-emerging suburbs which developed along the train and tram tracks. Clubs before this time, such as Sydney's Albert, Belvidere and National clubs, had no suburban link or residential qualifications. By the late 1890s the Sydney Electorate Club of Glebe had recorded crowds of 10,000 on several occasions, at its home ground of Wentworth Park, and crowds in the thousands were commonplace at other ovals.

Such was the interest in the game that Tests not only drew good crowds but there were also several thousands who watched the *Sydney Morning Herald's* scoreboard, outside its King Street branch during the Fourth Test in the 1897–98 series which was played at Melbourne. New scores posted from time to time brought applause and there was a great deal of bantering between the majority who supported the home side and 'a good many supporters' who expressed sympathy for the Englishmen. Six years later there were almost as many people by the *Herald* scoreboard, by then moved to the corner of O'Connell and Hunter streets, as at the ground. Some 11,451 spectators attended the fourth day of the First Test at Sydney but an estimated 8–10,000 occupied all the available space in front of the *Herald* office and extended back along O'Connell and Hunter Streets for a considerable distance. Office boys who waved straw hats, carters, loud in their comments, rubbed shoulders with phlegmatic businessmen. When Trumper reached his century the 'great surging crowd roared its approval, drowning the rumble of lorries and cumbersome vans that now and again rolled along'. Long after stumps were drawn several thousand remained behind to analyse the day's play. Productivity must have been reduced drastically in the central business district of Sydney, and other major cities of the country which also had their scoreboards. This tradition has continued ever since as indicated by one 1983 Sydney Hill banner: 'Sorry, at the cricket, Boss.' It was likely that the boss himself was either watching the game from the Members' Stand or on television.

It is not known how frequently scores were telegraphed from one city to another to be posted up on newspaper or shop-front boards, but it is likely that the messages were frequent. When the ABC organized synthetic cricket, a simulated cricket broadcast based on cables, in the 1930s, it received cables from England and at the end of each over. Communications had certainly improved since the 1850s, when no telegraph existed: first news of the Victorian defeat at Sydney in 1857 was brought by the team days after the match.[1] The establishment of an inter-city telegraph link soon after enabled cricket news to travel much faster and to a much wider audience. Improvements in communications, notably radio and television in the twentieth century, played an important role in the establishment of a mass audience for the game.

It is significant that the revival of cricket took place against the backdrop of severe depression and a bank crash which affected the colonial economies for much of the 1890s. This suggests that hard times bring greater crowds to sport, and to popular entertainment in general providing entry charges are not too high. There are several possible reasons for this. Sport provides an escape from harsh economic realities. It is also true that in difficult times people turn back to and can gain consolation from their traditional cultural roots, such as the established and epic struggle against the mother country on the sporting field. Within the sporting arena there is no depression, or it is forgotten, as the spectator reaffirms his suburban, urban or national identity or attends the game simply as a diversion.

Cricket's advance in the 1890s was achieved in part because the game became more democratic and more 'Australian'. It was not that the patricians left the game — ladies and gentlemen were still to be found in the members' enclosures, and those who ran the game still came from the Establishment — it is rather that the plebeian presence became so numerous that it came to

Hats and canes were thrown into the air at the SCG in 1892 rather than cans. Note the crowd outside the *Herald* office waiting for scores to be posted.

Ladies and Gentlemen play cricket in the bush: Cooroy Show Grounds, Queensland.

dominate a large part of the game. The social impact was not lost on Prince Ranjitsinhji, 1897–98 tourist, who wrote of Australian grounds that, 'It seemed a pity that during the different intervals of the match the ladies were prohibited, *from want of space*, [italics mine] from promenading, as they do at Lord's and the Oval... a sight that is at all times attractive and picturesque.'[2] This comment was probably, and certainly still is, less true of Adelaide where the socially prominent, and members in general, can stroll behind the Members' Stand on beautifully manicured tennis-court lawns or enjoy strawberries and champagne under gaily coloured umbrellas. It is not known whether the patricians welcomed a greater plebian presence but after the crowd slump of the late 1880s officials appreciated that big cricket could not survive without a wider base.

Whatever the cause it had become cheaper to attend Test cricket by the 1890s by which time entry to the Outer was 1/- at all grounds — a price more within the pocket of the ordinary spectator. Along with this development came improved facilities in the Outer: graded mounds, hills, and even covered seating, such as Sydney's Bob Stand which had room for 4,000. By the 1890s the three Test centres also had turnstiles and the newspapers were provided, for the first time, with precise daily figures for paying and non-paying (members) customers. Clearly, administrators had become more number conscious. Prior to this time newspapers had given out rounded crowd estimates which varied considerably from paper to paper.

Large scoreboards were another important addition to Australian grounds which indicated further an official interest in the welfare of the ordinary patron. Before this, Australia had followed the English lead with printed scorecards, revised during the day, which amounted to an additional charge on the spectator. By 1896 the SCG had an Australian-style scoreboard, constructed by Ned Gregory, which was three metres high and 20 metres wide: it set out details of the fall of wickets, the figures of bowlers and scores of the batsmen at the crease together with those already dismissed. In fact it contained all the information that the now unused scoreboard, built further up the Hill in 1924, provided. Gregory's scoreboard also had another Australian touch: it listed 'sundries' rather than the English term 'extras'.

The MCG followed suit with a large four-columned board in 1895: two wings were then added to the existing board, which dated from the 1870s, and the entire structure was placed on top of a shelter. Unlike Sydney it retained the English term 'extras'. Melbourne added a more modern edifice in 1901 which became the No. 1 Board because the 1895 board was not dismantled until 1936 with the construction of the Southern Stand. The 1901 board was removed to Manuka Oval, Canberra, in 1981 when the MCG opted for a giant video matrix. The new scoreboard has proved popular but one wonders why this marvel of technology has reduced 'extras' to 'extra' given that extras often advance more rapidly than a batsman's score at the start of a match to-day.

Adelaide's first board was built in 1885 and was replaced in 1911 by one of the most beautiful and comprehensive edifices of its kind in the world. It not only lists all the information spectators might want to know about batsmen, bowlers and team totals but it also includes the names of the umpires, one of the few boards to do so. The building also has a clock, weather vane, flag poles and an attractive colonial-style verandah-enclosed bar, the 'boozer' as Ron Hamence called it, which has become a focal point for some of the louder and thirstier patrons. Only Hobart retained until 1983 a small English-style scoreboard which was classified by the National Trust. However, there is talk of replacing it now that an electric scoreboard has been built.

The capacities of Australian grounds were expanded in the

The Melbourne Cricket Ground Outer still had a rustic quality in 1900.

Ladies and Gentlemen promenade at Lord's during an interval, Second Test, 1909. Photograph by Frank Laver.

1890s in response to a growing public demand for the game. By that time the SCG was able to handle a cricket crowd of over 36,000 (36,222 attended in 1898), and a football crowd of over 50,000 in the next decade (52,000 saw New South Wales play New Zealand in 1907). A crowd of 32,000 turned up at a Melbourne Test in 1904 and 54,463 attended a Victorian Football League Final in 1912. English administrators, by comparison, were far less innovative partly because cricket and football were played at separate venues: they did not have the incentive and financial backing for ground expansion which was provided by fast-growing football in Australia. By 1900 Lord's could accommodate almost 30,000; the Oval could hold more than 25,000; and there were other grounds with capacities between 20–30,000. (Leeds ground may have been an exception because a crowd of between 35–40,000 turned up to watch the opening day of the match between the Australians and Yorkshire in June 1902.) Consequently England has had no Test crowd of over 40,000: the largest match total listed by *Wisden* was over 158,000 for the Fourth Test at Leeds in 1948; this represents an average figure of 31,600 per day.[3] It is also revealing that this Test lacks a precise match total which suggests that English officials may have been less number conscious and concerned with facilities for the ordinary person than their Australian counterparts. There was also no comparable move in England to replace old-

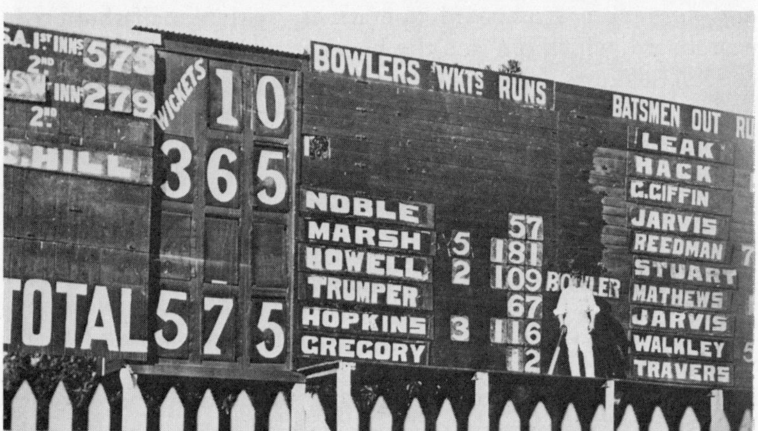

The evolution of scoreboards
Centre: The Adelaide scoreboard, 1893, South Australia vs New South Wales
Below: The Adelaide scoreboard, 1900, South Australia vs New South Wales featuring triple centurion, Clem Hill.

fashioned scoreboards — one has to buy a card to identify a player who is represented on the board by a number. No English ground has yet announced plans to install a video matrix though a temporary board was set up to provide replays for the 1983 Prudential Cup matches at the Oval.

The grand scale of early twentieth-century Australian cricket operations has left a legacy of problems in an age of escalating labour costs, particularly because many of the football co-tenants

The MCG ground staff and scoreboard, 1920. This more elaborate board operated from 1895–1936.

have since moved to their own grounds. It took six men, working at three floor levels, to operate the SCG scoreboard which operated until the 1983–84 season when it was superseded by a giant video matrix. It is also costly to operate the many turnstiles at the ground particularly with the advent of Sunday play in the 1960s with its higher labour costs. It was not surprising then that Sydney officials decided to close the Hill for Shield play in the 1982–83 season (which reduced both labour and cleaning costs) and to reduce scoreboard operations: with a half-shuttered scoreboard, which omitted the batsmen out, fall of wickets and the full fielding side, the SCG cut the board staff from six to three.

The Press also contributed to the democratization of Australian cricket in the 1890s. The 1890s and the 1900s witnessed a growth in Australian nationalism, and an important element of this spirit was the emergence of working-class sporting heroes, with whom the ordinary person could identify. Journalists such as W. F. Corbett in the *Referee* and the Sydney *Sun* consciously recognized this popular yearning for indigenous stars and helped to build up an heroic image for sportsmen and women, notably Victor Trumper in cricket, Dally Messenger in Rugby League, Les Darcy in boxing, the Cavills, Barney Kieran and Annette Kellerman in swimming, and many others.[4]

Among all the new stars no one was elevated more than Victor Trumper. The great reverence for the 'Immortal' (Jack Fingleton's phrase) Victor Trumper — for in Australian cricket writing he has been a saint, no more and no less — has made it difficult for historians (and no one has done it successfully yet) to convey some of the humanity of the man. Among other things he has been described as humble, self-effacing, loving, a person with an unchanging demeanour and someone loved by children. No one doubts that he was a most artistic, graceful and extraordinary batsman with immense personal charm and style but all accounts of him have a mythical and unreal quality. Professor Max Howell is now attempting to demythologize Trumper: he believes that the man who helped to found Rugby League and who was involved in the 1912 Board–player dispute was more hard-headed and far shrewder than previously thought, nor was he without failings: he could be stubborn, he had numerous rows with the authorities and, on one occasion, refused to play for his State when he was not made captain. However, no one can doubt the great crowd-drawing ability of the man especially when he put on such great performances as his 335 in 165 minutes at Redfern Oval during the 1902–03 season: there were about 10,000 at the ground, 20 deep everywhere, which meant that traffic had no chance of getting past. So many of Trumper's strokes landed on the adjacent bowling green that bowls play was suspended while the players lined the bank to watch him. No one could dispute that he was regarded with great reverence by Australian crowds.

An interesting comment on the appeal of Trumper to the Sydney crowd was made by Albert Knight, who toured Australia with Warner's 1903–04 team, and who was the most literary of all professionals and an active Christian: he used to stand for a moment in silent prayer after taking his guard, an action which Walter Brearley, Lancashire and England fast bowler, regarded as unfair and worth reporting to the MCC:

> Trumper they [the larrikins] may have misunderstood, but they loved him with the great love to which much is forgiven. Saint and savage and critic alike 'wondered with a foolish face of praise'. It was a rare and moving sight to look upon that crowd as it arose *en masse* to watch the ball strike the fence; to see those people standing in hushed expectation ere breaking into unrestrained delight. Never was the 'glow and glory of the game with the beautiful name' more freely scattered than by the charm of the incomparable master batsman.[5]

The Barracking 'Evil'

During the 1890s not only were the facilities transformed at various grounds but also Australian crowds became much less English in their behaviour, or perhaps the Hill, rather than the Members' enclosure, became the dominant feature of the Australian crowd. It was in the 1890s too that the Australian tradition of barracking came to the fore and the first-full scale debate took place on the 'evils' of barracking. Barracking, some used to think, was a football term dating from the 1880s. There are various theories about the origin of the word but there is no doubt that one of the word's usages remains uniquely Australian. The word 'to *barrack*, meaning to *jeer at or taunt*, has had a currency both inside and outside Australia but what is uniquely Australian is to *barrack for* in the sense of *support*.'[6] Cricket writer Philip Derriman argues that the tradition of barracking may have become popular first in Melbourne, however, 'barracking and barrackers have always found a more natural home in Sydney'.[7]

It is likely that the tradition of barracking pre-dated the word because banter at cricket — advice, sarcasm, wit — seems to be as old as the game itself in this country. With larger crowds, and a greater audience for the barracker, the practice became more extensive. By the early 1880s at least, barracking had become a concern of the Australian Press. The *Age* reported on 23 January 1883 an 'unpleasant feature' of the Second Test at the MCG was 'a cowardly attempt by a small knot of roughs to prevent Barnes catching Garrett, by jeering at the fieldsman as he was preparing for the catch'. The only consolation for the *Age* was that the 'unmanly behaviour' of 'these small-souled fellows' was far outweighed by the sporting behaviour of the majority who heartily cheered the visitors. More than a decade later the *Australian Cricket Annual* of 1895–96 deplored the increase in personal barracking over the previous few years which it described as 'regrettable, reprehensible and selfish'. This J. C. Davis-edited annual believed that barracking was sometimes prompted by partisan feelings but at other times by a 'sheer desire to be abusive'. The 1897–98 tour brought the barracking question to the front page of the sporting Press.

Reviewing the 1897–98 series on its completion, English captain, A. E. Stoddart, vented his anger on the Australian barracker and spoke at length on the 'evil of barracking' which he declared was 'no good to man or beast'. Stoddart had been a very popular figure on the previous tour and had handled spectator comments with aplomb but the strain of the 1897–98 tour, which brought out a tendency towards melancholia, coupled with the progressively worsening relationship between Ranjitsinhji and the local crowd and the Press, finally led to this outburst against the barracker. The English team, he contended, had met with jeering and hooting on all grounds and in every match of the tour, and even though they had been advised to take no notice of it when it occurred game after game he felt it his duty to speak out and deplore the lack of official action to curb it. Stoddart's idealistic solution was to appeal to the better nature of the barracker and he practised what he preached when he buttonholed one surprised Brisbane barracker who had hooted his own team. Stoddart recounted the conversation which was printed in the *Referee* of 9 March 1898:

> I... went up to him and said: 'Now, why did you hoot your own side?' He replied: 'Because they fielded badly.' Then I said: 'Do you consider that hooting them will make them field better?' He replied [with refreshing honesty and perhaps astonishment]: 'I don't know.' I talked to him very quietly and seriously for about ten minutes, during which he gazed at me and seemed to wonder what sort of person I was. At the end of the time he said 'he was damned if he would ever hoot them again.'

Unfortunately we do not have a record of this spectator's version of the encounter which might well be a revealing document. Stoddart added that colonial players themselves were 'as frequently the victims as the visitors': for example, in the New South Wales vs England game the barracking of T. W. Garrett, a fine sportsman, was considered 'disgraceful'. Stoddart also cited another unfortunate case of barracking when New South Wales batsman Donnan, normally immune to crowd comments, had been 'bustled out by the crowd'. Donnan himself later confirmed this fact.

The situation from Stoddart's point of view, worsened as the series progressed. During the Third Test at Adelaide there was a demonstration against Ranjitsinhji, reported the Adelaide *Observer* of 22 January 1898, which included hoots, hostile comments such as 'Get him out for a duck' and 'Bowl him, Jonah' [Ernie Jones], and some rude, personal and insulting remarks which were not repeated in the Press. The comments were felt very keenly by the prince though both he and Stoddart were quick to point out that they emanated from a small minority of the crowd.

Worse was to follow in the Melbourne Test. After an appeal from the English bowler and keeper for a catch behind was disallowed 'the crowd set to work and howled' at them even though the appeal 'was legitimate' because the batsman later admitted, so Stoddart contended, that he was out. Stoddart was further peeved, a little later, that when the Australian keeper appealed for a catch and unsportingly threw the ball high into the air before the umpire's verdict 'the crowd did not hoot Kelly' — which rather suggests that Stoddart believed that the barracking was more directed against the visitors than the home side. Cricket morality has changed so much since then that no one would ever quibble at Kelly's action to-day.

Finally in the last Test in Sydney the Englishman Hearne received a 'severe blow' batting against Jones at which the crowd in the pavilion laughed. After this Richardson bowled a full toss over Darling's head and the crowd 'howled'. Amongst the barrackers were three men who stood in front of the dressing-room; they were lectured by Stoddart who told them that they ought to be ashamed of themselves. Stoddart believed, at the time, that England was in a good position but that much depended on the bowling of Richardson. He was distressed that the crowd then set on Richardson: 'They hooted and howled at him to such an extent that when he came into lunch he had lost his head and his bowling.' There was no doubt in Stoddart's mind that the crowd played a very significant role in the subsequent English defeat.

The events at Adelaide are worth exploring in more detail because, unlike Sydney or Melbourne, Adelaide traditionally had a 'quiet crowd' where, as favourite son George Giffen put it, 'One does not hear one tithe [tenth] of the barracking which is indulged in Melbourne and Sydney.' No crowd disturbances had ever occurred at Adelaide. Yet even in this conservative city there was some barracking even before 1898 particularly when the popular idol 'Jonah' [Ernie Jones] was involved in the play. His appearance at the crease would bring a 'chorus of yells' which would also occur when a chance went his way. While the barracking was good-humoured Jones admitted to Giffen that crowd barracking could unnerve him. After grabbing a chance on the second attempt he complained: 'Do you know, George, I was nearly missing it. How can you expect a fellow to catch with a lot of small boys howling at him?'[8]

The barracking of Prince Ranjitsinhji in 1898 occurred because Ranji made some disparaging remarks about the local grounds and players — he questioned the action of Jones — and as the tour progressed his relations with the Press deteriorated. Ranji later complained that Press reports of his statements were exaggerated and taken out of context. Whatever the merits of the case, Ranji, in the minds of Adelaide people, had committed the cardinal sin of adopting a patronizing and lordly attitude to local cricket: Australian crowds have always been quick to cut any 'tall poppies' down to size and to pillory any Englishmen judged to have pretensions. Ranji was deeply hurt by his Adelaide reception and vowed never to play in that city again.

While Stoddart hoped to appeal to the better nature of barrackers, Ranji believed in a more drastic solution. 'Why not, then,' he later wrote, 'prevent a few — whether they be hundreds, scores, or tens — from making themselves a nuisance to both players and the spectators?' The *Referee* of 9 March 1898 spelt out the implications of this view when it stated that a seven-day stint in gaol was a more feasible solution to the barracking problem than any number of well-intentioned lectures.

After the series the Australian crowd came in for some stinging criticism from Surrey professional, Brockwell, who had toured Australia in 1894–95. While he admitted that the Australian crowd had its good points, 'the spectators are good critics and much of their banter is good-humoured', he concluded that, 'The Australian spectator is apparently overstrung, and as a consequence is impatient and intolerant.' An English crowd, on the other hand, took the game 'far more seriously' and it encouraged players by applause rather than putting them off with disconcerting banter. This was not the first occasion on which Brockwell had made an uncomplimentary remark about the Australian crowd. Long after a match had finished at Sydney during the 1894–95 tour and when a big crowd had lingered in the hope of gaining a glimpse of the players, Brockwell had, as David Frith noted, 'eyed the gathering with suspicion' and declared, 'It is a demonstrative, ribald crowd that, especially the boy section of it, has so much to say in a way that is personal that even a big man like Lyons won't face it alone.'[9]

It is surprising that most Australian players accepted and endorsed, admittedly in a much muted fashion, the English criticisms of the Australian crowd. For when the debate surfaced again, in 1911–12, prominent Australian players such as Clem Hill answered the English critics and defended the Australian barracker. In 1898 the only replies to Stoddart, Ranji and Brockwell came from one section of the Australian Press. The bulk of Australian cricket writers, however, supported Stoddart. The *Australian Cricket Annual* of 1897–98 endorsed Stoddart's comments and pointed out that, 'For some years Australian players have frequently, though quietly, complained of barracking.' Stoddart received further support from the leading colonial cricketers, George Giffen and Jack Lyons, and 'in a manner of speaking' by the Australian captain, Harry Trott himself. After Stoddart's press statement at the end of the series Trott's views were also reported in the *Referee* of 9 March 1898:

> I quite agree with Mr Stoddart's remarks about the crowd. They are a perfect nuisance. [Cheers] And yet we can't do without them. [Laughter] I think barracking should be stopped, and they could easily do it by sending a few private detectives among the crowd. They did it in Melbourne once and three men were taken to gaol. I think they got about a week, and there was no more barracking there for about six months.

There are a number of possible reasons why Australian players did not hurry to defend their crowds in 1898. One is that barracking was worse in 1898 than on subsequent tours. This, however, is an unlikely explanation, as we will see. A more likely explanation is that an English amateur captain, under considerable strain, and an Indian prince, totally unfamiliar with this tradition of public criticism, which could be abusive and vulgar, were less equipped to cope with the phenomenon of barracking than any subsequent English team which learnt, with experience, better ways of dealing with the Australian barracker. Stoddart became quite neurotic about Australian spectators and even allowed himself to become embroiled with a section of the Australian Press. The end result of the debate was that 'Mid On' writing in the *Age* accused Stoddart of making his criticisms 'out of the bitterness of defeat' — perhaps the first statement of the 'whingeing Pom' syndrome. It is also likely that Australian players were embarrassed by an over-sensitive English captain and an Indian prince and thought better of inflaming the situation. Perhaps, too, the limited defence of Australian crowds against the extreme comments made, represented a cultural cringe in cricket at this time.

The barracking 'evil' again surfaced as a major issue on the 1911–12 tour. There were a number of incidents in the New South Wales vs England match of late November. After being hit on the hand, later found to have been broken, Englishman George Gunn, noted the *Argus* of 1 December 1911, became the target of some 'raucous-voiced witticisms' as he soldiered on one-handed. Bill Hitch was also singled out for derision: his 'peculiar run before delivery' was greeted with 'roars of laughter'. Another Englishman, Foster, was jeered when he appealed for an lbw decision against Gregory. Barracking was, as usual, also directed against some of the home side: Barbour who took 30 minutes to score was the target of the crowd's satire.

This outbreak of barracking was denounced in a number of quarters. Early in the season, on 4 December 1911, the *Argus* deplored such 'American' behaviour and declared that the purchase of a ticket 'confers no right to make oneself a nuisance'. English captain, P. F. Warner, pointed out that cricket was a 'serious business' and that barracking was both unfair and unethical. The NSWCA was praised by the *Argus* of 1 December 1911 when it announced that it would attempt to 'evolve some scheme either to eradicate or minimise the evil, for it is an evil'. Meanwhile English batsman, Jack Hobbs, cabled back some critical comments on Australian crowds to a London paper. He later claimed that his views were simply 'intended as a more or less humorous pen-picture' but the Australian public thought otherwise. When Hobbs batted in the Third Test he was given a 'hot time' throughout the day — he batted all day for 187 to a backdrop of shouts such as 'Crying Englishman'. Hobbs tended to subscribe to the Brockwell view of Australian crowds and he wrote of them as 'thin-skinned' and 'inclined to be touchy'; but he learnt to live with them and even became a popular figure on later tours. In fact by the time of his fifth tour, in 1928–29, he had earnt the respect and affection of the Hillites who presented him with a gold-mounted boomerang and a wallet — full of money.[10]

The worst incidents occurred during the Second Test at Melbourne by which time the cricket authorities had declared war on the barracker; and the police had been issued with new orders to deal with the problem. On the Saturday of the Test, with the ground packed, the Englishman Barnes had bowled brilliantly for 90 minutes to dismiss four of the top home bats: at one stage he took four wickets for just one run. Towards the end of his spell, Barnes appealed for an lbw decision, whereupon the crowd, no doubt bitterly disappointed by the sudden collapse of the home side, erupted with cries of 'No, no.' Shortly after some of the Outer patrons took exception to the slow and deliberate manner in which Barnes set his field. A few hooted and one yelled, 'You're wasting time.' This was too much for Barnes who threw the ball to the ground and folded his arms. The hooting instantly became a roar.

Fortunately England had a shrewd captain in J. W. H. T. Douglas, who had some appreciation of Australian crowd psychology and, in this instance, instructed Barnes to get on with the job of bowling. Douglas was immensely popular in Australia because the more he was barracked — and when he took three hours to score 33 runs against Victoria his initials were declared to stand for 'Johnny Won't Hit To-day' — the more he smiled or waved at the crowd. All irritation vanished and the crowd responded with shouts of 'good old Johnny'. Douglas, unlike

Stoddart, understood that Australian crowds wanted to be recognized and responded to, and that the cardinal sin was to appear superior by ignoring them. Douglas helped further to defuse the Barnes incident by his tactful post-game comments reported in the *Advertiser* of 3 January 1912. He stated that, 'Some of the hooligans had become rowdy, but the Englishmen did not regard the matter seriously.'

There were now two quite divergent patterns of response to barracking. Some players let it affect them: Richardson in 1898, and Barnes in 1912. Bill Hitch was another sensitive player. During the match against Victoria Hitch was struggling to gain a wicket. After the crowd comments, 'He's no good' and 'Give him his passage-money home', Hitch all but lost his temper. However, as Hobbs put it, 'It does not pay to be touchy', and it is advisable to 'keep cool and take no notice' for 'if you keep cheery you are all right; but if you show the slightest temper they rub it in.'[11]

Commentators and authorities were equally divided about the so-called barracking menace. The Australian Cricket Board announced its determination to rid the game of the evil and was applauded by many papers in England and Australia. A number of veteran English players described the practice as a blight, but some others defended the Australian crowd. In 1906 Albert Knight questioned the 'nasty things' which had been written about Sydney larrikins. He said of them, 'Sarcastic and severe maybe, but delightfully impartial are the Sydney larrikins . . . they are far too cynical to be intensely bigoted, or what is much the same thing, intensely patriotic.' English wicket-keeper, A. A. Lilley, writing in 1912, endorsed this view: he stressed the impartiality of the barracker and praised the Australian crowd as 'thoroughly sportsmanlike'. He felt that most of the criticisms were done in 'good humour'.[12]

The strongest defence of the Australian crowds came from Clem Hill who took Hobbs to task for his published comments. The *Referee* of 10 January 1912 reported that Hill believed the Melbourne barracking was essentially 'good-humoured' and was not intended to be hostile to any players. While Hill could appreciate that Barnes might find the situation a 'little annoying', Hill claimed that Australian crowds in 1912 were 'as well behaved' as at any time during the past twenty years. Hill added that objectionable comments came only from a very small section and the removal of one or two persons would easily solve the problem.

P. R. Le Couteur, a former representative for Oxford University and his home state of Victoria, reviewed the debate in the *Referee* of 2 January 1912 and, made some perceptive comments about Australian crowds and the English and Australian perceptions of barracking. He pointed out that the very word barracking had taken on quite different meanings in the two countries. A man is said to barrack in Australia when he cheers on his own side, but in England, he barracks only if he cheers on his side 'with obviously disagreeable intentions towards the other side'. The word in England had come to mean 'gibing, in the nasty, objectionable sense'.

Behind these two perceptions was a fundamental difference of opinion about the role of a crowd at a cricket match: 'An English cricket crowd rather gives one the impression that it has come to see a spectacle, and be entertained. An Australian crowd has come to play,' wrote Le Couteur. He added further that comments such as 'Get a bag', which always followed a dropped catch, did not represent an expression of ill-will but rather arose out of a sense of disappointment coupled with a sense of humour. H. V. Hordern, who played for Australia in 1911–12, developed a similar point: 'The cricketer plays for pure sport and the honour of representing his country, whereas the Hillite pays his good money and not only wants but demands the best.'[13] Barracking, in this sense, was often a display of resentment that spectators were not getting the best. However, the Australian crowd, as Le Couteur further maintained, was 'essentially humorous' which was an Australian reaction to an often impossible situation. On a broiling hot day, with a hard ground, the bowlers and fieldsmen tired, and the visiting batsmen triumphant, a lull in play would bring out again a well-worn joke, to 'put the umpires on' which was 'always funny'. This was a characteristic of the Australian crowd and its humour. Le Couteur advised, 'a player must obviously laugh with it — if he is humorous he cannot help himself — but he is merely foolish if he allows himself to be annoyed.'

Le Couteur's views help to explain the intensity of the barracking debate. Englishmen, particularly some middle-class amateurs, could not fathom Australian humour with its earthy, droll and self-deprecating character — it was totally alien to them, which is not surprising given the class, educational and cultural gulf between the world of the English amateur and the Australian Outer patron. Some Englishmen only made the situation worse for themselves for by taking such comments to heart they were setting themselves up, even further, as the butt of colonial satire.

While Australian cricket has produced many original gems of barracking wit, and some celebrated and original characters, it is also true that much of the crowd humour is copied and derives its impact from the action of the game; the timing of the comment is of the essence. Comments such as 'Arrest that man for loitering!' (to a slow batsman), 'Put the umpires on' (when the home bowlers are being thrashed) and 'Give him his passage-money home' (made to a frustrated tourist) must have been repeated many times in later matches. One of the enduring comments, 'Get a bag', dates back at least to 1899 according to Philip Derriman and was heard regularly for sixty years. Even older was the commonest cry at Australian grounds, 'Have a go, you mug' or, more frequently, ''Ave a go, yer mug' which went back at least to 1880 and retained prominence until the 1960s. Both expressions have now gone out of fashion to some extent but ''Ave a go' can still be heard around the country.

A few other remarks have become dated more quickly such as the pre-1914 shout, 'Go home to Mother.' However, for the most part, there is a great continuity in cricket comments. During the 1950s, for instance, Les Favell spent a difficult twenty minutes before tea trying to put bat to ball and was informed that he could not even play a piano. More than twenty years later Graham Yallop was struggling to come to terms with Dennis Lillee at the MCG and a spectator advised Lillee to bowl down a piano and to see if he could play that.

Smashed Bottles and Rain-Related Disturbances

Barracking was not the only crowd problem in the two decades before 1914: disturbances continued to plague cricket. A number resulted from interruptions due to rain. During the Second Test at Sydney in 1892 players left the ground on several occasions due to rain. On both occasions the crowd hooted the players and after the second break 'several rough-looking characters jumped over the fence' but left the ground quickly when the police arrived. A more serious disturbance occurred at a 1903 Shield match at the MCG when light drizzling rain prevented play for almost four hours. By mid-afternoon the 14,000-strong crowd had become fed up and after 'hooting' and 'groaning' for some time several hundred youths jumped the fence and rushed the wicket: 'the

Bottles were smashed on this ashphalt cycle track which existed at the SCG in 1904.

first youth to reach the pitch pulled up the stumps at the railway end, and one venturesome individual deliberately dug his heels into the pitch.' The youths, the *Age* of 29 December 1903 commented, could have been easily stopped if a couple of policemen had gone out to meet them, for when the police finally arrived a little later, the youths quickly dispersed. Play finally began at 3.20 p.m. but the big crowd witnessed only 20 minutes' play before the rain set in again.

Just five days later Melbourne had another rain incident on the second day of the Test, 2 January 1904. Rain again prevented play before lunch but this time play did start at 1.15 p.m. and lasted until 4 p.m. when bad weather set in again. At about 5.30 p.m. a couple of men jumped the fence and headed out to the pitch but this time the authorities were well prepared and 16 policemen headed out to the centre to meet the intruders and then escorted them back to their seats.

The Fourth Test at Sydney brought the worst rain incident of the series. The scenario was familiar. A large crowd of almost 35,000 did not appreciate two breaks in play (for ten and eighty minutes) due to a very light drizzle. During the second break spectators threw watermelon skins and bottles, and some of the latter smashed on the asphalt cycle track which at that time circled the SCG perimeter. It started as a humorous diversion, according to Sir William McKell, a regular Hill spectator from his youth and occasionally in his maturity, when one spectator rolled a bottle down the bicycle track and some time after it was removed by an attendant. Shortly after another bottle was rolled down the track and, after it too was removed, the crowd sensed that it could make some fun out of the situation, and the trickle became a torrent. The ground staff continued to remove the debris but as their actions only created more rubbish they wisely retreated. McKell believes that there was no malice in the crowd action which was perhaps a way of making some entertainment out of a disappointing day. Some English scribes and players, he added, with an eye more to good copy rather than facts later made a 'great fuss' about an ugly bottle-smashing incident. Perhaps one local paper too wanted to gain some reader attention when it suggested that the police arrived just in time to prevent another invasion of the ground.

The worst demonstration of the whole series had nothing to do with rain. It took place earlier in the season when Clem Hill was adjudged run out by umpire Crockett on the fourth day of the First Test at the SCG. It happened just after tea when Hill and Trumper were well set in an important rearguard stand to stave off defeat. The trouble began when Hill, without uttering a word of protest, conveyed to the crowd by his 'heavy looks' and walk back that the umpire had made a mistake. Immediately the crowd began to chant 'Crock, Crock, Crock', which some observers thought sounded like 'Crook, crook, crook'. Abuse was hurled at Crockett and continued for the rest of the day: comments included, 'How much did you pay Crockett, Warner?', 'Have you

No women were to be seen in this area of the Members' enclosure at the MCG in 1904 presumably because it was a Smokers' area. Note the awnings to shelter the crowd in front of the stands.

got your coffin ready, Crockett?', 'Which gate are you leaving by, Crockett?' and one waggish and very Australian piece of advice that Crockett 'should stand for the Senate'. The din was so deafening that play was held up for some time. The English captain, Warner, later claimed that the demonstration 'started' in the Members' Pavilion and added that when Crockett left the ground at stumps, escorted by two detectives, he was hooted more fiercely than ever by some members. Some other members, disassociated themselves from the protest and applauded the umpire loudly. However, Warner was no apologist for the Hill for it was after this tour that he wrote his celebrated and 'probably only half joking' comment that he could amost envisage the British Army being called in to protect the players from the crowd on the Hill who were 'armed to the teeth with umbrellas, bottles, melon-skins and rude language'. He added that the troops would need a battery of Maxim guns to 'sweep the hill on the Sydney ground, whence in the past so many onslaughts on the players and umpires have issued'.[14]

It was not clear whether the two disturbances in Sydney were liquor-related but one report after the Crockett incident implied that drink might have been a factor. The crowd had swelled after lunch and 'empty bottles rolled wonderingly down the slope, impelled by the feet of spectators on the Hill. Black bottles most of them were, and they smelt not of milk', noted the *Sydney Morning Herald* of 16 December 1903. Possibly then the bottle-smashing incident of the Fourth Test is one of the first drink-related cricket disturbances.

District and club cricket usually mirror senior cricket so it is not surprising to find crowd violence at other levels of the game. Two were described in the *Argus* of 3 and 4 December 1914. Umpire Crockett was again the centre of an incident: this time he incurred the wrath of North Melbourne supporters when he no-balled their opening bowler three times in the first over in a 1914 match against Fitzroy at the North Melbourne home ground. After this the crowd became 'excited and angry' and abused him throughout the afternoon. In the same year a fight broke out at Mayor's Park, Clifton Hill, Melbourne, where several matches of junior cricket were in progress. During the mêlée the Secretary of the Clifton Hill Cricket Club was punched and knocked down and a policeman, who intervened, was 'followed by a crowd of shouting hoodlums, and was jostled and kicked to such an extent [that he] hardly knew where he was'. Three youths were convicted at Collingwood Court and fined a total of £50.

English Crowds

While it is true that pre-1914 Australian crowds were often unruly and violent, such disturbances need to be placed in perspective. Australia had no monopoly on cricket unrest: England too had its demonstrations and abandoned games — a fact which many critics of colonial crowds often conveniently overlooked. Hugh Trumble recalled that a lame Joe Darling, suffering from a bruised heel, was once batting very cautiously at Lord's and even this conservative crowd made its feelings evident: someone started to whistle 'Poor Old Joe' which was taken up around the ground; it was followed by 'We Won't Go Home Till Morning' and then the 'Dead March' from *Saul.* Frank Laver also wrote of the bedlam which broke out when Essex beat the Australians in 1899: 'The ground became covered with surging mass of howling humanity [and people] threw their hats in the air, cheered and yelled and cheered again.'[15]

Historians Wray Vamplew and Keith Sandiford have analysed sporting crowd disorder in Britain from 1840–1914 and found many examples of cricket disturbances though they also suggest that cricket disorder was comparatively rare and that cricket crowds behaved themselves better than soccer or horse-racing crowds. However, during a game at Lord's in the 1860s between Eton and Harrow play was abandoned after a clash between supporters. 'The disorder was precipitated by a spectator fielding the ball, throwing it to an Harrovian fielder who then ran out the Etonian batsman who had stopped running on the assumption that the umpire would have indicated a dead ball. When the umpire gave the batter out the playing area was filled with a seething mass disputing or supporting the decision according to their colours. So acrimonious was the temper of the crowd that stumps were drawn.' Another infamous event took place at the annual university fixture between Cambridge and Oxford at Lord's in 1896: it was made possible by a rule at the time which made following-on compulsory for any side more than one

CRICKET.

FINAL TEST MATCH.

25th FEBRUARY, 1898.

ENGLAND V. AUSTRALIA.

PICK THE RESULT AND WIN THE

WOLFE'S SCHNAPPS, £50.

The Proprietors of Wolfe's Schnapps will present the sum of £50 (Fifty Pounds sterling) to the person who gives the result (as per coupon in this advertisement) of the Final Test Match between England and Australia, to commence in Sydney on February 25, 1898. Should no one give the actual result, the person who guesses

NEAREST WILL RECEIVE THE WOLFE'S SCHNAPPS £50

presentation. If more than one person becomes entitled to the prize the amount, £50, will be divided proportionately amongst the lucky guessers.

COUPON.

I SELECT THE .... TEAM TO WIN THE

FIFTH AND FINAL TEST MATCH BY .... INNINGS,

.... WICKETS, ... RUNS.

FULL NAME ....

ADDRESS ....

....

Selections must be written plainly on the above coupon, with the full name and address of sender, and THE WHOLE OF THIS ADVERTISEMENT CUT OUT from the Sydney Morning Herald AND FORWARDED so as to reach us not later than the 18th FEBRUARY, 1898. Coupons will not be considered if received after that date. All envelopes must be properly stamped: outside Sydney, 2d; Sydney and suburban radius, 1d; and must be marked "WOLFE'S SCHNAPPS £50," and be addressed to the

SOLE AGENTS FOR WOLFE'S SCHNAPPS—

M. MOSS AND CO.,

WYNYARD-LANE, SYDNEY, NEW SOUTH WALES.

All the results will be sealed before the match commences, and deposited with the Manager of the Sydney Daily Telegraph, who has kindly consented to hold them during its continuation.

Commercialism, 1898 style.

hundred runs behind on the first innings which meant that a team which had performed well in dismissing its opponents were forced to bowl again and possibly be penalized by having to bat last on a crumbling wicket. In order to avoid this the Cambridge captain gave away 12 runs, three balls were bowled straight to the boundary, which put Oxford fewer than 100 runs behind. The result was a 'very hostile' demonstration with 'angry scenes' in the pavilion during which many members lost 'all control of themselves'.[16]

In his article on English cricket crowds Sandiford also refers to a rare occasion when a crowd became upset by 'improper conduct' of players such as the uproar which resulted when E. M. Grace, the champion's brother, dislodged a tenacious Henry Jupp with a high underhand full toss which sailed over the batsman's head and fell on the bails. Because such tactics were considered 'underhand and ignoble', the situation grew 'somewhat tense'. Sandiford also mentions a number of instances in the late 1870s when ground facilities were inadequate for the crowd which turned up, causing play to be stopped when spectators encroached on the field and leading, on one occasion, to a 'raid on the reserved seats'.

Many believed that there was a marked decline in the behaviour of English cricket crowds in the 1890s which included increased hooting, yelling at mistakes on the field and the practice of 'guying' at slow play. Vamplew believes that it was caused by time-wasting, poor facilities and a general official failure to come to terms with the wishes of the spectator. Possibly, too, it was due, as it was in Australia, to a greater plebeian presence at the game for English cricket writer, E. H. D. Sewell, blamed the Press for 'endeavouring to encourage the football element [the working class?] among spectators at our crickets grounds'.[17] The same comment continues to be made to-day although it is now directed more against the one-day crowd.

There was always a significant difference in England between the more working-class crowds of the industrial north and the more conservative crowds of the south. The former barracked players in much the same way as Australian crowds. It is Bill O'Reilly's belief that players from the south of England have always had much more trouble adjusting to Australian crowds than, for instance, Yorkshiremen.

Shrewd Shilling Spectators

The vast majority of the Hill patrons were neither violent nor objectionable. We know this because all the major newspapers from about 1900 on carried regular and detailed features on the Outer crowd, usually at the time of a Test. This in itself represented a significant change in the media accounts of the crowd because in the 1870s and 1880s the papers were rather more dominated by the comings and goings of the more fashionable crowd in the stand. There were a number of reasons for this change. It reflected not only the greater plebian presence at the game but also a belief that the Hill was the most colourful, interesting and above all most Australian element of the crowd. By this time the subject of Australian identity had been a matter of interest to both the Australian Press and the public.

The Adelaide *Advertiser* of 3 January 1908 began its discussion of the 'shrewd shilling spectators' by contrasting them favourably with the pavilion crowd. It believed that a number of ladies in the grandstand turned up 'to display a new frock or to criticise Mrs So-and-so's new hat' and that much of the feminine pavilion talk was 'fashion and scandal'. Nor did all the gentlemen devote their primary attention to the cricket: there were a number 'whose greatest wish is to take someone else's sister down to afternoon tea'.

By contrast the more philosophical watchers on the southern mound, near the scoreboard, didn't miss much because every ball was watched and discussed and they exhibited great patience as they were grilled all day by a blazing sun. 'The hum of talk subsides as the bowler runs to the crease, and a breathless moment follows as the ball flies down to the wicket only to be broken by cheers if a boundary is scored or an English wicket

The link between cricket and tobacco was not contentious in 1911.

taken.' It was on the southern mound that every person was 'brimming over with cricket information' and 'any titbit' passed from end to end of the mound with the greatest speed. The *Advertiser* quoted with some pride the rather more positive statement of P. F. Warner that, 'The Australian crowd knows more about cricket than any other crowd on earth.' This new-found pride in the Hill, rather than the stand, patron was a revealing development in attitudes towards crowds and the further emergence of an Australian nationalism in sport.

Ladies were not merely spectators in 1911. The Memerambi (Queensland) Ladies Team — 1911.

Such was the Hill spectator's concentration on the game that anyone who might pause on the path, and obstruct a view, was quickly advised to 'Git off the earth', or 'Move along sonny, or sit down', or informed, 'You ain't a window.' The shilling crowd revered past and present cricketers. 'That's John Hill Clem's father,' a boy once pointed out to the reporter on the Hill. 'The old man was the first to score 100 on this oval.'

Melbourne and Sydney papers made similar comments about their Outer patrons although there were some differences from ground to ground and paper to paper. The Outer crowd at the MCG, the *Argus* of 1 January 1912 reported, was almost 'entirely men and boys', ladies were 'as few among the outside crowd as daisies on a well-trimmed lawn'. Nine-tenths of the outer crowd carried brief-bags or kit-bags or brown paper parcels with their lunch and a bottle. Hundreds of scorebooks were evident and the keenest spectators could be observed keeping score. Early arrivals bought or brought magazines and buried their heads in them while waiting for the game to begin. Men staggered on to the ground carrying great loads of old issues of illustrated London papers and yelled: 'Here y'are. The best London literatoor by the greatest living writers. Only a penny each.' Many spectators never left their seats despite a fierce sun: the only concession to the weather was a handkerchief under the hat to protect the neck. It was not surprising that such stoic watchers of the game resented a short interruption to play due to a few drops of rain. The umpire was often asked, 'Why didn't yer bring yer umbrella with yer?'

On January 2 1912 the same paper contained a description of the grandstand crowd and a feature on 'Women at Cricket', a subject of perennial interest to journalists as it enabled them to add a certain amount of colour and humour to crowd stories. Perhaps indicative of a change in the female section of the crowd, but possibly also reflecting a change in the media perception of women at cricket, the *Argus* stated that there was 'one type' of woman, the 'lady enthusiast', who had a thorough knowledge of the game: some of them 'can keep scores, and they can interpret the signals from the umpires [so that] there can be no doubt that their brothers play cricket, and that they sometimes play with their brothers.' Perhaps some were even among cricket's first groupies: the writer of the article went on to state that the ladies knew the players by their first names and sat in a position in the stand where the players passed 'directly beneath them as they proceeded on to the ground'. As they came in or went out they might have observed these ladies 'with their bashful heads bent'.

On the other hand there was another 'type' according to the *Argus*: there were also hundreds of women who 'went to see people and to see how they dressed'. The holidays, the paper added, attracted the 'celebrity-watchers', though both male and female. There was also one young lady at the 1912 Test, who sat under the awning in front of the public grandstand, who read a novel and 'never raised her eyes' when Hearne was dismissed after a celebrated innings of 114 and was cheered all the way to the pavilion. However, the *Argus* could not resist the popular Australian pastime of satirizing the female spectator. There was a lady from the country, it added, who protested loudly, 'Of course, I understand cricket... At home I used to go to all the matches. I helped to make afternoon tea for the players!' Such comments fitted in with the popular male belief that the finer points of the inscrutable game of cricket were, and always would

A segregated crowd at the SCG in December 1901: the majority of spectators in the Ladies' Reserve (in front of the Ladies' Stand) were women.

be, incomprehensible to women; the persons who subscribed to this view also contended that the mysteries of the English game were unfathomable to a German or a Frenchman.

It was said, in two *Sydney Morning Herald* features on the Hill on 5 and 16 January 1903, that the best place to watch cricket at the SCG was behind the bowler on the southern side, that is, if one was a critic. Many patrons there were regulars, as were some of the characters who acquired nicknames and built up reputations; they were instantly recognized and acclaimed as they filed in. 'There's Johnny the scaler,' a Hillite was heard to call out, 'as a well-dressed chap with a general appearance of prosperity walked along the path.' Johnny was greeted by a few 'derogatory remarks' about his personal appearance from a group 'to whom he was known', but he walked on 'imperturbably'.

The Sydney Hill was no respecter of persons and status. At one stage a 'jovial, red-faced clean-shaven minister' outraged a section of the Hill when he paused on the path oblivious to the fact that his very large umbrella which was shielding his face from the sun, obstructed the view of a number of persons. 'The roar behind him gathered in intensity' and a number of sarcastic comments filled the air: 'You wouldn't think the sun could burn him, by his face', and 'He oughtn't to be afraid of the 'eat.' The cleric only became aware of the situation when a 'small shower' struck his umbrella. He then looked round, 'moved on gracefully', and received the applause of the crowd which indicated that the tough-minded Hill could forgive also.

On another occasion two sailors obstructed the view of a large group of spectators and were advised, 'Full steam ahead and drop anchor on the grass.' They knew that they must obey the Hill because 'everybody obeys the crowd on the Hill when its requests are reasonable'. Earlier in the day a young man from the country paused in front of the Hill and peered into the crowd as if looking for a friend. The comment, 'Hullo! Lookin' for cows', brought a roar of laughter and the embarrassed youth moved on.

The occupants of the Hill knew their players and always addressed them in personal, and even affectionate terms. Bill Howell was referred to as 'Billowell' or 'Blowell' by the Hillites. Monty Noble, a much-respected captain and enforcer of discipline, was always referred to by his nickname 'Mary-Ann'.

A small happening could greatly interest the crowd during a slow passage of play for on such occasions the crowd created its own entertainment as it did, to a lesser extent, throughout the day. During one Test at the SCG a straw hat was blown off a spectator's head and 'bowled merrily along on its rim for a hundred of yards or so' before one of the Englishmen fielded it, to ringing applause. As the hat was bowling along one of the wittiest comments of the day was made: 'Look at the donkey's breakfast training to race Major Taylor.' Such comments were remembered, and retold time and time again, and embellished in the bar, long after the batsmen, the bowlers and the scores of the day — the 'real play' — were forgotten. The patrons on the Hill could enjoy the drama on both sides of the fence and the interplay between the chorus (the Hill) and the performers.

Sydney vs Melbourne Rivalry

Another symptom of changing official and media attitudes towards the crowd was that more attention was paid to the quantity as distinct from the quality, of the assembly. Records, for instance, were given more prominence in the Press.

During the 1890s and 1900s matches in Sydney and Melbourne drew comparable crowds. Melbourne produced a Test match total crowd of over 90,000 (newspaper figures varied between 92,659 and 95,023) in 1895 which was eclipsed by a Sydney figure of 96,339 in 1903. In the New Year Test of 1912 Melbourne found an additional 116 spectators (96,455) to wrest back the crown. Given the keen inter-city rivalry which existed then, and still continues to this day, it was natural that officials and the Press in each centre should gloat when the record of the rival city fell. The moment could be savoured because it could be announced not just as an Australian but as a world cricket record.

While most of the match and series records were claimed by Melbourne by 1914, Sydney remained superior to its southern rival in terms of daily Test crowds. Perhaps the capacity of the SCG was larger then than the MCG's. The six highest daily figures were all recorded at the SCG:

Daily Test Crowd Records before 1914 (all vs England)

37,997	15 February 1902 (SCG)
36,222	26 February 1898 (SCG)
35,526	16 December 1911 (SCG)
35,499	12 December 1903 (SCG)
34,606	27 February 1904 (SCG)
34,167	14 December 1901 (SCG)
32,000	1 January 1904 (MCG)
31,750	10 February 1912 (MCG)
31,453	1 January 1912 (MCG)

Melbourne enjoyed a marginal superiority over Sydney with Sheffield Shield crowds. In the 22 seasons from 1892–1915 Melbourne had a season average total of 44,228 compared with 38,859 at Sydney.

Sydney could compete with Melbourne by the turn of the century because much of the city's population lived close to the ground and Sydney's transport was adequate to move crowds of more than 30,000. However, with the suburban sprawl later in the twentieth century, the comparative disadvantages of the SCG location in relation to public transport and, later, parking facilities and the supporting road network became more and more apparent. The MCG, on the other hand, was ideally placed at the hub of the city transport system and road network — a point proudly featured in the *Members' Handbook*, which is issued to all new members:

> No major stadium in the world is better situated than the MCG to promote sport and to serve its community in terms of easy access, comfort, shelter and overall accommodation.
>
> The MCG is within 15 minutes' walking distance of the city centre, has two adjacent railway stations and tramway links with all suburbs. The surrounding parkland accommodates 12,000 vehicles; crowds in excess of 100,000 are cleared from the ground within 14 minutes.

The Challenge from Football

Cricket crowds were not the only sporting assemblies to grow after 1900, there was an even more spectacular expansion in football crowds. In fact football crowds rapidly re-wrote the cricket records of the 1890s: the SCG had a rugby crowd of 52,000 in 1907 (New South Wales vs New Zealand) which was bettered by the 1912 VFL Final crowd of 54,463. This development had a number of implications for cricket. VFL crowds were, as we will see, a significant factor which led to improved facilities and an expanded capacity for the MCG after the First World War. Cricket officials, too, had reason to ponder why the hitherto-most popular team sport in the country was in danger of losing its dominance even though the winter codes did not compete in any direct sense. No one has yet explained why football crowds overtook cricket ones at this time but it is clear that football clubs were closely tied to the newly emerging suburbs which were spreading out along the tram and train tracks, and played a part in developing each suburb's identity. Of course cricket clubs did too. Possibly also cricket was still regarded by some as an English, fashionable and cerebral game, run by the middle class — as indeed it was — whereas there was no question that football was more easily understood and had more roots with the working class. With its shorter time span, and more convenient time of play (Saturday afternoon) and rules which were easier to understand it could count on a much greater audience. Some codes, notably Rugby League, were more democratic in leadership and epitomized working-class values. While cricket closed up shop during the war and put its weight behind the war effort, Rugby League officials and supporters made strenuous efforts to continue competition.

However, there's no question that there were deeper reasons for cricket's eclipse by football because it was a pattern which was repeated in England: in fact it was far more dramatic there. While there was limited growth in cricket crowds in the last decades of the nineteenth century, the F.A. Cup Final crowd increased, for instance, from only 2,000 in 1872 to 112,000 in 1901 which was above five times the normal (daily) Test crowds. Sandiford argues convincingly that soccer's advance in this period was due to greater enterprise, initiative and marketing of the game particularly to the urban working class. Cricket officials by comparison were less willing to modernize the game, to alter

The crowd at the SCG at the Fourth Test, February 1895. Note the awning which covered the Outer crowd where the Bob Stand was soon to be constructed. The Paddington terraces were yet to be obscured by stands.

the rules and to make it more accessible to the public by changing match times. Sandiford concludes that:

> By refusing to tamper with the traditional rules and tools of the game, the Victorians preserved Georgian cricket in a more or less mummified form. It thus became a somewhat quaint and rustic anomaly in a highly urbanized age. It remained too much a leisurely and protracted affair geared to meet the needs of pre-industrial gentlemen-farmers. This reactionary approach on the part of cricket's administrators was accompanied by an almost dogged refusal of the leading county cricket club committees to sell the game to the rising urban proletariat as aggressively and as effectively as the first division soccer clubs so obviously did.[18]

Australian officials were probably less reactionary than their English counterparts: after all they built more modern scoreboards and provided better facilities for Outer patrons. However, on more substantive issues relating to the format and the presentation of the game, there was limited change in Australia. In fact it was not until the late 1970s that there was a concerted attempt to market cricket aggressively and to compete with football and alternative sports by placing a much higher premium on 'attacking strategies' and the 'explosive excitement' of a football game, and by completing an entire game within a single day.

Whatever the reasons for the rise of football crowds, it is clear that while club cricket continued to attract its thousands, football club followers had now begun to be numbered in the tens of thousands.

However, despite the greater increase in football crowds in the two decades prior to the Great War, this was also an expansionary period for cricket crowds and a formative period in the development of a uniquely Australian tradition of behaviour. It was in this period that the more ordinary spectators made their presence felt — a presence which left a lasting imprint on the game.

CHAPTER THREE

Bumper Well-Behaved Crowds Between The Wars

Record Crowds

The 1920s and the 1930s witnessed spectacular growth in cricket crowds. Mammoth attendances were recorded at all levels of cricket; almost all the Test and Shield records date from this period. In fact most of these records, such as the 350,534 who attended the Third Test at the MCG in 1937, and the 89,386 who turned up for the New South Wales vs Victoria clash at the MCG in the December–January 1923–24 holiday period, are unlikely ever to be broken. Record daily totals at Sydney (58,446 in 1928), Adelaide (50,962 in 1933) and Brisbane (30,598 in 1936) will never be surpassed because the ground capacities have since been reduced. The only record to fall in recent decades was the Test daily total: the 1937 MCG total of 87,798 was bettered in 1961 when 90,800 came to that ground.

The Shield competition was also well patronized between the wars and on six separate occasions crowds passed 30,000. The 1920s and 1930s were undoubtedly the heyday of cricket crowds even though crowds in earlier times may have been larger in per capita terms as a proportion of a city population. The population increase between 1900 and 1930 of 2.7 million was more than adequately reflected at the cricket ground.

The war, more than any other factor, created a leisure boom. The work of war had been constant and onerous and so it was not surprising that after the hostilities ended, Australian society, which had had the 'stuffing knocked out of it' and had been wracked with serious political crises, craved for some light entertainment and embraced, among other things, Hollywood's escapist fare and rediscovered the popular traditional pastime of watching cricket. When Test cricket was resumed in 1920–21 it was the first series for nine seasons, and from 1915–19 the public had gone without Shield cricket.

War also helped to loosen social bonds and change attitudes. Women, who had played a significant role in war work, were just as keen as men to demand their leisure rights. They became enthusiastic movie-goers and constituted a majority of the audience by the late 1920s. This trend was also reflected in cricket crowds. Test players of this era claim that women made up between 30–40 per cent of the grandstand Test crowd by the

1930s. Although there are no official estimates of the number of women in pre–1914 crowds general comments suggest that it was probably less than 30 per cent. What is clear, however, is that the women who flocked to cricket by the 1930s were not just socialites, there were many ordinary women to be seen at the game. Jack Badcock observed one such woman at a Test in the 1930s; she was sitting in the stand during the afternoon sessions shelling peas for the evening meal.

'Why Women Attend Big Cricket Matches' was the subject of a *Sydney Morning Herald* feature article on 24 November 1936 in which it was argued that, 'While there are still many women who accept such cricket terms as "silly point" and "square leg" literally, the great majority of them are well informed by husbands, fathers, brothers, or sons about the finer points of the great game and are thus able to take an intelligent interest in play.' Women at this time were found in all sections of the SCG including the Hill which was 'dotted brightly with colour — the colour of bright dresses, scarves, and gay hats'. Family groups could also be observed there. The *Herald* believed that there were a number of reasons behind women's interest in cricket and included in these was the fact that 'it is a quiet game — a game that is alluring in its uncertainty, and many changes of fortune' and that the game provided women with a number of options: to follow the game closely, to score, to knit, and to enjoy a day out with the family.

There is no question that affluence enhanced crowds not just at cricket but also at horse-racing, football, cinema and theatre. In fact the attendance pattern at all forms of popular culture in the 1920s and 1930s is remarkably similar. There was a steady growth in crowds during the 1920s with attendances peaking in the heady days just before the Depression. Crowds dropped by 30–40 per cent over the next four to five years but picked up again by the mid-1930s. By the late 1930s, when people were willing to spend freely again, crowds reached the heights of the late 1920s. Shield attendances reflected this trend. The Bodyline series, however, was an exceptional one, as we will see, which went against the Depression trend.

Another reason for the expanded audience at all forms of popular culture was cheaper gate entry charges. It cost only 6d to attend the cinema and a VFL game in the 1920s. Cricket was more expensive — perhaps indicative of its still more middle-class base — but increases in Shield prices were well behind rises in the basic wage. Between 1907–37 Test entry charges to the Outer doubled (from 1/- to 2/- or just over) but this cost was on par with charges in the 1890s: it represented 15–20 per cent of the daily minimum wage.

Administrators capitalized on this enthusiasm for cricket by expanding ground facilities. The Cresswell Stand, with a capacity for 4,800, was built at Adelaide Oval in 1924. Sydney's M. A. Noble Stand, seating 5,330, was opened in 1936 and there were plans for another 10,000-capacity grandstand on the site of the

When the Englishmen played at Geelong in January 1921 many spectators viewed the match from vehicles. While some spectators chose to study the game studiously, others posed for the camera.

Bob Stand which were later shelved. Almost fifty years later the idea was revived and the new Hills Stand built.

However, the most impressive ground development took place at Melbourne in the mid-1930s. Following complaints of overcrowding at the 1933 Bodyline Tests — 68,238 attended the Monday (New Year) holiday and thousands were turned away — and, more significantly, following the regular growth of VFL Finals crowds in the 1920s and 1930s, the MCC announced that it would add a new Outer stand which would accommodate 35,000 and increase the capacity to 105,000. An important dimension of ground improvements at the MCG was that they were improvements both in quantity and quality: unlike Sydney, Brisbane and Adelaide some 70 per cent of MCG Outer patrons (which invariably was the entirety of the cricket crowd) could count on having a seat and the vast majority of these seats were under cover: when the ground capacity was later increased to around 120,000, it provided seating for 85,000 which included 55,000 seats under cover.

There is a more general reason for the spectator boom between the wars: the relative dearth of leisure facilities and opportunities at the time. Such an argument cannot be proved but can be inferred from leisure developments after 1945. After the Second World War there was a marked decline in spectator attendance at cricket, horse racing and many other major sports, with the possible exception of football; the movie industry was also affected. The cause, without doubt, was the expansion of leisure facilities and alternatives. The 1950s witnessed a boom in home tennis courts which was followed by a proliferation of private swimming pools; then there were many technological innovations, such as cheaper and lightweight surfboards which enabled individuals to pursue their own inclinations; there was also an endless variety of air, land and sea-borne leisure vehicles; more tourist activities; and, of course, television and the home-entertainment industry. The result has been that mass public entertainment, which dominated the scene for want of competition, has now been challenged by a variety of home-based individualistic leisure opportunities.

It is precisely for this reason that it is rather misleading to compare the crowds of one era with our own. Many old-timers refer nostalgically to the bumper Shield crowds of the 1920s and 1930s and a time when the Shield was both viable and profitable. In terms of numbers they are quite right. However, the comparison ignores the very much reduced opportunities for watching major cricket in the 1920s; Tests, for instance, were only played in four of the first eleven seasons after the First World War. Regular patrons could only watch two Shield matches in the other seven seasons which might represent seven to ten days' play. (The situation improved a little in 1926–27 when Queensland entered the Shield since this led to three home matches per year.)

It is the unanimous view of players from this era that the crowds were well behaved, intelligent and never invaded the field to protest or to congratulate a centurion. Victorian all-rounder,

The *Brisbane Courier* noted that 'many thousands cheerfully stood throughout the day', including ladies, at the First Test played in Brisbane at the Exhibition Ground in 1928.

A full view of the unusually-shaped palm-lined Exhibition Ground, December 1928. Many of the Outer patrons had to stand too.

Ted a'Beckett, recalled that there was a 'pin-drop atmosphere' at the start of a Test and there was never any slow handclapping. There was some barracking, even abuse and booing, but the overwhelming response was appreciative of the game and supportive of the players. Fast bowler, Harry Alexander, and batsman, Jack Badcock, suggested that there were very few, if any, police in attendance: so the crowds must have regulated themselves. More down to earth was the comment of Victorian batsman H. L. 'Stork' Hendry: 'They knew their cricket unlike the galahs that go to Packer one-day cricket.'

Bill Brown, who played for New South Wales and Queensland, provided a more detailed picture of the Sydney crowd of the 1930s:

> The crowd there was caustic, critical but knowledgeable; it was vocal, humorous, and had great insight; they could pick a show pony or a malingerer; what they wanted was a sincerity of purpose. By the time you had finished there, they had cut you down to size, but having survived this 'rough treatment' you could face crowds anywhere in the world. The crowd was always quick to see through flashy showmanship.

Such claims are remarkable given the pre–1914 history of spectator violence. If this picture is correct, it represents a significant change in the disposition of crowds especially since between-the-war crowds were often crammed into ovals and had to watch their cricket under far-from-comfortable conditions. For example, over three-quarters of Sydney's record crowd of 58,446 had to stand for the entire day on 15 December 1928 — as pictures of the crowd attest.

The memory of former players is selective: while they remember some of the major crowd controversies, such as the Larwood incident of 1929, they underestimate, or fail to remember, the continuing tradition of crowd unrest. However, if they are hazy on some of the details, they are correct in a more general sense: crowd incidents occurred regularly but crowd violence — invasions of the pitch, interruptions to the game, and actual attacks on officials and players — was greatly reduced.

The Gabba and Other Grounds

Queensland had to wait a long time to get Shield and Test cricket; a campaign had been initiated as far back as 1903. So when Queensland was finally admitted to the Shield, in 1926–27, and was granted a Test, two years later, Queensland was gripped with cricket fever. Photographs of the first Test played at Brisbane, at the Exhibition Ground, reveal the extent of this interest: not only were the aisles of the stand packed but there were people hanging off the edges of the stand, or crouched on the rim of the iron balcony. This enthusiasm carried over to the city. The *Brisbane Courier* posted Test scores in its vestibule, for the subsequent Test, but the practice had to be discontinued because the police found that large crowds were interfering with the traffic. Proprietors of wireless shops and other premises were also requested to stop the broadcasts and the posting of scores because of similar problems.

Facilities at the Exhibition Ground, venue of the first two Tests in Brisbane, and the Gabba, Brisbane's Test centre since November 1931, were primitive if not rudimentary when compared with other grounds. Keith Dunstan remembers the Gabba from the 1950s — it had not changed much from the 1930s — as an 'amiable shambles of wooden stands and bare red earth' with a 'draughty primitive Press box'. The 'outer cognoscienti' used to gather under the third Moreton Bay fig tree at the Stanley Street end and would sit there in 'shorts, bare feet, and red dust between their toes'. At the Gabba there was only one small grandstand, seating 1,200, and several other even smaller buildings; over 80 per cent of the spectators sat or stood in the

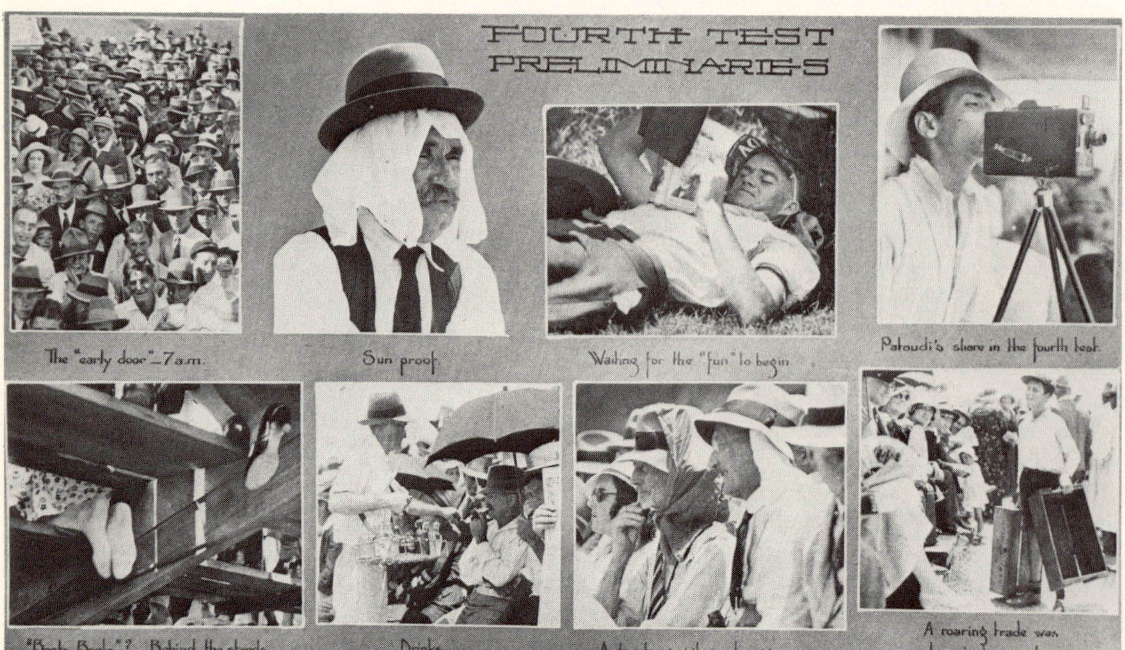

Keeping cool in Brisbane was a problem at the Fourth Test, 1933, since some spectators wore ties and even coats.

open. Hats and handkerchiefs to cover exposed necks from the blazing sun were common sights.

Conditions were also fairly basic for players too. Victorian batsman, Len Darling, remembered that players changed in a modest two-roomed bungalow with a simple partition which separated the two sides. The bungalow had an iron roof so that when a thunderstorm hit the ground the noise could be deafening. Outside was a wide verandah where the players sometimes sat and draped their clothes to dry. Inside there was an ample supply of pineapples, beer and soft-drink — Larwood, Darling added, used to live on beer and pineapples during a match. Perhaps this was because lunch at the Gabba was reputed to be the worst at any ground in Australia: the same corned meat and salad was served up day after day.

By the early 1950s some players were no longer willing to put up with this menu and according to the *Courier Mail* of 8 December 1952 during the series against South Africa several players boycotted the lunch. The South Africans requested that fruit be added to the menu but this request was denied. With a more progressive administration in the past few years the situation has altered to such a degree that the Gabba along with the WACA has the best Test lunches in the country.

However, for all its shortcomings, the Gabba had a great deal of character. As Keith Dunstan noted, 'Somehow it was a reflection of Brisbane itself — blousy, suffering from a lack of paint, quite hideous and full of character.'[1] Queenslander Frank O'Callaghan admitted that the old Gabba was Brisbane's 'ugly duckling' and had a 'general air of drabness' which was augmented from time to time whenever a pall of smoke drifted across the ground from a steam-engine as it passed by. But there was a 'brashness, even a rusticity' about the Gabba together with an 'atmosphere of mateship' that had a special appeal. Cricket at this ground was further shaped by the heat, humidity and spectacular thunderstorms which brought 'breathlessly exciting sticky wickets' in the Tests of 1936, 1946, 1947 and 1950 before wickets were covered in 1954.[2]

The Queensland crowd in the 1930s, not surprisingly, was less knowledgeable than those at the other Test centres. Bill Brown described the Gabba crowd as 'much rougher, cruder and more partisan'. The same point was stressed by Peter Burge, Test batsman of the 1950s: he regarded many of his home crowd as 'rude' and having 'no idea of cricket'; the Gabba was one of the toughest crowds in the country. Comments there were not very memorable but occasionally there was one. When an overweight Burge, in the twilight of his career, bent over to field a ball which he missed by 30 centimetres he was the butt of an earthly comment: 'Burge, I got a sheila like you at home. She won't work, she can't bend over, she wears corsets and she's about the same bloody size and as useless as you are!' South Australian, Ron Hamence, was also given some basic advice when he dropped a skier: 'Get a 40 tonne truck, Hamence.'

Another problem for visiting players was, according to Len Darling, the parochialism of the umpires, at least in the first years of the Shield there: they seemed reluctant to give any decisions against the home side. Even the sportsmanlike New South Wales captain, Kippax, was perturbed by the Queensland umpires and on one occasion he refused to go on with the match and sat on the pitch. Darling admitted, however, that the umpires there improved after a few years as they gained more experience.

The Gabba was totally inadequate for the crowds which turned up for the first Tests there and hundreds watched the game from adjacent roofs and tree limbs. Considering the limited facilities the crowd was well behaved. It must have been difficult for some spectators to reach food outlets, or even to get a drink of water; small boys made a profit by selling water bottled from the irrigation system. During the Test against South Africa in 1931, spectators by the pickets in the Outer were pushed against the fence by thousands behind them according to the *Courier Mail* of 30 November 1931 and 'in desperation they began knocking out the palings of the fence with empty bottles and their bare fists'. When a groundsman appeared with a hammer to repair the gaps in the fence he was pelted with 'orange peels and other rubbish'. His attempts proved unsuccessful because the crowd 'spirited away the loose palings'. Saturday at this Test proved too dreary for some youths who began a 15-minute pillow fight at the end of the day. Cushions, rented at the ground, were thrown at spectators or high in the air. This largely good-natured adolescent demonstration was watched by the South Africans from their reserve: 'Their feeling was not of disgust, but first, amazement, and then amusement.' Administrators were less amused and by 1933 cushion-throwing had been defined as a 'penal offence'.

After each Test in Brisbane there were regular complaints of overcrowding. N. Butler wrote to the *Brisbane Courier* on 13 February 1933 complaining of the 'disgraceful overcrowding of the grandstands':

> Hundreds of spectators were imprisoned in the stand from 8 a.m. until stumps at 6 p.m., owing to every gangway being blocked by a seething mass of humanity. Many who had seen advertised that full catering was available on the grounds were without food or anything to drink.

Queensland's problem was not a unique one in the early 1930s. Hundreds of pickets were torn off the SCG fence by a Bodyline crowd which became wedged against the fence and simply wanted a better view of the game. On the Hill there was the usual crowd warfare: orange peel, tomatoes, refuse and even grass were thrown at spectators who blocked the views of others. At one point the *Sydney Morning Herald* of 5 December 1932 noted, 'A young woman, by a clever bit of headwork, dodged one of the tomatoes' but when it splashed with a resounding crash on the back of a faultlessly-attired young man in front of her she felt responsible for the mess and offered him her handkerchief.

The Melbourne Cricket Club was the only authority to come to grips with the problem of overcrowding and spectator comforts with its greatly expanded capacity after 1935. Sydney added the Noble Stand but plans for another stand to seat 10,000 were scrapped. A 1948 plan of the SCG indicated that there were only 16,420 fixed seats at the ground out of a stated capacity of 63,420.

Better facilities and access to the ground enabled the MCG to jump ahead of the SCG as the sporting crowd capital of Australia in the 1930s — a position which it has never lost. Facilities continue to play a vital role in the size of cricket crowds and the game's ability to keep old spectators and attract new ones.

Crowd Incidents

When cricket resumed after the First World War it was clear that crowds had not forgotten how to barrack. F. G. Smith complained to the *Argus* on 23 December 1919 that 'insulting and disgusting abuse' was hurled on a regular basis at players in Melbourne pennant matches. One season later there was a sustained demonstration against English vice-captain, E. R. Wilson, and team member, Percy Fender, in the Fifth Test at Sydney, which was reported in the *Sydney Morning Herald* on 1 March 1921. It occurred after the Englishman had cabled messages back to English newspapers critical of the crowd for jeering at a lame Hobbs who fielded with the handicap of a strained thigh muscle. When Wilson came to bat in the second innings there was 'vigorous and sustained hooting' and cries of 'liar', 'squealer' and 'Wilson, the squib'. The crowd set out to make Wilson as uncomfortable as possible and succeeded in unnerving him: after he was dismissed cheaply he returned to the pavilion looking 'profoundly aggrieved'. He was riled further by abuse from some of the members and after one comment he adapted a 'menacing attitude' towards one spectator. The situation was defused when a veteran cricketer intervened. Wilson later explained his indignation and astonishment at his reception: he claimed that he had not blamed the entire crowd, he had merely criticized a section of the Hill.

Wilson learnt a lesson, which Ranji had learnt several decades before, that it could be hazardous to comment on Australian crowds in the English Press. In addition to the problem of misquotation, there was the very real possibility that a statement would be distorted, oversimplified or just simply condensed by the time it was reported in the local Press. English players, too, may not have appreciated Australian sensitivity to criticism — a manifestation of the cultural cringe — and the intense local fascination with English comments on Australia.

Fender was also hooted, abused and counted out by the Sydney crowd but he did not allow them to get under his skin; he went on to score a brisk 40 by which time the crowd had almost forgiven him. Since much of the barracking is a response to dull play, an entertaining innings is always an effective way of answering critics. Fender had been barracked in the Test before this when the crowd redefined his four initials and chanted in unison, 'Please Go Home Fender.' Rather than being peeved by this demonstration, Fender responded appropriately, by conducting the shouting.

Apart from the Fifth Test of the 1920–21 series there were very few incidents on this tour, and the next, 1924–25, was almost trouble-free. There are two likely explanations. Australia won both the series handsomely and the two visiting captains, Douglas and Gilligan, made an effort to get on with Australian crowds. Just before the Third Test, for example, Gilligan went out of his way to praise Australian spectators. He told the *Argus* on 14 January 1925, 'They were enthusiasts, and knew every point of the game. They applauded both sides, and had given Sutcliffe the finest reception he had ever seen accorded to a batsman.' It was not surprising that there were many more incidents during the next two tours when the home side was beaten comprehensively and when England was led, on the second occasion, by a man who remained aloof from and publicly critical of the crowd.

However, the Englishmen were not the only target of spectator abuse in the 1920s: it was also directed against home players on some (although probably fewer) occasions, as was the case in the pre-1914 period. During the 1921–22 season a number of Australian players recently returned from England and South Africa, notably Mayne, Ryder and McDonald, were subjected to continuing abuse over two days of a Shield match at the MCG. The *Argus* of 27 and 28 December 1921 declared that the crowd took a 'dead set' against Mayne because he had been preferred as captain to Park and Ransford. Mayne was jeered every time he touched the ball and he was advised frequently, in insulting and obscene terms, how to handle his team. When he was dismissed there were cat-calls and jeers. This paper added that with the high stands around the ground 'every word is heard by the players on the field'. The Victorian Cricket Association (VCA) held a special meeting to discuss the problem and decided to send extra police to the Outer to 'repress the evil'.

The Kippax incident took place on the first day of the Second Test at the SCG in 1928 when he was given out bowled, 'by the square leg umpire on a second appeal'. The *Sydney Morning Herald* of 15 December 1928 stated that the decision was correct in that the ball 'struck his pad and the spin assisted it to curl on to the leg stump', a view which was shared by some of the Englishmen. However, the umpire at the bowler's end, George Hele, 'was convinced the ball came off the pads of the wicket keeper, George Duckworth, and rebounded on to the stumps'. Kippax, like most of the players and the crowd, was totally confused by what happened and remained at his crease for some time while the issue was debated. (Kippax was admired as a great sportsman who never questioned a decision.) The situation was complicated when he was given out by the square leg umpire, Elder, whereas he should have been given out by the other umpire, Hele. The Englishmen could not appeal to Hele because by this time he had called 'over' and moved away to square leg. So it was Elder who sent Kippax back to the pavilion.

The chain of events convinced the crowd that the decision was unfair and there was a demonstration against the Englishmen. When the visitors returned after the interval there was further hooting and Duckworth, the keeper, was singled out for special abuse. Some even accused Duckworth by innuendo of having steered the ball on to the stumps even though he had been at least two metres away from the stumps when the bails were disturbed. More than three decades later Larwood admitted, 'The Hill was right, though it is doubtful whether they saw exactly what happened. They sensed rather than saw.'[3]

Duckworth later stated that he had no idea why he was singled out for abuse at the time of the Kippax incident and why, in the following Test, the Melbourne crowd subjected him to a hostile demonstration for his 'role' in the incident. Possibly it was because he was such a keen player — his high-pitched raucous appeal could be heard all round the ground and he expressed his joy when he participated in the fall of a wicket by throwing the ball high into the air. The *Sydney Morning Herald* of 30 May 1929 also reported that Duckworth believed that Australian umpires might have been 'frightened by the barrackers' and consequently reluctant to uphold some appeals. From early on in the tour he had decided that he would not allow the crowd to upset him and would not show the 'slightest sign of being troubled by their attacks'. He later admitted that his stiff upper lip might have added to the barracking. Duckworth, like Brockwell, had a rather negative image of the Australian crowd. He believed that the unusual amount of barracking in 1928–29, when compared with previous tours, was due to the crushing defeat of the home side.

On the following day a record crowd turned up at the SCG and there was considerable violence on the Hill arising for the most part from the cramped and uncomfortable conditions. People who arrived at 10 a.m. to secure the few seats along the fence were pelted by jealous spectators behind them who threw fag ends of ice cream bars, apples and soggy plums. And when the seat-dwellers stood up for some relief from the hard benches the crowd behind 'screamed horribly' and showered them with 'bags of dirt, fruit skins, pies, bottles, sandwiches, an old boot, peach stones and tins'. Liquor, too, flowed freely on the Hill. The *Sydney Morning Herald* of 17 December 1928 reported one spectator's impressions:

> He had seen hundreds of heads tilted under beer bottles, and thick earthenware drain pipe necks gurgling like stormwater channels in

> flood time. He had seen little fat men fighting spider like up the stairs, always pushed back and trampled on and insulted. And, finally, he had seen men crushed in the middle of a vast, sweltering block of people, far from the bar, gradually growing thirstier and thirstier till their tongues became incandescent.

T. K. Martin wrote to the *Herald* on 18 December 1928 and complained of the utter disregard of the Trustees for the 'safety, convenience and enjoyment' of the Hillites who were compelled to sit or stand in 'cramped inhuman positions to be bombarded with every available piece of refuse' while the Trustees lounged in their easy chairs:

> After 2.15 p.m. we were forced either to sit down and witness no play, on account of those standing in front, or to stand up and become a target for the anger of those behind. The only course open to discretion was toward the gate. One poor unfortunate near me received a blow on the head from a thrown bottle, and he, too, retired, but with blood streaming from the wound.

Martin went on to warn the authorities of the possibility of a future 'brawl of magnitude' and complained that 'nothing had been done for the Hillite for the past thirty years or more. The situation on the Hill was made worse by heavy rain which reduced play to three hours and must have drenched most of the crowd. Mud pies began to be thrown along with the other rubbish and whenever a drunk fell over the fence the police threw him back. Many people believe that the Hill degenerated in the 1970s but there were clearly some ingredients of this tradition in the 1920s; and an overcrowded Hill was probably as comfortable then as it is now. The Hill may have been a good place to watch cricket on an uncrowded day but it was certainly not when bumper crowds turned up.

By far the worst incident of the 1920s occurred in the England vs Victoria match in 1929 because this was the one occasion when the crowd interrupted a game so that it forced a captain to declare his innings. Prior to the incident the crowd was in an excellent mood: Woodfull had made 275 not out in nine hours and was close to a record — that of carrying his bat through an innings for three times in a season against the Englishmen. The crowd fairly 'roared with amusement' noted the *Sydney Morning Herald* of 4 March 1929 when Chapman threw the ball to his strike bowler, Larwood, in an attempt to dispose of Ironmonger, one of the premier 'rabbits' around. After Ironmonger cut the first ball for two, and then repeated the shot the crowd 'increased its noise' and when he survived another ball 'the noise could be heard a mile away'. Up to this point it was 'all comedy' added the *Argus* of the same date but the situation became too much for Larwood who allowed himself to become rattled. Larwood then ran in to a 'perfect babel' to deliver the next ball but stopped at the crease and waited for the din to subside. The noise did not abate and Larwood threw down the ball. Three times Chapman coaxed his bowler to run in again but each time Larwood baulked at the crease. Woodfull and Chapman then walked over to the 'storm centre', the Wardill Stand, and addressed the crowd but without any effect. To defuse the situation Ryder declared the innings and denied Woodfull a unique record.

The English Press was again highly critical of the Melbourne crowd and, as usual, the most vehement and lurid comments were regurgitated in the Australian Press, on this occasion in the *Argus* of 5 March 1929. The *Daily News* headed its story, 'Baby Cricket' and argued, wrongly, that this protest about fast bowling against a rabbit was 'scarcely credible in the children's cricket in a match on the sands'. *Sporting Life* declared the event to be a 'blot' on the game and the *Daily Sketch* denounced the 'outrageous action of churls' who had brought the game to a halt.

Larwood later associated himself with Duckworth's comments when he castigated Australian barracking as 'ugly, unnecessary, and unfair' and 'deliberately planned'. There were even reports that he would not tour Australia again — which could have denied history its most famous cricket controversy, Bodyline. However, when he reviewed the incident more than three decades later, Larwood had clearly mellowed in his attitude to the Australian barracker:

> I didn't know what hit me when I struck the Aussie barrackers Down Under. I took it personally. It upset me and definitely put me off when they counted me out and called out personal remarks. I didn't understand the Australian character. Especially when, two days after the experience, they stood and cheered me when I went to bat.[4]

Reviewing the event a few years later, Melbourne journalist, R. W. E. Wilmot described the incident as 'ridiculous' because an event of high comedy had been turned into tragedy simply because some of the Englishmen lacked a sense of humour:

> This episode was quoted in England as an exhibition of disgraceful barracking. The only people who did not see the humour of it were the Englishmen. Had Larwood sent up a slow ball Ironmonger would probably have been bowled, but to refuse to go on was only courting trouble. Had the Englishmen entered into the joke the laugh would have been with them. A lack of sense of humour caused all the bother.[5]

While regretting the Larwood incident the English Manager, F. C. Toone, tried to pour oil on troubled waters but even he could not resist some paternalistic comments on the reasons for barracking. He described it in the *Argus* of 19 April 1929 as 'essentially Australian' and 'usually good-natured'. In his opinion the climate was responsible for the barracking. 'The Australians must do something to keep up their spirits,' he opined.

Not all Englishmen, however, found the Australian barracker hard to cope with. Some players such as Patsy Hendren played along with the crowd. Among other things he used to jump over the fence and enjoy some liquid refreshment with spectators.

It was convenient for an English official to ignore the phenomenon of English barracking which was a sufficient problem to surface twice in *Wisden* editorials in the 1920s. First, *Wisden* of 1920 disapproved of the behaviour of a section of the Lord's crowd which hooted J. W. Hearne who was playing the innings of his life attempting to save Middlesex from defeat at the hands of Yorkshire. Later, noted *Wisden* in 1925, a rather more serious outbreak occurred, not surprisingly in the industrial north, when the 'Sheffield public — false to all their old traditions of good sportsmanship — barracked for three days in most unseemly fashion'. New South Wales batsman, C. G. Macartney, came to the defence of the Australian barracker and disputed the point that barracking represented intimidation. 'Surely,' he wrote, 'no visiting Test match player is so nervous that a few words of advice from outside the boundary fence will seriously interfere with his batting or bowling.' He also made the point that barracking *did* occur in England.

'Demonstrative barracking' in England was admittedly rare but during the 1921 Test at Old Trafford there was a hostile demonstration against the Australians: 'when Armstrong ran up to bowl, the yells were so loud and personal, that after three tries he gave it up and sat down.'[6]

Barracking continued to occur at all levels of cricket in Australia and no one seemed to be immune from public criticism. According to the *Argus* of 25 November 1929 Bill Ponsford, record-breaker and popular idol of the 1920s, was baited on one occasion at his home ground, St Kilda, by a group of Richmond youths who shouted 'insulting remarks' and generally made themselves a 'nuisance'. Several years later the *Sydney Morning Herald* of 15 February 1932 reported that barrackers at the Marrickville 'Hill' were blamed for taking the wicket of Randwick, and New South Wales, batsman Dr E. P. Barbour. Barbour usually had no problem in dealing with barrackers, but was disconcerted by a section of the crowd who were silent as the bowler ran in but who shouted 'Hit it' just after the ball left the bowler's hand. He appealed to the umpire and the home captain but no action resulted. When the barracking continued Barbour stepped away from his wicket, just after the ball was delivered, and was bowled. Barbour remained at the wicket for a minute discussing the matter with the umpire, who had given him out, and left for the pavilion: the scorecard read 'b. Amos' but it could have read 'b. Marrickville barrackers'.

Barracking was not a uniquely Australian form of behaviour, or even an American trait, as some commentators thought. Nor was it a specifically Australian problem. Barracking became a natural activity for the less-restrained working-class crowds, for soccer crowds in England, and the more working-class cricket crowds in Australia. The critics of the barracker were found both in England and Australia and were mostly middle-class upholders of the amateur tradition: they believed that crowds, like players, should conduct themselves in a sporting manner.

The Barrackers

Concentration on incidents and disturbances puts too much emphasis on the negative elements of crowd behaviour in the 1920s. On more normal occasions the crowd was, particularly by more recent standards, well behaved, knowledgeable and appreciative of the game. It is also important to remember that people then watched cricket in far-from-comfortable conditions. Overcrowding was the most obvious, although not the only, problem. For example, the *Sydney Morning Herald* of 26 November 1932 reported that when New South Wales played England under a blazing sun those on the Hill not only took off their coats but 'hundreds ignored sartorial proprieties by taking off their shoes and boots for added comfort. Some of the males even took of their socks.' Obviously this daring move was not a common practice. It was not until well after the Second World War, possibly by the 1960s, that the t-shirt, shorts and thongs (and an optional beer belly) became the uniform of the Hillite.

Some pickets were pulled off at the SCG by the mammoth crowd of 58,058 at the Bodyline Test in December 1932.

Most commentators of the time confirm the views of Bill Brown that the ordinary spectator knew the game. Journalist Alex Scott, however, acclaimed the Sydney Hill as preeminent and wrote in the *Sydney Morning Herald* of 28 November 1928:

> For knowledge of its beloved game, however, the Hill stands alone. Keen-eyed and watchful, nothing that happens in the arena escapes the shirt-sleeved enthusiasts seated on that grassy slope. And when they choose to be reminiscent what memories they have, what an encyclopaedic store of dates and details. Giants of the past reappear before us as we listen on the Hill.

Scott added that the Hill could be generous to its favourites but it could also exhibit a malicious glee such as when Kelleway, overlooked for the Australian team, got Ryder's wicket in the Macartney Benefit game and when Hobbs got a duck in his last Test at Sydney. The crowd roared its delight on both occasions.

However, when it came to the Hill's reputation for humour Scott had some reservations and claimed that it was overrated. When he analysed the 'loud-voiced comments and criticisms' they boiled down to a 'few hardy annuals, probably invented in the days of Bannerman and Spofforth'. The same point had been made, in a different and probably more correct form, by a number of writers including Jack Fingleton. Many of the barrackers, they contended, were unoriginal and unimaginative, the 'men of real humour' were comparatively few and far between.

Fingleton divided barrackers into three types. First there was the 'blah' type who repeated hackneyed comments ad nauseum, such as 'Get a bag', and 'Get the fire brigade to get him out.' This type, in Fingleton's opinion, should have been drowned at birth. Keith Dunstan encountered one such barracker at the Gabba in Brisbane in the 1950s: he distinguished himself by calling out, "Ave a go, yer mug' 1,032 times in a single day!

Another type was the 'baiter' who would 'join in to make a chorus with anybody to rag a person susceptible to barracking'. He too was unoriginal and monotonous and placed a greater premium on abuse than wit.

Then there was the barracking 'genius' who would save his 'flash of humour' for the right moment: his comment would sum up a situation, cause people to 'rock with merriment' and help many survive grim and slow passages of play. He was a self-appointed, unpaid actor who understood both the game and the dramatic possibilities of a large and often-hushed audience waiting for some inspiration. His lines were unscripted and unprompted.[7]

Fingleton might have added a fourth category, the 'one-issue' barracker. Jack Perryman, a night-cart worker, made a name for himself at the SCG in the 1950s when he became fixated on Keith Miller and repeated at regular intervals during the game comments such as, 'Keithie, you cham-pee-an, I love you, Keithie.' Perryman had a stentorian voice which could be heard around the ground no matter what way the wind blew. At one time this adulation used to embarrass Miller but he got used to and accepted it along with the annual Christmas card which always had the same message on it, 'From your old mate on the Paddington Hill.'[8]

No one knows how many original barrackers were around but it is likely that each ground always had a few, some more prominent and lengendary than others. Ted a'Beckett recalled that the MCG had one such character in the late 1920s with a 'deep penetrating voice' — an essential asset. He once called out: 'Hendry, Ryder and Blackie, the three old colonials. To get in the side you have to make 100 ten times in a row, but the only way to get out of it is to die.'

When extras reached 12 in another match at Melbourne the *Argus* of 23 December 1929 noted a 'megaphone voice' bawled out to the English keeper, Duckworth: 'Twelve extras, that's one up against your duck-house, Duckworth.' Puns based on players' names and nicknames have always been a feature of cricket comments since the time-span of a game allows ample opportunity to work out all the linguistic possibilities in a name.

The Celebrated Yabba

There is no question, however, that by far the most celebrated and legendary barracker of the era was Stephen Harold Gascoigne (1878–1942), better known as Yabba, who was as much a part of the game at Sydney as the players themselves. When he took up his seat, usually by the fence in front of the

Sometimes players, rather than barrackers, had the final word. An Arthur Mailey view of a possible exchange between Yabba and Englishman, Patsy Hendren.

scoreboard, hundreds of Hillites gravitated towards this born entertainer. Yabba was no less than the Hill's own expert commentator: he added to the excitement, relieved the tension and helped the crowd to participate actively in the game. He was also unofficial coach and mentor to the players.

Yabba was born in Redfern but in his adult life hawked rabbits around Balmain in his pony and cart — he supposedly acquired his name from a corrupted version of his call, 'Rabbo, wild rabbo.' He was a large man, just under 1.82 cm (6 ft) and around 89 kg (14 stone), with a fleshy face and close-cropped hair which was usually covered by a felt hat or a cloth cap. He had a 'coarse and penetrating voice' which rose above the 'nondescript yells' of

Yabba in his habitat: Darling Street, Balmain. Since he skinned and gutted the rabbits on the job, he was always popular with the cats.

lesser lights. Carol Badcock, who was based in Adelaide for part of the 1930s, recalled that such was the power of his voice that it could be heard over the radio commentary. Yabba arrived at the game with his lunch and a couple of bottles of beer but he seldom drank more than that. He rarely missed a major match and was a regular follower of grade cricket: he knew the game intimately. No one knows when he established himself as Sydney's number one barracker — some have claimed that he was prominent before the First World War — but there is no doubt that between the wars he 'stepped forward from the ranks of the chorus', as Ray Robinson put it.

A number of Yabba's comments were variations on themes which had been called out many times before but with Yabba they were sharper and more pithy. When a slow batsman scored after a period of inaction he yelled: 'Whoa there! He's bolted.' Then when a bowler strayed too far from the stumps he delivered a classic, and much-repeated, comment: 'Your length is lousy but you bowl a good width.' On another occasion he advised New South Wales captain, Herbie Collins, to declare when a new batsman had added only five runs in half an hour and the side had passed 500 runs: 'Hurry up, Herbie, declare the innings before he gets set and scores a century.'

Yabba differed from the run-of-the-mill barracker in that his range of comments was much wider and was based on a very close knowledge of the game. When the Nawab of Pataudi remained scoreless for half an hour he advised the umpire, who was a gas-meter inspector: 'Put a penny in him George, he's stopped

While Yabba was a tough character whose rough humour and coarse language could cut 'tall poppies' down to size, he also had a soft and even sentimental side as this picture shows.

registering.' Then there was another occasion when an umpire had to hold his hand aloft for some time waiting for the attendant to move the board: 'It's no use, Umpire; you'll have to wait till playtime like the rest of us.' Because he knew the game so well Yabba's comments were fairer than most other barrackers. When a Sydney grade crowd laughed when a North Sydney tailender had his middle stump smashed first ball Yabba consoled the dejected batsman: 'Don't worry, son. It would'a bowled me.' According to the *Sydney Morning Herald* of 17 December 1934 Yabba was also reluctant to join in the patronizing remarks made to women cricketers in the first international match at the SCG (New South Wales vs England, 1934). When the teams were late to return after lunch there was a stream of comments such as, 'Shake it up with your powder puff in there, girls!' and 'Don't get impatient, old chap. Women are never on time these days. Anyway, it's a woman's privilege to keep a gentleman waiting.' One spectator then turned on Yabba and yelled, 'Hey, Yabba, why ain't yer yowling?' Yabba replied, 'Why should I? The ladies are playing all right for me. This is cricket, this is. Leave the girls alone.'

Yabba was not only a celebrity, he was also the subject of a Cinesound newsreel. When Jack Hobbs played his last match in Sydney the members of the Hill chipped in to buy him a Testimonial, an ornate boomerang: when Hobbs walked round the Hill to receive his gift he asked for Yabba and then shook hands with him — the one-time critic of barrackers acknowledged the number one barracker. After Yabba died the

The complete Yabba: hat, pipe, braces, butcher's apron, rabbits, basket and cart.

NSWCA stood in silence before its next meeting in memory of a man who probably added not only to the entertainment but also to the very size of the crowd itself. Recently Yabba has achieved another distinction, an entry in the *Australian Dictionary of Biography* and joins a select band of Test cricketers — a minority of them — who have been similarly honoured.[9]

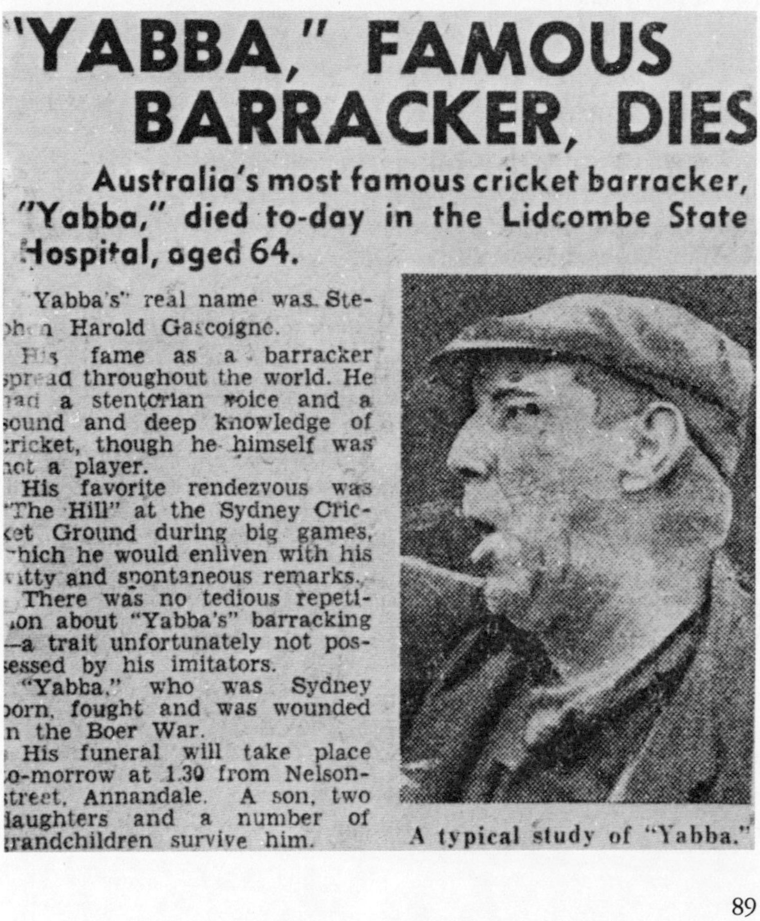

"YABBA," FAMOUS BARRACKER, DIES

Australia's most famous cricket barracker, "Yabba," died to-day in the Lidcombe State Hospital, aged 64.

"Yabba's" real name was Stephen Harold Gascoigne.

His fame as a barracker spread throughout the world. He had a stentorian voice and a sound and deep knowledge of cricket, though he himself was not a player.

His favorite rendezvous was "The Hill" at the Sydney Cricket Ground during big games, which he would enliven with his witty and spontaneous remarks.

There was no tedious repetition about "Yabba's" barracking —a trait unfortunately not possessed by his imitators.

"Yabba," who was Sydney born, fought and was wounded in the Boer War.

His funeral will take place to-morrow at 1.30 from Nelson-street, Annandale. A son, two daughters and a number of grandchildren survive him.

A typical study of "Yabba."

The celebrity in full cry.

Bradman, Bodyline, Broadcasting and the Depression

Cricket's audience was greatly expanded in the 1930s due to the emergence of a new superstar, the furore created by the most controversial series ever, expanded media coverage and the Depression.

Cricket has always had its crowd-drawing stars. Bill Ponsford, for example, with his record-breaking scores, was a great attraction in the 1920s. After one Ponsford scoring spree of 133, 427, 202, 38 and 336, the NSWCA capitalized on his name when it featured him prominently in advertisements for the 26–31 January 1928 New South Wales vs Victoria game. The Association was not disappointed with the result: Sydney had a record crowd of 30,386 for the Australia Day holiday, most of whom came, in the opinion of one paper, to see 'the record breaker and maker'. Ironically, it was in this match that Ponsford did not bat well and was dismissed for only two and six in a high-scoring game.

The greatest crowd-drawer of the 1920s and 1930s was Don Bradman. No one before or since has matched his appeal. His reputation was based firmly on his unparalleled deeds such as his two Test double-centuries and one triple-century-in-a-day on the 1930 tour. Next season, not surprisingly, he featured prominently in match advertisements for the Test series against the West Indies.

There is no doubt, too, that the Bradman legend was a product of the Depression. Australians needed sporting heroes at this time because their success provided one of the few notes of cheer amidst the gloom.

Bradman became, as Brian Stoddart put it in the *Sun-Herald* of 15 December 1982, a 'god-like' figure whose 'trips across the country were like those of a saint; people made a pilgrimage to see him'. He was also seen, noted Philip Derriman of the *Sydney Morning Herald*, to have 'almost superhuman' powers and was the object of 'hero-worship almost amounting to idolatry'. While Bradman appeared to have magical and even divine powers, he was probably regarded more as a film star and a sex symbol than a saint. Bradman received 'Hollywood-star treatment' wherever he went after 1930, which did not endear him to his team-mates, although the 1930 team as a whole was the subject of one of the first Cinesound talkies. Bradman's sex appeal was noted by an English journalist, William Pollock, who wrote that Australia had become 'Bradman mad' and that people, women in particular, who knew nothing of the game, flocked to see him. When Bradman toured England women fought to get near him, 'to kiss him or touch his sleeve' even though Bradman never flaunted or exploited his enormous popularity.[10]

There are countless stories of the phenomenal drawing-power of Bradman. Many contemporary players have described how disconcerting it was for a batsman to follow Bradman; once Bradman had been dismissed many of the crowd filed out.

Victorian and Australian batsman Len Darling, who claims that he must have fielded some 5,000 Bradman runs, tells the story of how he was about to catch Bradman on the boundary at the SCG, after Bradman had chalked up yet another century, and how spectators — greedy for more Bradman runs — yelled at him to drop the catch. A Bradman duck was even reported in the *Sydney Morning Herald* of 3 January 1933 to have saved the lives of three children. When Bradman was dismissed for a first-ball duck at the 1932 Melbourne Test, a man at Launceston was so disgusted that he left the commentary and went for a walk along a river. He was just in time to rescue three young children who had fallen in to deep water.

Bradman crowds have been studied at length by Irving Rosenwater but it is worth exploring one Bradman-inspired crowd. Cliff Winning, former Balmain first-grader and historian of the club, tells of how Bradman agreed to play in a charity match at Gladesville Mental Hospital in January 1933 when he was at the height of his powers. The crowd was 'so dense that traffic problems never experienced before in the area were created in Victoria Road' (the oval was then adjacent to this road) and for a while it seemed that the match would have to be abandoned. Play was only able to proceed when the authorities 'allowed the spectators to encroach on the playing area'. After all this trouble it was with 'utter disbelief and great disappointment' that the huge crowd watched Bradman dismissed by Mailey for just a couple of runs. No crowd ever dispersed as quickly but it still led to a thirty-minute delay in the match while the crowd streamed through the exit gates. Winning, who had partnered Bradman in his brief innings, went on to score 80 runs, one of his best-ever innings, but it was witnessed by just a few officials and some of the hospital's patients who were seated in the special reserve.

The next grade match was a promoter's dream because it pitted Bradman's team, St George, against Mailey's team, Balmain, at Birchgrove Oval. Many believed, at this time, that Mailey had a hoodoo over Bradman. Special trains were put on for the two Saturdays to transport the record crowd which provided the Balmain Park Trust with sufficient operating revenue for 12 years. Bradman did not disappoint the crowd this time as he scored 134 and in the process 'massacred' Mailey, who had dropped a 'sitter' at the beginning of his innings. Such was the crush at the ground when Bradman was batting that he decided it was better to remain at the wicket during the tea interval rather than fight his way back to the stand. As the Balmain side trooped off the oval at tea Winning thought it only polite that someone stay with the visiting captain and the umpires. He moved towards Bradman but ended up nowhere near him because he was elbowed and pushed aside to somewhere near the boundary by the huge crowd which swarmed on to the ground attempting to get close to Bradman, to get his autograph, or to touch him or his bat.

It is possible to work out in more precise terms Bradman's crowd-pulling potential. The 1930s were a period, apart from the Bodyline series, when bat dominated ball so it is reasonable to assume, given the good wickets and large scores, that most spectators came to see the great batsmen of the era. A 'Bradman factor' can be calculated from Shield matches at the SCG and the MCG from 1930–40.

The Bradman factor was worked out by considering the daily crowds of the 74 days of Shield cricket which involved Bradman at the SCG and the MCG as a New South Welshman (1930–34) and a South Australian (1935–40): the average attendance on the 41 days when he batted was 14,557, whereas the average when he did not bat was only 7,627. Therefore the Bradman factor amounted to 6,930, an additional crowd of 91 per cent.

THE BRADMAN FACTOR

(Shield matches involving Bradman at the SCG and the MCG)

Season	Days Bradman batted	Crowd total	Days Bradman did not bat	Crowd total
1930–31	6	55,926	4	19,909
1931–32	4	25,417	3	21,829
1932–33	5	67,674	4	37,656
1933–34	6	100,957	6	48,473
1935–36	3	50,682	3	15,566
1936–37	3	42,902	5	22,681
1937–38	5	74,918	3	29,677
1938–39	3	41,528	3	38,937
1939–40	6	136,830	2	16,964
Total	41	596,834	33	251,692
		Av. per day 14,557		Av. per day 7,627

Bradman factor = 6,930 (the difference between the average daily figure of when he batted and when he did not)

Radio provided another boost for the 1932–33 series. At this time radio really established itself as a popular medium. Cricket broadcasts in Australia dated from the First Test at Sydney in 1924 but listeners had to be content with scores at fifteen-minute intervals on 2BL (Broadcasters Limited) and a five-minute lunch-time report, direct from the ground and a resumé in the evening on 2FC (Farmer's Service). The first continuous ball-to-ball description was initiated by 2FC in a trial match between Australia and the Rest at the SCG on 4–8 December 1925.[11]

By the time the next home series was played, 1928–29, cricket followers in the major capitals could follow the ball-to-ball commentaries when the Test match was played in their city. After each day of the First Test at Sydney they could also listen to a ten-minute summary of the day given by M. A. Noble on 2BL. In that season none of the Sydney commercial stations — 2GB, 2UE, 2UW, 2KY — had cricket coverage. The 1932–33 series

Officials were well aware of the Bradman factor in the 1930s.

was the first in which a national hook-up enabled listeners to follow the Tests broadcast from each city.

By 1932 sport, and cricket in particular, dominated the airwaves: almost every Sydney radio station devoted some time to the game. In addition to an expanded coverage of the cricket there was a much larger radio audience by 1932: in 1924 there had been only 1,400 license holders but by 1932 this figure had increased to 370,000.

Surprisingly cricket authorities and sporting interests in general were wary of radio suspecting that it would affect attendances at matches. For example cricket administrators of the Sheffield Shield were worried by the sharp drop in Shield crowds from 1930–34 and thought that radio was, at least in part, to blame. Attendances for the five seasons from 1930 were about 50 per cent down on the five seasons before 1930 as the table shows:

Shield attendances 1925–35

1925–26	267,777	1930–31	206,972
1926–27	389,883	1931–32	191,673
1927–28	423,159	1932–33	184,339
1928–29	237,779	1933–34	298,132
1929–30	280,686	1934–35	207,068
Total	1,599,284		1,088,184

The drop in crowds, however, had very little to do with the introduction of radio and was caused more by the Depression. In fact it is more likely that radio helped to expand cricket's audience, a point which a number of journalists sensed rather more quickly than officials. The *Argus* pointed out, as early as 4 January 1929, that 'if the V.C.A. loses anything by having Test matches broadcast, it gains also, because thousands rush to the ground when news goes forth that interesting events are imminent. This was especially noticeable when Bradman was nearing his century.' The ABC endorsed the same view in its 1932–33 Report commenting that 'experience has repeatedly shown that the broadcasting of descriptions is a most efficient method of stimulating public interest and has almost invariably greatly increased the average number of spectators present on similar occasions thereafter'. The *Sydney Morning Herald* suggested that cricket's audience was further swelled since in 'thousands of homes, the housewife who never went to a match is being educated while the radio is turned on in the points and personalities of cricket'.[12] Overall the expanded media coverage, rather than harming a sport, seemed more likely to whet the appetite of the fan for more.

Cricket benefited from radio more than most sports. With its imperial links and long-established traditions, Test cricket quickly gained a 'right of way', as Ken Inglis put it, over other ABC programmes, a position which it has largely retained to this day. The game also attracted to its commentary team some of the most gifted and articulate radio personnel such as Charles Moses and Michael Charlton. Cricket, with its extended playing time was able to dominate the airwaves for a much longer period than other sports. In addition Test broadcasts from England were at a convenient time to catch a large audience, which further improved their popularity.

Bodyline

Bodyline more than any other issue before or since, brought the question of barracking and Australian crowd behaviour to the fore both in Australia and England. The *Sydney Morning Herald* reported on 11 November 1932 that at the beginning of the 1932–33 season the English Manager, Pelham Warner, appealed to barrackers to create a 'different atmosphere' at the game and asked them: 'Do you think that it is quite dignified that the greatest cricket match between the two greatest cricketing powers should be interrupted by a certain amount of noise?' But the Bodyline controversy and an austere and aloof English captain, Douglas Jardine, ensured that this was to be one of the noisiest seasons ever; and in its wake there was another full-scale debate on the barracking question. The Depression, which entered its worst phase at the time of the tour, made the situation even more volatile.

From the time Bodyline was unveiled Englishmen became the objects of sustained and abusive barracking. It reached a peak during the Third Test at Adelaide. Two days before the game the ground authorities adopted the extraordinary and probably

One view of the Bodyline debate.

unprecedented step of removing the crowd from net-practice because of barracking. Such was the interest in the game that many had arrived before noon to secure prime positions for the Wednesday 3 p.m. practice. By the time it began a crowd of 4–5,000 had gathered. When Jardine came to bat there was a 'running commentary of barracking and cheering' and when Bowes bowled Jardine such a great cheer went up that it startled players at the other nets. All this was too much for Jardine who ran off to get the Secretary who then removed the crowd. Net practice on the next day was closed to the public.

The events of the Test proved even more dramatic. After England had occupied the crease on the first day, a record Saturday crowd of 50,962 turned up to see the end of the English innings and the start of the Australian on a typically hot January day. Judging from the cramped conditions which prevailed when 34,897 turned up on 30 January 1983 (the sixth largest cricket crowd at Adelaide) conditions in 1933 must have been very uncomfortable, even unbearable for some. Even with the much-smaller 1983 crowd many members had to sit in the aisles, which made access to the stand difficult, the open bitumen area in front of the stands was packed, and the path round the Hill vanished

Barracking features prominently in this collage published in March 1933.

although the police tried to clear it. Clearly the additional 15,000 spectators in 1933 must have stood for the entire day. When Woodfull was hit over the heart there was a stunned silence for a moment followed by boos and cat-calls, and when Jardine signalled to Larwood to adopt Bodyline bowling in the next over the crowd 'went wild'.

The third day of the Test brought the much-discussed Oldfield incident when Oldfield was felled, glancing a short-pitched ball on to his face. Sylvester Phelan, then 19, and later a sporting writer for the Adelaide *Advertiser*, was a spectator on the eastern mound and remembers what happened. When Oldfield was hit there was a tremendous 'crack' — one player in that game can still 'hear' the sound of the crack — and for an instant there was an 'absolute silence' followed by an angry murmur which swept the ground. It appeared a prelude to a hostile demonstration. By the time Woodfull ran out to pick up a prostrate Oldfield a full-scale demonstration was underway and Larwood was counted out. Radio took this demonstration round the country: listeners could hear the shouts and jeers clearly. Had anyone jumped over the fence thousands would have joined in. Larwood for one moved towards the stumps so that he could grab one for self-defence. The demonstration came as much from the members as from the Outer.

SACA had prepared itself for violence and 40 mounted police

Cricket helps to sell radios in the 1930s; and radios helped to widen the cricket audience.

had been marshalled at the No. 2 Ground and another 400 were stationed on foot near the oval pickets. However, whether they would have intervened to stop a popular protest against Bodyline tactics is not certain. It was fortunate perhaps that the worst incident of the series took place in conservative Adelaide: had it occurred in Sydney, or Melbourne, there might have been a recurrence of the 1879 riot or worse.

Jardine was the focus of much barracking, some of which was very abusive, because he was seen as the mastermind behind Bodyline. One such incident occurred at Adelaide where a large horse-drawn roller was in use. After the horse relieved itself by the side of the pitch one of the groundsmen brought out a shovel and picked up the droppings. He then paused briefly, with his loaded shovel in the air, as if he didn't know what to do with it; whereupon a lone voice advised him: 'Take that back to Jardine.' In the same Test another spectator yelled out during a drinks break: 'Don't give *him* a drink! Let the bastard die of thirst!' It

Adelaide's record Bodyline crowd of 50,962. Few women are evident in the hatted Outer crowd.

was also common for Jardine to be referred to as 'Sardine' and once when Jardine had been scoreless for an hour a wit advised: 'I say, Woodfull, get a tin-opener and extract the Sardine.' Perhaps the most-repeated Jardine story stems from an instance when he was brushing away flies. The barracker advised him: 'Leave our flies alone; they're the only bloody friends you've got.'

Jardine may have made the situation worse because he appeared to goad the spectators into heaping more abuse on him. Perhaps this helped him confirm his dislike of Australian crowds. The crowd too disliked Jardine's Harlequin cap, with its hint of class distinctions, and they laughed at his stiff-legged running when he was forced to chase a ball to the outfield. On one such occasion Yabba called out, 'Mind your stays, old man!' his tone mocking the English Public School accent.

By the time of the last Test at Sydney relations between Jardine and the crowd had reached rock bottom. When he was struck a 'sickening blow on the side' by new strike bowler, Alexander, a large section of the crowd 'howled with delight'. During this Test every short-pitched ball bowled by Larwood drew a 'tremendous

The non-paying crowd in Stanley Street at the Gabba, February 1933.

roar' so much so that Yabba could not be heard above the din.[13]

However, not all the 1932–33 English team were unpopular; the youthful Nawab of Pataudi, for instance, adopted different tactics towards barracking than Jardine. Pataudi was barracked in the First Test for slow play according to the *Sydney Morning Herald* of 6 December 1932 but he saw the humour of the situation and now and again raised his cap in acknowledgement of a mock ovation. Pataudi became a popular figure with the Adelaide Hill because he took their 'chaff' in excellent spirit. When one spectator called out: 'Hullo, Mr Gandhi. Where's your goat?' Pataudi brought a laugh from the crowd with his reply: 'He has broken his string and got among the crowd.' On the other hand there were some occasions when Pataudi was reported to be 'deeply hurt'.

Herbert Sutcliffe had developed another technique on a previous tour for winning over the crowd: after he had been heckled on one occasion for slow play he put his bat to his shoulder and pointed it like a gun at his tormentors and from that moment the crowd took him to its heart.

During the tour, and particularly after, there was the usual English criticism of the Australian barracker and crowd which was noted in the *Sydney Morning Herald* of 8 and 9 May 1933. One English journalist stated that the behaviour of crowds was sometimes 'nightmarish and frightening' and there were moments 'when the players felt that thousands would break through the fences and pour on to the field'. Larwood complained of the taunts and abuse of the crowd and the concerted attempts to put the Englishmen off their game. He also criticized Woodfull for not trying to quieten the crowd. Jardine added his own caustic comments on the Australian barracker. It is hard to avoid the conclusion that the old chestnut of barracking provided a convenient English answer to the Australian Cricket Board's criticisms of unfair play. Many Englishmen countered the criticisms of Bodyline by suggesting that not only were Australian crowds unfair but that their actions were condoned, to some extent, by Australian players.

The English cricketers practice in Sydney, November 1932, watched by a large crowd.

English critics found support in some Australian quarters. Journalist R. W. E. Wilmot, who had defended the Melbourne crowd at the time of the Larwood incident, was critical of a section of the Australian crowd in 1932–33 — it was probably only one per cent but unfortunately they made 99 per cent of the noise. These spectators believed that it was their 'inherent right' to 'deride an opponent, to be personal, to be rude, to hurl insulting epithets across the boundary fence, and generally to become a public nuisance'.[14]

Many Australian players and officials came to the defence of Australian crowds. M. A. Noble, for example, described them as an 'asset to cricket' and argued that the practice of barracking was a worldwide phenomenon. The same point had been discussed at length at the beginning of the Bodyline season by *Sydney Morning Herald* writer, Alex Scott, on 21 November 1932. Somewhat ingeniously he added a new dimension to the debate by tracing the practice back to Biblical times. He cited the case of children who followed the prophet Elisha calling, 'Go up, thou bald-head.' He contended further that there were 'undoubtedly instances of barracking during the Olympic Games in Ancient Greece, and there are obscure references to a tense silence during a javelin-throwing contest'. Perhaps Scott was on safer ground when he added that barracking was not unique to Australia and was commonplace in English football. Clubs there had organized bands of barrackers who armed themselves with banners, bugles and deafening corn-crake rattles, their prime aim being to intimidate the referee and the opposition. Australian barrackers, he argued, were much more moderate in their behaviour.

There was some support for this view from Indian visitor, S. P. Foenander, who published his impressions of Australian crowds in *Field-Madras*. He thought that, for the most part, the Adelaide crowd was knowledgeable and impartial. However, when Bodyline was introduced in the Test the crowd 'saw red'. Even so, much of the crowd behaviour was good-natured:

> In the cheaper enclosures, where food and fruit are carried in paper bags, as a rule the spectators collect all the remnants, crumbs, orange peels, etc., and store them in the bags for use later in the day. When play becomes very dull and listless, as often happens in Test cricket or someone in the crowd on the mounds stands up 'to stretch his legs' he is a target for those behind who pelt him with the contents of their paper bags. In this way an amusing battle is often waged . . . To the spectators in the grandstands the fight of a 'pitched battle' of orange peels, bread crumbs, banana skins, etc., is most diverting . . . I have seen a hugely exaggerated account of these innocent pranks given in Larwood's articles, making one who has not been out in Australia believe that the crowd attack the players in the field with missiles! I never once saw such a thing occur.[15]

Such was the interest created by the 1932–33 series that it defied effects of the Depression which had reduced attendances at all forms of popular entertainment from one-third to one-half. The five Tests drew 761,163 spectators — the sixth largest Test total in history. Admittedly this figure was lower than 1936–37 (948,498 spectators) and 1928–29 (857,600) but allowances need to be made for the 1932–33 programme. There were only four days of Test cricket at Melbourne in this series, which drew 200,635, whereas there were 15 days of Test cricket at the MCG in 1928–29, for a total of 476,261, and 11 days in 1936–37, for another 574,650. The two most crucial Bodyline Tests, the third and the fourth, were played at Adelaide and Brisbane respectively. Record crowds flocked to these Tests, but the ground capacities were very much less than Melbourne and Sydney.

While Australian crowds were often criticized by English players and the Press, it is clear that much of the criticism was unfounded and was a convenient red herring promoted by the initiators of Bodyline. Given the size of crowds in 1932–33 and the relatively poor facilities in most of the Outers, which resulted in many patrons having to stand all day without any cover, there is no doubt that Australian crowds were surprisingly well-behaved. The only violence perpetrated on the Englishmen (by a minority of spectators) was verbal.

Synthetic Cricket

Tests played in England presented special problems for radio authorities in the 1930s since short-wave was not yet clear or reliable enough to be the basis of a continuous description. To cater for the public demand, radio stations developed synthetic, or ghost, broadcasts, and by the 1934 series had captured a very large audience.

The most professional synthetic broadcasts, which emanated from the ABC, have been described by historian Ken Inglis. The system was based on the transmission of brief cables at about five-minute intervals, after each over or the fall of a wicket. 'From time to time the cables carried information about the weather, changes in field placing, and anything else that might help the broadcasters in Sydney. A team in the studio turned cables into notes for the commentators, made up-to-date maps of the field, and posted the latest score on a board similar to the one at the Sydney Cricket Ground.' The simulated broadcasts were enhanced by sound effects which included applause, the sound of the ball on bat (a pencil tapped on to a 'hollow hemisphere of wood'); and the thud of a defensive shot (made by the other end of the pencil which had a rubber-band wrapped around). The greatest challenge for the commentators was to deal with the lulls due to interruptions in the flow of the cables; they then had to draw on their own imagination perhaps 'sending Larwood off to change his boots, having lunch papers blow on the pitch, or as a last resort making it rain'. In such situations Moses was 'brilliant'.[16]

The commentaries were a pretence which fooled many

listeners even though the ABC went to some pains to explain that the broadcasts came from Sydney and not from England. Even so many refused to believe that the commentary was not real and bets were laid on the subject.

Synthetic cricket distorted the game in a number of ways. Not only were fictitious happenings invented to cover a break in the cables, the commentary even falsified the game itself on some occasions: Ted a'Beckett recalled one farcical situation in 1934 where a commentator provided a vivid description of a regulation caught behind; whereas in reality the batsman had skied the ball which was taken by the keeper in the middle of the pitch. Radio also made cricket appear to be a faster-moving, more exciting game than it actually was (at least for many

Not everyone appreciates the first complete national ball-to-ball description of the Tests in 1931–33 which took cricket into the living rooms of the country.

people): commentators filled in the many gaps and dull passages, with reminiscences, anecdotes about players, or discussions of the crowd, the weather and the morality and ideology of the game. Radio began a tradition which was taken up even more by television with its zoom lenses, slow-motion replays and 'speeded-up' match highlights which make the game appear as if it is all fours, sixes and wickets. The tradition has been further embellished with the addition of Melbourne's electronic scoreboard which enabled December 1982 spectators to watch replays rather than the tedious return to the bowling-mark of yet another fast bowler. It is significant that the replay often brought louder cheers than the event itself.

Many commercial stations did not pretend to have men at the ground and 'created instead the atmosphere of a party at the studio'; new cables were greeted appropriately with joy or dismay. Some stations, such as 3DB in Victoria introduced synthetic broadcasts but they were not as polished as the ABC; however, there were some popular elements. 3DB had a doll, Ricketty Kate, who used to perform at appropriate occasions, such as when an English wicket fell. The station made no attempt to fool the public when the cables failed, rather they handed over to the whimsical Charlie Vaude who amused the crowd with songs and jokes. The same station organized an open-air type broadcast outside the Atheneum in Collins Street which thousands came and watched. The same night there was a huge crowd outside the *Age* office in Collins Street which cheered every English wicket to fall as it was posted on the make-shift scoreboard.[17]

Synthetic broadcasts continued until 1938 but by that time short-wave could be heard through the static after midnight and Australians were able to listen to comments from Woodfull and Oldfield from the ground itself. Technically the broadcast of live cricket in 1938 must have been much inferior to the synthetic descriptions which the public had come to know and like.

Radio provided cricket with a wider audience than ever before. It consolidated support within the cities and expanded interest by taking the game to remote country areas. Test batsman of the 1960s, Brian Booth, recalled the impact of radio on his home town of Perthville, a small settlement about ten kilometres from Bathurst. His family happened to own one of the two wireless sets in the town just after the Second World War. Throughout a Test winter his father opened the house to 20–30 people who sat round a fire right through until stumps, 3.30 a.m.

CHAPTER FOUR

Television, Tin Cans and Transistors: The Impact of Technology on Crowds

'Declining' Crowds and the 'Brighter Cricket' Campaign

Cricket boomed after the Second World War, as it had in 1918. Despite an uneven contest between a strong Australian side and a depleted English team, the 1946–47 series drew the third-largest series audience in history, 846,942. The Third Test at the MCG drew 343,675 just short of the 1937 record of 350,534.

This time, however, the boom did not last long and by the 1950s officials began to worry about a slump in cricket crowds. Cricket's problem in the 1950s was that for once it failed to grow; in fact cricket crowds appeared to decline. On the surface Shield attendances in the 1950s were on par with the 1920s and 1930s (the average Shield season attendance from 1919–40 was 235,102 which was virtually the same as the average figure of 235,099 from 1945–60.) From 1921–61 the Australian population had almost doubled from 5.4 to 10.5 million, so in maintaining its numbers cricket fell behind, or as a proportion of the population, cricket crowds declined by up to 50 per cent. It is also important to remember that even though the Shield season during this period was expanded from an average season of 39 playing days between the wars to 61 playing days from 1946–60 and Western Australia was added to the Shield competition in 1947–48 the average daily attendance figure dropped from 6,021 to 3,836. There was also a decline in Test aggregate figures in the 1950s: the two series against England in the 1930s had attracted an average total of 854,831, while the three series against

England in the 1950s averaged only 693,760, a decline of approximately 20 per cent.

The expansion of other sports in the 1950s, notably tennis, highlighted cricket's relative stagnation. With the success of its youthful stars in the Davis Cup and at Wimbledon, tennis began to challenge cricket's glamour and its monopoly of the summer. No longer was cricket assured of dominating the airwaves on Boxing Day and subsequent holidays because more often than not Australia was defending (usually successfully) the Davis Cup. The expanded following of tennis translated into real growth in all facets of the game: there was a boom in home tennis courts and a large increase in coaching classes and the number, particularly of boys and girls, playing the game.

The 1950s did see some high points for cricket, for example the dramatic bowling of 'Typhoon' Tyson and the return of the Ashes in 1958–59 attracted wide public interest and media attention. However, in some of the other seasons, cricket had to struggle for media attention against tennis, and in 1956, the Olympic Games. (During the 1955–56, and 1956–57 seasons there was no cricket at all on the MCG — it was transferred to St Kilda.)

No doubt 'winning' and 'age' were factors in the decline of cricket in the 1950s. For while Australians dominated the world tennis courts in the 1950s and even more youthful competitors won a record number of gold medals in the swimming pool and on the track, the cricketers lost the Ashes in 1953 and were humiliated by speed in 1954–55 and spin in 1956. The team was led by 'elderly' captains, Lindsay Hassett and Ian Johnson, and a Lindwall–Miller pace attack which now appeared past its prime. Only in 1958 were there signs of a national cricket recovery under the leadership of Richie Benaud.

Officials, who had long assumed that interest in the game would expand as a matter of course — the formula was a tried and tested one — were confused by the apparent decline in public interest. Many believed that there was nothing 'wrong' with cricket, the 'decline' was a temporary trough, which would level out in due course. Others, however, believed that cricket had become too negative and too defensive and spoke of the need for 'brighter cricket'. Such people argued that if more runs were scored per day, ideally a run-a-minute, crowds would be more likely to come back to cricket.

During the 1950s Queensland Cricket Association (QCA) officials discussed a number of proposals for 'brighter cricket'. In 1952 T. S. Redgrave linked the decline of crowds with changing rules and slow wickets: he argued that 'brighter cricket' could be promoted by more 'organized practice' and the encouragement of players 'to widen their scope of strokes with consequent brighter play'. Q. F. Rice, however, suggested that the remedy lay in encouraging junior cricket and admitting children to representative matches free of charge. In 1954 the QCA obtained 'Negative Cricket Reports' from five 'ex-internationals',

Hornibrook, Brown, Hartigan, Tallon and Lindwall — though the latter still had a lot of Test cricket left in him. In 1955 Rice added a further dimension to the debate when he spoke of the need to 'speed up the game by players, particularly in taking the field after an adjournment'. Two years later there was another discussion of 'brighter cricket' and G. Hornsby enquired whether the Executive intended to arrange for the players to have physical exercises. Just five months before the historic Tied Test there was yet another QCA debate. V. C. Schafer argued that cricket was not offering 'entertainment value' to attract people to the game and also expressed concern that newly introduced television might have an adverse effect on crowds.[1]

Even in the 1950s there were a few serious attempts to grapple with the problem of cricket's 'shrinking' audience. Q. F. Rice of Queensland concerned himself with the question of children, defined at cricket grounds as 'under 14', at cricket; and produced a set of statistics of daily attendance at the Gabba at representative games from 1947–53; children–adults breakdown at the New South Wales vs Queensland matches for nine seasons from 1947–55; and the number of children and adults who took advantage of the cheaper gate entry after 4 p.m. This research indicated that children constituted about 10 per cent of the Shield audience. Rice believed that cricket should attract more children and added that they should be admitted free to representative games. The idea was not taken up in Queensland though they did introduce a pensioner concession in 1960; they were admitted to the Outer for the same price as children. However, South Australia introduced free admission to the ground for children in 1952 and continued the practice for a decade. It has continued off and on at various grounds ever since: children were admitted free, for instance, to sections of the ground at the SCG for Shield matches from 1975. So, even in the 1950s, there was some recognition in some quarters that cricket officials needed to woo certain groups and provide them with incentives.

During the 1950s Australian sport underwent a period of rapid transformation. Big money had made an impact on golf and altered the shape of tennis. This led to a crisis of professionalism in tennis, and the 'open' tennis debate, which was not solved until a decade later when Wimbledon went open. There were also the first signs of a television-led technological revolution in sport which would create new arenas of competition for the leisure dollar and the spectator. The 1950s demonstrated that cricket would have to compete with other sports for the allegiance of the young, the support of sponsors and for media attention, but officials were unable or unwilling to face up to the realities of the situation. They believed that they could ignore the problems. Somehow, they thought, cricket would be different from other sports: it would be immune from the winds of change and would always prove attractive to its patrons in the long run, come what may.

It was hardly surprising that the part-time amateur-inclined officials of the 1950s were reluctant to make any radical change in the game to increase its competitiveness with other sports; they were conservative both in background and temperament. The 'brighter cricket' campaign amounted to not much more than an ephemeral tinkering with the presentation of cricket which resulted in very little real change to the public face of cricket. Furthermore the impact of some reforms was undone by the very people who had brought them about. For example, the decision of the QCA to set up a public relations committee in 1952 'to secure a better understanding with the Press' was applauded by the *Courier Mail* which pointed out that most sporting bodies appreciate the need for publicity. As a result of this decision, the *Courier Mail* sent a photographer to the Gabba, it was noted on 10 December 1952, to get a pre-Test picture. The photographer entered the ground through an open gate but 'was promptly ordered out' by a QCA official. There was no pre-Test picture in the paper. During the same match social writers were barred from the Members' Stand so that there was no frocking news in the *Sunday Mail* social columns.

According to the *Sydney Morning Herald* of 1 December 1947 the public was not impressed with the arrangements for the December 1947 Test at the Gabba. Play had not begun on the Saturday until 4.50 p.m. and the crowd of 10,890, who had waited patiently all day saw less than an hour's play and 36 runs. Bradman was booed — a rare event — when he appealed against the light. Earlier in the day spectators had been issued with pass-out tickets which would be valid for the following Monday in the event of no play on Saturday and signs were posted outside the ground to this effect. After a very brief session of play on Saturday the QCA decided that their legal obligations had been met — the crowd had witnessed some play — and declared that the pass-out tickets would not be valid for Monday. This decision aroused strong public reaction in Brisbane and it was thought that it would affect future gates at the Gabba.

Cricket officials in Brisbane, as elsewhere, were also reluctant to modify dress codes which dated from another era. For example, in the course of an MCC vs Queensland match at the Gabba in 1950 the *Sydney Morning Herald* of 27 November 1950 noted that a Brisbane businessman, W. Steward, was rebuked for being 'inappropriately dressed' whilst in the Members' Reserve. He was attired in 'khaki shorts, long stockings, and grey shirt with tie and carried a sports coat'.

The stuffy conservatism and narrow horizons at Brisbane were repeated in other States. The VCA published an extraordinary match advertisement published in the *Age* on 24 December 1948 which wrote off about one-quarter of the population, girls, as potential spectators. Given that the advertisement appeared in the very same season that the English women cricketers made a well-patronized tour of Australia, it seems clear that the VCA had a limited, and sexist, view of the market. The advertisement read:

Victoria vs NSW
at
Melbourne Cricket Ground

Dec 24, 27, 28, 29 [1948]

Stand: Adults, 3/3 (inc. tax)
boys, 1/3 (inc. tax)
Ground: Adults, 1/11 (inc. tax)
boys, 9d

One wonders whether girls were turned away from the gate or charged adult rates. The category, boys, was advertised for only a couple of seasons after which the VCA returned to the more usual category of children.

Controversial player Sid Barnes had his own idea of brightening up cricket during a drinks interval at an Adelaide Shield match reported the *Sydney Morning Herald* of 30 November 1952. 'Dressed in a grey suit, with a carnation in his buttonhole, and sporting dark glasses' and with a 'towel folded over an arm' twelfth-man Barnes escorted the uniformed steward on to the ground. He then proceeded to brush the players with a clothes brush, comb Keith Miller's hair and then hold up a square mirror, before he sprayed both players and umpires with a scent, offered round cigars and chocolates and towels soaked in iced water. In some respects Barnes anticipated the gaily adorned accessory-laden trolley of the late 1970s but officials at this time were not amused and this behaviour adversely affected his selection prospects. The crowd of 9,155, on the other hand, roared with laughter and some of the players thought the event was very funny. A few of the spectators became impatient with Barnes when it took him a long time to remove his gear from the wickets but, after the event, Barnes received many phone calls of appreciation: many said it was the most humorous event that they had ever witnessed on a cricket field.

The expanded Shield programme in the 1950s coupled with the decline in daily gates meant that individual cricket match profits fell after the 1930s. This comparative 'poverty' provided officials with a convenient excuse to hold the line on player payments, which declined markedly in real terms after the 1930s, and to defer any major programmes of ground improvement. Spectators benefited in one sense because entry costs were lower in the 1950s and 1960s than ever before or since. Test ground entry fees dropped to one-tenth of the daily earnings under the basic wage. However, along with 'reduced' entry fees came the decline in facilities at some grounds, notably the SCG and the Gabba. Parking became extremely difficult and prompted some patrons to make their own arrangements. One motorist trying to get to the Third Test at the SCG on 11 January 1963 was caught in a jam and moved only 400 metres in 45 minutes. He decided to abandon his car and walk the last 800 metres to the ground. The gates on that day were opened at 8.53 a.m. and by 9.30 a.m. signs were put up advising 'standing room only'. No new stands were built at Sydney, and for that matter at Adelaide and Brisbane, in the 1950s and 1960s. It was not until the 1970s that another era of significant ground improvements and stand construction emerged at the Test centres. Melbourne was an exception to the general rule: the Olympic Games and ever-increasing VFL finals crowds provided the incentives for the construction of a new public stand, completed by 1956, which increased the ground capacity to 120,000.

Another factor which adversely affected attendances was the timing of the Shield programme. Many games were played in October and November when children were still at school. In a typical season at this time children could be denied access to as much as half, and even more on occasions, of the Shield programme. Office workers, with much shorter annual holidays, had even less opportunity to watch major cricket. The cricket programme of the 1950s was still geared to men and women of means and leisure. The gradual expansion of the Shield programme from the 1920s, with more teams involved and more matches, meant that many more games were played at times inconvenient to the general public. When a state side used to play only two or three home games it was easier to schedule more of the season around the holiday period. No serious consideration was given to the presentation of cricket at a more convenient time until the 1960s, when Sunday play was introduced, and the late 1970s, when night cricket was begun.

One experiment which tried to cope with 'decline' was the introduction of a restricted Shield season in 1954–55. By halving the Shield programme administrators hoped, presumably, to reduce costs and avoid the danger of over-exposure of the game in a season dominated by an English tour. In 1954–55 each Test centre had just two Shield games and Western Australia, in the competition on a restricted basis, had just one match. Unfortunately two days of this game were washed out by a rare intrusion of rain in the West and WACA patrons had to be content with a home Shield season of just two days. It was a very lop-sided programme of cricket at Perth; following the tourists match against Western Australia, in mid-October, Perth patrons had to wait until mid-February for another two days of cricket. This experiment was never tried again.

A Short Recovery in the 1960s

By the early 1960s cricket had righted itself. The recovery was what officials had hoped and prayed for, because they had discovered no real solution to the 'decline' of the 1950s. It began with a player-led revival in 1960–61 which owed much to the flamboyant West Indians who batted with reckless daring, fielded brilliantly, and who had an explosive and well-balanced attack which stretched a good home batting side to the limit. Led by the personable and much admired Frank Worrell, they were one of the most attractive and positive sides ever to visit Australia. Equally responsible for the success of the series was the Australian team and its adventurous and attacking captain, Richie Benaud.

The series got off to a slow start with only 4,100 attending the last day of the First Test at Brisbane, the day of the historic tie. However, with an even and exciting contest right to the last Test the series drew ever-increasing crowds culminating in a world daily record of 90,800 on the Saturday of the Fifth Test at Melbourne. This was a more than impressive figure because it occurred on 11 February, far outside the traditional peak period of the Christmas–New Year holiday.

The West Indians were an immensely popular team and after the Fifth Test were given a rare tickertape reception as their motorcade proceeded through the streets of Melbourne. One of the unique features of this series was that Australian crowds supported the visitors as much, or almost as much, as the home side. Good cricket was applauded irrespective of who won. In fact Benaud was jeered by a large section of the MCG crowd in the Second Test when he appealed successfully against Solomon for hit wicket after Solomon's cap had fallen off and disturbed the wicket. The appeal, however, was a legitimate one as it occurred after Benaud had surprised Solomon by a wrong-un and had forced him into a hurried shot.

Nine years before another Australian captain, Lindsay Hassett, had been booed by his home MCG crowd after a successful appeal against West Indian batsman, Sonny Ramadhin. There were several reasons for the demonstration: the appeal for caught behind was a very belated one, not made until after the ball had been returned to the bowler, and the attitude of at least one of the fieldsmen suggested that there was an element of doubt involved. The most significant reason, however, was the crowd inclination to support the underdog West Indians.[2]

Cricket officials must have been pleased when the excitement of the 1960–61 Test series rubbed off on to the next Shield season, 1961–62, which attracted 363,360 spectators, the largest season total since 1927–28 and the third largest season total ever. The presence of West Indians Hall, Sobers and Kanhai must have added to spectator interest in a domestic season without Tests. The Shield competition was still a viable entity at this time because international cricket was restricted (apart from a lone Test against Pakistan in 1964) to six of the ten seasons in the 1960s. 1961–62 was one of the four seasons when Shield cricket was the top level of cricket available.

Public interest and media coverage remained high in a much-heralded 1962–63 series between a successful Benaud-led home side against a Dexter-captained English team. During the Third Test, for instance, Sydney viewers had no choice but to watch cricket between 4–6 p.m., the time allocated to live coverage, because all three channels focussed on the game.

Radio followed suit. Listeners were able to choose between the complete ball-to-ball description of the ABC and an alternative service provided by 2UE which had lured away Alan McGilvray. 2UE had not broadcast cricket in 1961 but 2UW then had significant, but not complete, ball-to-ball segments.

The media interest in cricket during the 1960–63 seasons repeated a pattern which had occurred in 1932–33. Whenever cricket produced an exciting series which generated great public support the commercial stations fought among themselves to jump on the bandwaggon. When times were lean and ratings were modest, the commercials left the field to the ABC, the long-term and trusted media patron of cricket.

During the 1950s and 1960s the ABC did not forget its close association with cricket which dated from 1932 and the benefits that flowed from this relationship. Cricket, even in its less popular times, still had a very wide audience and provided the ABC with a popular image. The ABC was also advantageously placed in periods of cricket resurgence in that it had a greater fund of expertise in cricket broadcasting to draw upon and listeners were more used to tuning in to the cricket on the ABC than to the commercials.

The bias towards cricket manifested itself in several ways. First, by covering major matches in their entirety the ABC determined that cricket would dominate the summer airwaves. Second, it capitalized on and contributed to expanding public interest in the game because it gave alternative sports little opportunity to establish themselves.

Cricket also continued to attract to its commentary team some of the most articulate and highly placed personalities in the ABC. The tradition established by Moses in the 1930s was maintained after the war by commentators such as Michael Charlton, founder of 'Four Corners', who spiced his commentaries with quotations from the Bible and Shakespeare, and visiting South African broadcaster, Charles Fortune, who entertained listeners both with his cheerful commentaries and his vivid and colourful descriptions of the behaviour of birds at cricket.

Birds and the weather have always provided the most promising subjects to fill in the gaps in the game so it is not surprising that Channel 9 in Sydney has institutionalised the weather in its 1982–83 cricket commentary by making it a regular feature of the game with its 'weather wall'. Perhaps the birds too have themselves contributed to the spectacle of a cricket match. Actress Kate Fitzpatrick, a knowledgeable cricket follower, has confessed to being fascinated by the field placings of the seagulls at the SCG for years: 'The amount they [the seagulls] understand about cricket is probably not so remarkable when you consider how much close-up time they spend at the ground. They stand solemnly at fine leg and gully, re-group after every ball and instinctively mass on the safe side. If I were a captain I'd be tempted to check the gulls.'[3]

The following season, 1963–64, only moderate crowds turned

out to watch the South Africans although this was followed by another successful Shield season: 313,147 attended in 1964–65. From then on the revival in cricket crowds quickly petered out and for the rest of the 1960s when there was a return to the 'slump' of the 1950s. The next series against England, 1965–66, was a dull and defensive contest which saw a drop in crowds of more than 20 per cent over the previous English tour. Worse was to follow in 1967–68 when a four-Test series against India drew only 121,735, less than one-third the number who had turned up to the last five-Test series against India in 1947–48. The return of the champion West Indian team in 1968–69 also proved a disappointment: the crowds were less than 60 per cent of the 1960–61 figures. The decline was mirrored in Shield attendances. Despite an expanded programme — Western Australia was now a full Shield participant — the season average from 1965–70, 235,356, remained at the level of the 1950s.

The decline in cricket was reflected in the media coverage. During the 1968–69 series the ABC alone provided live coverage of the Sydney Test. The three Sydney commercial stations preferred programmes such as 'Wyatt Earp', 'Blind Date', 'Jungle Jim' and 'Annie Oakley'. However, it was a different story when it came to television coverage of the Davis Cup, which began on Boxing Day 1968 in Sydney: it was covered in full by three channels, 2, 7 and 9. Only Channel 10 catered for the non-sports viewer with movies such as 'Sheena — Queen of the Jungle'.

By the late 1960s cricket's future as a major spectator sport looked far from certain. By this time Australians had more leisure alternatives than ever before and many opted for more individualistic sports such as tennis, surfing, motor car and cycle racing, rather than traditional team sports. Some faster-moving, less-time-consuming team sports, notably the various football codes, were less affected by this trend. Many must have wondered whether a more cerebral slower-paced sport could survive into a technologically transformed media-dominated future. Cricket seemed to have lost some of the glamour which once surrounded it. Officials were at a loss to understand the decline of the game let alone devise solutions.

Television eventually rescued cricket from seeming oblivion. This happened seven years before Kerry Packer implemented his programme of revitalization. In fact the television-led revival of cricket from 1970 created the environment in which such a takeover looked worthwhile.

Sunday Play

Although officials in the late 1960s had no effective strategy to arrest the slide in attendances they did make one positive marketing move, reluctantly on the part of some — the introduction of Sunday play. The change was an obvious move to make cricket more accessible to the public and consequently there was the prospect of larger crowds once the innovation was

A huge Rugby League crowd of 47,096 (Australia vs Great Britain, 1954) sits behind barbed wire at the Gabba. Note the primitive dividing fence and absence of cover.

accepted. The first Sunday game took place at the Gabba on 22 November 1964 between Queensland and Western Australia, the two States which had campaigned for this reform.[4]

Opposition to Sunday play amongst the older Associations was probably mostly due to an official conservatism but there was also the problem of escalating labour costs which were enhanced by Sunday penalty rates. It took a small army to stage a major cricket match at the SCG, for example, which was a legacy of colonial times when labour was much cheaper and there was more emphasis placed on social propriety and deference. In addition to the many who manned the turnstiles, the six who worked behind the scoreboard, the two who adjusted the sight-screen, and a number of others who kept the toilets in order, or who patrolled the stands to keep a watchful eye on the more exuberant younger patrons, there was one attendant whose function was to open the boundary fence gate for the umpires to enter or leave the field. With Sunday play this attendant's daily wage swelled from $22 to $41 in 1976. It was certainly an anomaly. Ray Robinson pointed out in 1976, that he received $107 for a four-day match (with a Sunday included) and State captain, Doug Walters, received a match payment of only $66 in 1975–76 and $80 in 1976–77.[5]

The move proved an instant success in Perth and Brisbane: between 1964 and 1982 Shield crowds on Sunday were 14.5 per cent higher at Perth than the next best-drawing day, Saturday, and the figure at Brisbane was almost as high. At a typical Perth Test, Sunday drew over a 1,000 more spectators, approximately 8 per cent more than Saturday. There were two main reasons for the success of Sunday sport at these two centres: Queensland and Western Australia had weaker anti-Sunday sport lobbies than other States and Sunday sport was not new in Bribane. For example, Sunday had been the major playing day in Rugby League since the mid-1950s. If anything, cricket officials were tardy in taking advantage of the wide social acceptance of devoting the whole weekend to sport.

In the other three States there was more resistance to change, particularly in South Australia. Sunday play at Adelaide was only partly successful: although the crowds were larger on Sundays than weekdays, Saturday outdrew Sunday by 16 per cent. Adelaide was and is one of the more conservative crowds: there has always been a section of the crowd there which prefers Saturday to Sunday play presumably for religious and traditional reasons.

Sydney and Melbourne fell mid way between the two extremes. For the first three seasons of Sunday play at the MCG the Saturday Shield attendance was invariably larger than the Sunday. However, during the 1970s Melbourne Test crowds at least came to prefer Sunday play: Sunday Test crowds from 1973–83 were 3 per cent larger than Saturdays.

During the last few years there has been a dramatic change in crowd preferences at Melbourne. The 'new' fans attracted to the one-day internationals have no prejudices against Sunday sport, in fact they have shown a clear preference for Sunday over Saturday play. The world record for a one-day international, 86,133, occurred on 22 January 1984. Melbourne officials were keen to capitalize on the superior drawing power of Sunday. Whenever there was a weekend double-header the best-drawing match (Australia vs England or the West Indies) was always set down for Sunday.

The emergence of Sunday play was an important development in the history of cricket crowds and Australian sport in general, because it signalled the triumph of promotion over official, and to some extent, spectator puritanism. Scheduling matches at more convenient and popular times gave many more people greater access to the game.

Expansion in the West

Western Australia entered the Shield competition in 1947–48 on a restricted basis. It achieved full status in 1956–57 but it had to wait until 1970 to earn a Test match. During this period there were a number of ground improvements at the WACA. After the old scoreboard was demolished during a storm in 1947 a new one was completed by 1954. A Players' Pavilion was constructed in the 1950s and there were improvements in the Farley (Members') Stand. The orientation of the Players' Pavilion is unusual, to say the least, because the stand does not face the wicket: spectators have to watch the game on an angle of at least 30 degrees; if they looked straight ahead they would miss the centre action by a fair margin. Sewerage pipes, apparently, were to blame for this architectural aberration. A new public stand, the Test Stand, was completed in time for the first Test there in 1970.

Some players from the 1950s and 1960s remember Western Australian crowds as conservative and rather quiet. Victorian and Western Australian bowler, Colin Guest, believed that this was because the Western Australians were almost always beaten. South Australian bowler, Eric Freeman, contended that the behaviour of the crowd was influenced by the distance between the players and spectators — the stands are a long way back from the fence. With the introduction of a reduced roped-off boundary in recent times, the WACA has a large wasted area within its fence, possibly a distance of 25 metres at some points. At the SCG, on the other hand, the recently introduced rope is just two metres within the boundary.

However, a majority of players, particularly in recent times, has made less flattering comments about the WACA crowd. Ken Meuleman, captain of the WA side in the late 1950s, described crowd members as 'parochial and immature' at that time and added that they had 'no real cricket knowledge' and an 'over-inflated opinion of success'. The words parochial and partisan crop up time and time again in descriptions of this crowd by players from the State and outside. New South Wales bowler, Gary Gilmour, put it more colourfully when he stated, 'You have to clap yourself on at the WACA.'

WA bowler, Tony Mann, has dismissed this criticism of his home crowd as ridiculous and others have pointed out that the WA crowd is now as appreciative of good cricket as any in the country. However, there is no question that the majority of players believe that there is more partisan feeling expressed at Perth than elsewhere. In fact some New South Wales players look with envy on their WA counterparts since they would prefer SCG crowds — who often abuse their home players as much as they applaud them — to be more partisan.

John Rutherford, WA's first Test player, has suggested some of the historical reasons behind WA attitudes to cricket. For many years the State was saddled with an invidious subsidy; it had to pay half the Adelaide–Perth return fare for interstate teams. When WA travelled east the State paid the full fare. The subsidy lasted until the mid 1960s. WA also suffered because it received only 1/13th of Test and tour profits: rather than assisting emerging and outlying cricket States the Board of Control maintained the privileged position of the established cricket States. New South Wales, for instance, had three Board members which entitled it to 3/13ths of national profits. Western Australia also had to wait until 1982 to have a Test selector, Lawrie Sawle, despite the fact that the State dominated the Shield in the 1970s and frequently dominated the Test side.

Rutherford himself had first-hand experience of discrimination against WA players. When he was selected for the 1956 Mailey–Taylor Testimonial match in Sydney he was left to make his own way — he was the only WA player chosen — from the airport whereas the three South Australians, who arrived on another flight, were met by officials. As a result he arrived a little late and by the time he padded up everyone else had finished.

Rutherford's problems did not end when he was selected for the 1956 tour. He was told by one official that he should join the team in Fremantle which meant that he would miss the first two matches of the tour which were in Tasmania. (Tourists in the

1950s still travelled by ship and played games along the way at Tasmania, Perth and other places such as Sri Lanka.) After discussions with captain Ian Johnson and Sir Donald Bradman he was permitted to proceed to Tasmania.

Former captain of Western Australian John Inverarity believes that Western Australians' strong desire for success, observable in players and supporters alike, results from an 'adolescent desire' to prove themselves. He remembers that on his first tour east, 1963–64, the side was 'soundly thrashed' in each game and out of this emerged a passion to reverse the situation which manifested itself in the attitude, 'We'll show them.' The highest West Australian priority was to 'stuff the Vics' because this State had consistently drained away the best football talent from the West. For a variety of reasons Western Australia has been able to retain its cricket talent and this, undoubtedly, is one of the reasons why the game is so prominent in the West. Inverarity also argued that in Western Australia there is a much stronger identification with the team, the town and the State than there is in New South Wales or Victoria.

There is no question that supporters in the West back their team more than cricket followers in the East. The Saturday–Sunday average Shield attendances for the past two decades indicate a superior attendance figure based on an aggregate basis. Western Australia's Sunday average from 1964–82 was 4,800 per game and Saturday average was 4,102 whereas the equivalent New South Wales figures were 2,824 and 2,633. The contrast would be even more impressive if the attendance was related to respective city populations. It can be seen that Western Australian Shield crowds represent about one-third of the size of the average Test crowd there whereas Melbourne Shield crowds were about one-eighth the Test average. Community support is also reflected in the level of sponsorship. In 1981 Perth millionaire, Alan Bond, pledged $100,000 to the State cricket association which was then a record for such a donation.

Western Australia's progressive administration has capitalized on the strong community support for the game. A 1982 match advertisement was headed: 'We'll knock the Vics for six to keep the Shield.' There was the added incentive of a $45,000 Shield sweep with a block of land and a holiday for two in London as well as many daily prizes. At least one former State player was critical of this promotion stating, 'It's no use bribing people to come to cricket.' However, the results suggest otherwise.

Many people think that there is a sameness in Australian crowds from one ground to another but this ignores the varied traditions at each ground and even the differences apparent in one part of the ground to another, and from one day to another. Adelaide, with its 'Lord's-type atmosphere', was universally described in the 1960s as the most conservative crowd in the country. This was not the case for the Queensland vs South Australia match which included play on Christmas Day and denied players Christmas dinner at home. The Christmas Day crowd was quite different from the usual quiet and fair-minded assembly which reflected the temper of a conservative city. The crowd did not turn up until after noon, and fortified with a festive lunch, was always boisterous. Woe betide the fieldsman who let a ball slip through his hands for bedlam would break out. And then around 5 p.m. the crowd vanished just as quickly as it arrived.

There was also a voluntary segregation practised by Outer patrons at Adelaide. Some of the rowdier and more thirsty spectators headed for the 'boozer' under the scoreboard. Other fans, who wanted to concentrate closely on the cricket, congregated on the half-dozen rows of seats in front of the Victor Richardson Gates. At this point the Oval is at its narrowest and the 100–200 people there were always close to the game. South Australian bowler, Jeff Noblet's father used to sit there. On one occasion Jeff chased a ball to the fence and as he picked it up looked up to see his father and said, 'Morning, Dad. How are you to-day?' After that his father was pestered with so many questions that he moved to the Members' Stand.

Adelaide, like any other ground, has its characters. One regular, christened 'the walker' by other patrons, used to walk from one end of the Outer to the other throughout the day scanning the crowd as if he were looking for an elusive friend who never materialized. He carried an Ansett bag and a towel loosely strung over his shoulder and made a point of never watching the cricket. Another, a thirtyish, undernourished man named 'the singer', used to (and still does) stumble out in front of the scoreboard in a very drunken state and sing the scoreboard in a liturgical style. Other grounds had their characters too. A bare-footed, freckle-faced boy became a great favourite of WACA spectators in the early 1950s. He made a tidy sum hiring out cushions which he carried round the ground stacked on his head.

The Impact of Television

Technology has always played a significant role in the spread of Australian cricket: cables, cheaper newspapers, bigger stands and scoreboards, and radio had all altered the shape of the game. However, after the Second World War almost every series brought some new invention or improvement which changed the way in which cricket was played, watched and perceived. For instance, 1954 witnessed the first transistor Test; 1958 saw the introduction of television and 1962–63 the first 'beer can' series. The opening of the Sydney–Melbourne coaxial cable by 1961 marked another milestone and enabled Sydney viewers to watch a live coverage of a Test played in Melbourne. Further advances in technology in 1970–71 allowed the nation to follow an entire series live for the first time.

Other changes came in more imperceptibly. No one quite knows when the lightweight cooler, known in Sydney as the 'esky', first made its presence felt at cricket but most players

Officials now have to replicate home comforts and replays at the ground to compete with television. Purists fear that this may distract the public from a real study of the game.

believe that it became a significant presence on the Hill, and a potential headache for administrators, from around 1970.

The 1970s continued this trend with colour television, live television coverage from England, night cricket and many innovations in television broadcasting, such as the use of zoom lenses.

Neville Cardus went to the first transistor Test in Sydney in 1954 'hoping to enjoy my first Test match in several decades, having had to write about them for more than a quarter of a century', as he put it in the *Sydney Morning Herald* of 22 December 1954. He found a quiet seat in the Ladies' Stand but had to move when he was disturbed by a 'squall of children'. Worse was to follow because he was 'at once encircled by a whole Australian family, complete with radio, which they turned on full blast and — believe it or not — listened to the ABC commentators even while looking at the actual play'. Having had this experience Cardus predicted that when television was introduced people would want to take their sets to the game and 'watch the screen vigilantly' to see if it corresponded with 'objective truth'. He was not far wrong. Spectators may not have taken their television sets to the ground because there have not been any lightweight equivalents of the transistor and also because television is only broadcast for part of the day in the city of origin, but the MCG authorities obliged spectators with a video matrix, a giant television screen, which enables spectators to watch both the cricket and the replays. Cardus, a purist, was concerned that the eye of the camera and the opinions of the experts would interfere with and perhaps one day become a substitute for the spectator's own assessment of the game.[6]

However, it must be remembered that not all spectators have an intimate knowledge of the game, as Cardus had; consequently they can benefit from and appreciate the comments of the experts. Not every watcher of the game was able to follow each ball as closely as Cardus obviously did and a replay, while not the real thing, was certainly better than missing out on a dramatic event. It is also true that even the keenest and most dedicated eye might miss out on the 'objective truth' of a dismissal and a slow-motion replay will enable a viewer to get closer to the truth. No doubt some spectators take the easy path and watch the replay rather more intently than the real thing but the purist can always study both the event and the replay intently.

It is significant that television sets were installed in Press boxes around the country to provide journalists with replays long before the MCG had its video matrix. Television replays have made the task of the journalist easier and have saved some from embarrassment such as occurred in 1934 when a number of pressmen took an early lunch and missed the dismissal of the top three English batsmen in four balls bowled by Bill O'Reilly. Unfortunately photographers cannot make use of replays and David Frith, editor of *Wisden Cricket Monthly*, was more than a little perturbed when the photographer, on whom he most relied, took an early lunch during the 1983 Sydney Test and missed a Greg Chappell catch on the stroke of lunch which was one of the best of the season.

Whatever the merits of the arguments concerning the transformation of cricket-watching through technology, there is no doubt that transistors introduced a new dimension to the cricket commentary, which has continued ever since: the regular request that radios which feed-back into the commentary be turned down, were and are still made. Players continue to be disturbed by the commentaries not only because of the noise but also because they receive an instant opinion, sometimes critical of their every move on the field.

Television was by far the most significant technological change to affect cricket. Television broadcasting began in Australia in January 1956 and by the following season the ABC was also broadcasting substantial segments of Shield play. Sydney viewers, for instance, were able to watch most of the two sessions of play in the New South Wales vs Queensland match in January 1958 and by the following season Sydney and Melbourne viewers were able to watch live Test cricket, from tea to stumps, when the match was played in their own city. (If the match was not played in their city they had to be content with a 30-minute film of highlights which was flown between the capital cities and screened mid-evening.)

Television coverage of overseas matches was much slower to develop. Films were made of the 1957–58 South African Tests and were shown within a matter of days to television audiences.

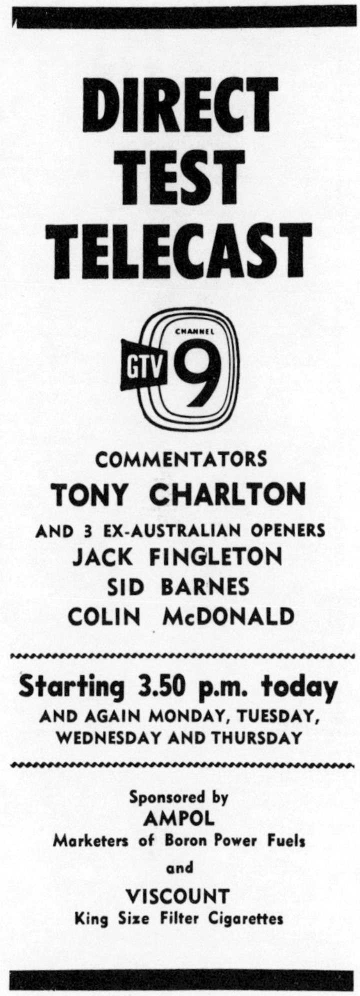

An expanding media opened up new career opportunities for former players.

Not much progress had been made by 1964. Radio listeners followed the first day's play on Thursday night–Friday morning live but the first day's play did not reach the television screen until Sunday noon (three days later) and the second day's play was screened on Monday at 6.30 and 8.30 p.m.

The impact of television on cricket was a much slower process than radio. It took just eight years for radio to progress from the first live broadcast to a full national coverage and another two years for a complete broadcast of the English Tests, even if this was simulated. With television it took 13 years to progress from the first live broadcast to a full national coverage in 1970–71 and it was another five years before an overseas match was broadcast live.

There were several reasons for the delayed impact of television, namely costs and the need to overcome a number of technical problems. However, an experiment conducted by the ABC during the 1960–61 series provided the incentive for a more extensive television coverage. After the coaxial cable was established between Sydney and Melbourne, Sydney viewers were able to watch the entire Fifth Test which decided the series. The experiment was an immense success: the annual report of the ABC commented that 'probably no programme — certainly no day-time television programme — has attracted so many viewers in New South Wales'. This was the first occasion that cricket followers could watch an entire Test on television. Cricket enthusiasts in other cities were not so fortunate and had to make do with filmed highlights.

Presumably the costs involved in televising matches limited live coverage in the 1960s to the final Test of the series against England. However, as the decade progressed the number of cities able to enjoy televised cricket increased. The Fifth Test in the 1962–63 series was shown simultaneously in three cities — Sydney, Melbourne and Canberra. By the next English series, 1965–66, the network had been widened and several Tests in the eastern States were transmitted direct in the State of origin from tea to stumps and relayed to all other States except Western Australia. In the lesser series against India, and the one-sided series against the West Indies later in the decade, there was no national hook-up for the final Test and viewers had to be content with filmed highlights and two hours of live transmission for the Test played in their own city.

Advances in television technology in the late 1960s, the satellite and a Western Australia microwave link, created a revolution in television broadcasting. During the 1970–71 series the ABC was able, for the first time ever, to provide a live telecast between tea and stumps in the State of origin and up to a full six hours of play in all other States, including Western Australia. Viewers throughout the country had the opportunity to watch an entire summer of Test cricket: 30 days of viewing, which included up to 180 hours of live Test cricket for country viewers, and approximately 160 hours for viewers in the major cities. The

ABC's Research Department estimated that the average audience for the later Tests was in excess of one million per day and that one person in four in the country watched the ABC's Test cricket telecasts at one time or another during the series.

The impact of this development cannot be overestimated for no series has ever attracted one million paid spectators. The 1936–37 series holds the record with 948,498 spectators in 26 days. The 1970–71 series drew 616,196 spectators which amounted to an average daily figure of 20,279. The television audience, at least for the later Tests, was approximately 50 times this figure. It is not surprising that television and television interests came more and more to dictate the shape of the game in the 1970s and that the cricket world was convulsed by a war, which was largely inspired by this huge television audience.

Crowd Behaviour and Barracking

Technology did not have an immediate effect on crowd behaviour, in fact crowds continued to be comparatively well behaved in the first decade after the Second World War. When Len Hutton batted through an English innings on a Brisbane sticky, he was accorded a 'magnificent reception' which was superior, noted the *Sydney Morning Herald* of 9 December 1950,

Umpire Lou Rowan took no chances with his bails and stumps when the crowd invaded the SCG prematurely, two runs before an Australian victory, Third Test, 1962–63.

Final year students from Sydney and Canterbury High Schools barrack at the SCG in 1958.

to any previous ovation given to an English batsman. The crowds too knew their cricket: they needed no prompting to applaud milestones in the game, such as the 50 partnership. Members continued to dress formally: though the coat was dispensed with and white shirts and ties predominated. This continued into the 1960s when the *Age* of 31 December 1962 commented that the (MCG) Members' Stand presented a 'united white shirt front'. By this time more informal standards prevailed in the Outer, for under the scoreboard at the southern edge of the MCG were the 'bare-back brigade'.

Women were prominent at the first series after the war and the media made its usual jibes about their knowledge of the game. The *Age* of 2 January 1947 commented that women provided 'comic relief' at the cricket and found their behaviour 'most amusing':

> Even the most serious-minded male cricket enthusiasts had to admit that women caused some comic relief to the day's concentration with their intermittent screams when a bump ball bounced high and seemed to the unitiated to be a threat to the Australian batsmen. On several occasions highly excited women jumped to their feet in false alarm, with piercing screams, to the amusement of other spectators. When a catch was dropped in front of the Members' Stand during

Very little must have escaped the keen eyes of the older generation of Hill barrackers at the SCG in 1958 who still wore coats, hats and even ties.

the afternoon, the women's cries of fear, then hysterical relief were most amusing.

Misogyny has been one of the enduring themes of Australian cricket commentary, though undoubtedly it was true that some women, and perhaps even some men, came to cricket for the glamour and the spectacle.

The main crowd demonstrations in the 1950s were directed against slow batsmen and defensive play. These tactics were rewarded with heckles, boos and the slow hand-clap (no one knows when this form of crowd behaviour emerged but players believe it was a post-war development). Slow play provided ample ammunition for the barracker. On one occasion in 1963 a Sydney spectator could take no more of Peter Parfitt's padding away to Benaud's bowling (this was before the amendment to the lbw law) and called out: 'Why don't yer tie yer bloody bat to yer pad, Parfitt? Then you might make a run!' Dour Jim Burke took an entire day to reach 85 in the match between New South Wales and the MCC on 14 November 1958 and prevented the SCG crowd from watching a Harvey–O'Neill partnership. When Burke narrowly escaped being run-out barrackers yelled, 'Let him go' and 'Give him out'. Burke inspired one of the classic comments of Australian barracking which has been repeated and

Sponsorship, 1947 style, maintained the close link between cricket and alcohol.

published many times, 'Burke, I wish you were a statue and I was a pigeon.'

Burke was one player who was acclaimed as a hero by the media and the crowd, after a century in his first Test, but who became a villain a few seasons later when he attempted to grind his way back into the national side. No one knows what affect sustained crowd hostility has on a player but the fickleness of the sporting public, who acclaim heroes one day and knock them the next, must leave some psychological mark on sensitive individuals.[7]

Anal comments, such as the one made to Burke, and other crude remarks may have become more commonplace after 1945 although there have always been some spectators who have made basic and earthy comments. Ron Hamence, who played before and after the Second World War, remembered there was always a lot of noise under the 'boozer' (the Adelaide scoreboard) in the later afternoon when the 'Fourex started to talk'. One such comment was made to English captain, Walter Hammond during the 1946–47 series when he batted very slowly using the England vs South Australia match for Test batting practice. Hammond at the time was being sued for divorce. Late in the afternoon one barracker called out, 'Why don't you belt the ball, like you used to belt your wife?' More innocuous was a comment made to Trevor Bailey in the 1950s at the SCG, 'Eh, Bailey, your bowling reminds me of a lavatory seat... straight up and down.' Later, during the 1960s, Sam Trimble was abused by one spectator at the Gabba, 'You can't bat, you can't bowl, you can't field, all you can do is root the selectors.'

Players have always had to endure personal comments because cricket crowds have such a long time to observe every feature and mannerism. Big noses and ears have been obvious targets: Bill Lawry has been called 'Pinocchio' (along with Wayne Clark) and a 'big-nosed pelican' while another spectator feigned astonishment at the nose of Dave Renneberg: 'That's not a nose, it's a banana.' Lindsay Hassett was often the recipient of comments about his ears such as 'Monkey!'. Hassett, late in his career, was also chided for his age by a Gabba wag: 'Eventide [an old mens' home] awaits you Hassett.' A Sydney spectator once noted that Les Joslin's creams were not as clean as they could be and asked, 'Don't they wash in Victoria?' A friend of Bill Watson's, a potato and onion wholesaler, who worked alongside Watson at the markets, always used to announce his arrival at the SCG and his link with Watson with the call of, 'Ay, ay, potaties.'

No one, however, attracted more comment than Tony Lock who had the double 'misfortune' of being both English and bald. In addition to 'nude nut' and the more banal 'Pommy bastard', Lock was the object of a classic comment at the SCG. With a great sense of the dramatic a barracker repeated the comment, 'Lock, I'm awake to you', a number of times in the space of a few overs. Then, with the audience in his hands, he delivered the punch-line, 'You're not actually bald, your head's grown through your hair.'

Relationships between players and the crowd were often complex and challenging particularly for those players posted on the fence in front of the Outer. In his first match at the SCG Gavin Stevens was singled out for abuse from an Englishman. 'Look what you South Australians did to Sid Barnes,' he yelled. 'You crucified him.' And with each fresh barb the crowd got more and more behind the barracker. Finally the Englishman went too far when he called out, 'Look what you did to Larwood...' Stevens had a ready reply for his tormentor which turned the tables in the argument, replying, 'My friend, I wasn't even born then.' From that moment the crowd turned on the barracker and pelted him with oranges and refuse; he left the ground soon after. In the same match Stevens almost created an Ian Chappell–dropped-pants incident. Impressed by the beautiful carpet-like surface of the SCG Stevens called out loudly to Duldig: 'If anyone misses the ball on this ground, he should drop his pants in the centre.' When the very first ball hit to Stevens went through his hands to the fence he felt there were 'ten pairs of eyes on me to see what I would do'. Shamefaced Stevens was shocked into inaction and was unable to practise what he preached.

Barracking has never been confined to the spectators, players too have made their quips and comments. When Badcock set out for a risky third run the wicket-keeper yelled out to him, ''eave her in, Evildick.'

One interesting exchange took place between players and spectators in the 1950s when Victorian State Liberal member, Sam Loxton, took on striking waterside workers who went to the cricket en masse. According to the *Sydney Morning Herald* of 31 January 1956 Loxton stirred up the crowd when he bowled a number of bumpers one of which New South Wales batsman, Burke, ducked into. Loxton, a colourful character, acknowledged the jeers by motioning with his hands, Fender-style, 'as if he were a cheer-leader asking for more noise'. He was greeted with comments such as, 'You've got Bob [Menzies] on your side, Sam', and 'If you get a wicket, Sam, we'll go back to work.' However, Loxton had the last laugh. During the second innings he developed a 'bad shoulder' and was fielding at slip. When he chased the ball to the boundary one of the wharfies declared, 'if you're thirty-five, I'm twenty-five.' Loxton then moved slowly and deliberately back to the centre and shouted his reply: 'At least I've got a birth certificate to prove it.' The wharfie knew that he'd lost the encounter with Loxton and like the Englishman he soon headed for the gates.

Good barracking stories are retold many times and embellished. Consequently there is more than one version of this story. Lindsay Kline and Ian Meckiff agree with Loxton on the punch-line but presented variations on the original comment. According to Kline it was: 'It says in this souvenir that you look thirty-five, but my God, you look fifty-three.' Meckiff thought it was: 'If you're forty, then I'm 140.' It seems the story has improved with age. Loxton was a popular figure with Australian crowds. He always made a point of chatting with the MCG Outer crowd and when he first arrived there each day he would call out, 'How are you? Everyone well?'

The tradition of cultivating Outer patrons was carried on by Max Walker and Alan Hurst. In fact Hurst's awareness of the importance of humouring the MCG crowd led to an amusing incident in a Test in the late 1970s. After bowling an opening over Hurst walked to the boundary and was confronted by a barracker, in the vicinity of Bay 13, with t-shirt, shorts, thongs, a paunch, a full cartridge (esky) of beer and a silly smile: he was, as Hurst described him, a 'dead-set Norm'.

'Have a drink', he yelled. 'There's plenty here.' Hurst turned down the offer but implied that he might partake later. The offer was repeated a number of times and not wishing to anger the barracker or arouse the crowd, Hurst decided to accept the hospitality but opted for a handful of ice, some of which he placed in his mouth. When he chanced to return to his host next over he was surprised to find him cooling his feet in the cartridge ice. 'How long have you had your feet there?' Hurst enquired. When the barracker replied, 'Right from the start of the game,' Hurst felt quite sick in the stomach.

Crowds continued to be well-behaved in the 1960s but there were some ominous warnings, as the decade progressed, of the more turbulent 1970s. Keith Dunstan has labelled the 1962–63 series as the first 'beer can series'. Cans had just come on to the market and they were rolled down the concrete steps of the Southern Stand to provide 'that most representative MCG noise'. Cans were also clunked together to provide a more modern and louder variant of the slow hand-clap. There was no record of thrown cans but it didn't take long for this to develop. Sydney spectators copied the slow can-clap to protest against dreary play. The noisiest demonstration occurred late on the first day of the Fifth Test against England in 1963 when cans were banged for ten minutes.

On the last day of the Third Test at Sydney in 1963 hordes of youngsters invaded the pitch thinking the match was over. They struggled with one of the umpires, who was attempting to protect the stumps and the bails. Two stumps were taken though one was returned. Television viewers saw a boy in white shorts pocket the ball and scamper away with it. With two runs still needed for victory and heavy rain threatening Simpson signalled frantically for another stump. When the match finally ended youngsters again invaded the field and shortly after, a squad of policemen turned up — too late to prevent either invasion. The *Sydney Morning Herald* of 16 January 1963 noted that many of the boys who jumped over the fence were armed with autograph books even though players were barred from signing books on the field of play. By the 1970s this rule had been abandoned. There was a greater police presence on the first day of the Fifth Test of the series: ten minutes before stumps there were twenty-one policemen ranged round the boundary who discouraged all but two spectators from jumping the fence when play ended.

By the late 1960s 'hooliganism' had emerged as a problem on the Sydney Hill and cans were not just rolled and clapped, they were also thrown. Many long-term Sydney Hill spectators declared that in future they would watch cricket on television only. They complained of being 'showered with beer cans and ice, and almost deafened by the drunken abuse hurled at players'. It is hard to believe that Trust members had not, as Arnold Furniss of Balmain commented, 'heard snatches of the screams of the mob, or seen the sun flashing on flying beer cans and the gay whirl of colour in the vortex of a brawl'. He made a suggestion to the Trust which has been made regularly ever since: why could the SCG Trust not ban alcohol from the ground, or at least set aside a small area for those who want to watch in peace? Although the Trust has investigated many complaints the problem remained unsolved at the end of the 1982–83 season.[8]

By the late 1960s crowd invasions of the field had become a regular occurrence. When Bill Lawry reached a Test century at the MCG in 1968, 500 spectators swarmed on to the field to congratulate him according to the *Sydney Morning Herald* of 28 December 1968. In the process Lawry and his partner were 'pummelled heavily' and Lawry was 'struck heavily on the ear by one over-enthusiastic spectator — perhaps a portent of the more famous Alderman incident of 1982. Umpire Col Egar almost came to blows with a heavily built man as he struggled successfully to retain the stumps; but the bails were stolen. The police presence seemed hardly adequate. It took officials a long time to evolve better techniques of crowd management and during this time cricket-watching on the Hill, or in the Outer at other grounds, became even more hazardous. Officials at some grounds seem to have taken the easy way out by turning a blind eye to invasions at major milestones in the hope that this action might limit intrusions to once or twice a day.

Sydney and Melbourne were not the only grounds to witness declining standards in crowd behaviour in the late 1960s. Ross Duncan recalls that in one of his first seasons at the Gabba in 1964–65, he was pelted with cans after he dropped a catch in front of a group of patrons who were swilling beer. His captain, Burge, decided to move him to a position in front of the Members' Stand and gave him some words of encouragement: 'Don't worry, son, you'll get the next', and 'They'll [the members] appreciate your situation and give you encouragement.' However, worse was to follow because Duncan dropped another catch and Burge was at a loss to know where to put him next. Fortunately for Duncan the captain dropped a catch soon after and the crowd criticism shifted from him to Burge.

Ian Chappell, a shrewd captain, capitalized on this principle to protect one of his players during a Shield match in the 1970s. Chappell was faced with the fact that one of his key bowlers, Terry Jenner, had allowed crowd comments to get under his skin and to affect his bowling. Chappell proceeded to rile the crowd with the result that they started to abuse him and forget about Jenner. The strategy worked admirably and Jenner settled down to take five wickets.

Players would be less than human if they were not affected by crowd comments, at least on some occasions. However, it seems clear that some players, such as the volatile and sometimes hot-tempered Jenner, were more affected than other, more phlegmatic individuals. It is also true that some players are more vulnerable at certain periods of their career, for example, when they are struggling to retain their places in a side, than at other times. The situation is particularly difficult for a young player who has had a rapid rise to the top but who then has had to struggle in subsequent seasons. Jim Burke was one such player and Peter Allan of Queensland was another. Allan experienced the fickleness of the Gabba crowd in the 1960s. After he had taken three South Australian wickets in an over he was cheered all the way to the boundary but one over later his feat was forgotten because he proceeded to drop a catch and was roundly booed.

During the 1950s and 1960s technology began to transform the way cricket was played, watched and presented. New conventions of behaviour emerged both outside and inside the boundary. With more gamesmanship in cricket from the early 1970s largely good-natured barracking was replaced with more concentrated and less humorous sledging.

CHAPTER FIVE

'Ugly' Ockers and Full Eskies

Revival in the 1970s

The early 1970s were a crucial watershed period in Australian cricket which marked an end to the crowd slump. Even more importantly, it marked the emergence of a more dynamic image for cricket which enabled it to appeal to a wider and more youthful audience, and to recapture the ground which had been lost to other sports, such as tennis, in the 1950s. There were a number of ingredients in this cricket revival. Extensive television coverage from 1970 added many new followers while the dramatic and exciting series of 1970–71 and those from 1974–77, and the emergence of a youthful and successful Ian Chappell-led national team provided cricket with a modern and vigorous image.

Members of this side contributed significantly to cricket's revival partly because they played such positive cricket but also because some of them, notably Dennis Lillee, quickly became skilled media performers in their own right. Lillee in fact built up such a following that Jack Fingleton headed one of his articles: 'Forget Arnie's Army — now it's Lillee's Legions'. In the *Age* on 4 January 1977 Fingleton described how an MCG crowd gave Lillee 'every support' and how they 'roared and rooted for Lillee, spurring him on, and it was just what he wanted after his other days of mixed experience.' There is no question that Lillee skilfully used the crowd in this Test (and in many others), which responded with the deafening chant of 'Lill-eee, Lill-eee, Lill-eee', to inspire himself and to intimidate the Pakistani batsmen who collapsed on the fourth day of the Test and set up an Australian victory.

For officials the most encouraging feature of the revival of cricket crowds was that it was solid and broad-based: it was not confined simply to the major series against England and the West Indies but it also rubbed off on to other levels of cricket. After the 1970–71 home series and the closely fought 1972 English tour there was a boom in Shield attendances in 1972–73 (319,409 spectators) and in 1973–74 (348,684) — the fourth largest Shield season total on record. Both figures were much larger than the average season totals for the 1950s and 1960s of just over 235,000. The 1972–74 Shield crowds were even more impressive given that there was competition from a three-Test series against Pakistan in 1972–73 (218,097) and a three-Test series against New Zealand (120,729) in 1973–74. Shield figures have plummeted since 1977 because there has been a major Test series in every subsequent season and there has been an additional round of one-day international cricket each season. The average Shield season total from 1974–80 fell to 203,802 even though more matches were played.

There is no question that cricket's popularity soared in the three seasons before World Series Cricket (WSC). The Lillee–Thomson blitz of the English team and the return of the Ashes in 1974–75 attracted the largest series crowd, 777,333, since 1946–47. Crowds were almost as large in the following two seasons. The West Indies drew 741,311 in a six-Test series in 1975–76 including a crowd of 85,661 on the first day of the Melbourne Test. Then, in the following season, there were encouraging crowds at the three Tests against Pakistan (324,657), more than 50 per cent larger than the last tour in 1972–73 (218,097) and the season was capped off with the Centenary Test which attracted 248,260 for a four-Test season total of 572,917.

Cricket-watching was also enhanced by the introduction of colour television in 1974–75 and by the addition of slow-motion replays so that spectators were able, as Rod Humphries put it in the *Sun-Herald* on 12 January 1975, 'to see the graceful slow motion action of Dennis Lillee as he rattled rib after rib at the SCG'. Before this time cricket replays had been at normal speed. However, it was not long before the slow-motion replay, originated in Canada to help audiences see ice hockey goals that the human eye simply could not see, was applied to less fast-moving sports to provide a viewer with a second or third view of a dramatic or controversial moment.[1]

For many it became a substitute for the real thing. The replay has now become so institutionalized in all sports that viewers can count on many versions from every conceivable angle of any significant happening. Such a development has placed an enormous strain on umpires who have to make a split-second decision on an incident that they might see, and occasionally even fail to see, just once. Umpires have been loathe to call on technological assistance even though the electronic eye is now well established in tennis and the photo-finish has long been part of more professionally organized racing, both animal and human. It now seems just a matter of time before there will be laser beams across the crease, to help reduce the number of controversial run-outs, or something else will be introduced to reduce the anomaly of 'human' errors (made by men who are paid only $1,400 per Test) which could affect the earnings of players on around $50,000 per annum. Another frequently made suggestion is that there should be a third umpire in the pavilion, who could study the replay, and provide further information for the men in the middle. However, it is unlikely that technology could ever cope with the complexities of the lbw law.

By the 1972–73 season 'back-pack' equipment for cameramen was an integral part of television coverage. The 'back-pack' is a portable video-recorder and since it was not locked into the game itself like the other four cameras it could be used for crowd pictures, interviews, close-ups and for shots of players coming on to the ground. Up to this time television cameras were located in one bank which meant that viewers saw the game from one angle and one end of the ground. This also meant that probably half, if not more, of the crowd could sit in their seats without fear of appearing on the screen.

There were also a number of technological advances which enhanced television coverage of overseas tours. During the 1972 tour to England a 30-minute segment of highlights was beamed back to Australia by satellite at the end of each day's play: it was then shown on the ABC at 6 p.m. on the following evening, several hours before the next day's play. Such was the interest in the Fifth Test, which Australia had to win (and did) to square the series, that the ABC arranged a live coverage of the last day's play which continued until 40 minutes after lunch. This was the first time an overseas match had been covered live. However, it was not until the final of the 1975 Prudential Cup between the West Indies and Australia that a match was televised in its entirety. It was thought the match which began at 8 p.m. (EST) would continue until approximately 3 a.m. In fact this dramatic and fluctuating final went well beyond the scheduled time — it lasted almost nine hours — and was not decided until 5.30 a.m. approximately. The game, the ABC later reported, created 'unprecedented interest' and 'viewer reaction throughout Australia indicated that this was probably the most popular sporting telecast ever undertaken'. During the 1975 Test series the ABC provided direct telecasts of each day's play up to the luncheon interval and it noted that viewer interest was 'intense'. The coverage of overseas tours was extended in 1977 when viewers were able to watch the first session and part of the afternoon session. However, it was not until 1980 that an entire Test series played overseas was televised live in Australia.

With cricket's new-found popularity the ABC found itself, not surprisingly, competing with commercial television interests. ABC television had capitalized on, and enhanced, the public interest in cricket: in the 1974–75 season it televised 170 hours of cricket which was more than a quarter of the time devoted to sport on the ABC, judging from the 1975–76 figure which stated that the ABC broadcast a total of 715 hours of sport. This meant that during the summer months more than half the ABC sporting coverage was given over to cricket.

During the 1974–75, 1975–76 seasons Channel 7's 'Sport Spectacular' televised cricket with assistance from its sponsors, Colgate Palmolive, National Ford and Waltons: its commentary team included ex-players Bill Lawry and Richie Benaud and for the West Indies series a current player not involved in the series,

Tony Greig. The ABC stuck more to its tried and trusted formula of integrating ex-players, such as Paul Sheahan and Frank Tyson — who usually gave the expert comments — with ABC straightmen, such as Norman May, who concentrated on the ball-to-ball description. The idea was that the ABC regulars were best equipped to describe the actual events, whereas the ex-internationals were best able to interpret them. By concentrating exclusively on recent ex-internationals the commercials were developing a different commentary formula: perhaps it was thought that some ex-player glamour would rub off on to the broadcast and appeal more directly to the growing band of youthful followers of the game. By the following season, 1976–77, the commercial team had moved to the Ten network: and Benaud and Lawry were joined by Bob Simpson and Ian Chappell. In the first year of WSC the commercial team, minus Bob Simpson who returned to the cricket field to lead the Establishment side, found a more permanent home at Channel 9.

Until 1977 the ABC held off its commercial rivals and continued to monopolize the television audience for cricket. In fact the ABC could boast that according to independent ratings surveys it captured 75–85 per cent of the audience across Australia during the 1976–77 Pakistan Tests and the Centenary Test. The commercial networks achieved a very poor rating of 15–25 per cent of the audience despite their galaxy of ex-internationals. The ABC still had the advantage of a traditional and loyal audience, a long and continuous experience of cricket broadcasting, and a wealth of experience which flowed out of this. The commercial networks had yet to devise an attractive alternative to woo the newer fans of cricket or even to wean away a few of the traditional supporters. 1977 was the highpoint of the ABC's domination of cricket television. It was ironic that this very success made the ABC's future position vulnerable; it assured that the commercial interests had even greater incentives to devise means to break its near-monopoly.

The Emerging Rift in the Cricket World

There were many signs of revolution, of division and debate, within the hitherto monolithic world of cricket well before 1977. In addition to the television battle for cricket ratings there was an emerging split in the cricket audience itself, between the long-term, traditional, and usually high-brow followers of the game and the newer, often younger, more low-brow fans. The latter group were less patient with the slower rhythms which punctuated some sections of cricket; they were more inspired by media-generated hype, aggression on the field and the excitement of cricket highlights, with the inevitable flurry of fours, sixes and wickets. After the Third Test of the 1974–75 series many cricket enthusiasts wrote to the *Sydney Morning Herald* putting forward their views. Former English women's team captain, Betty Archdale, came down on the side of the traditionalists on 4 January 1975 with pleas for 'more silence and less talk' in the television commentary. She complained of the 'incessant chatter of the announcers' and that remarks such as 'fifteen minutes in terms of time' did little to enhance the game. The case for the purist received further support on 8 January from former Liberal parliamentarian and Australian Ambassador to the US, Sir Howard Beale, who described how he 'groaned and gnashed his teeth at the verbose drivel perpetrated by some commentators'. Beale took exception not only to the commentators' 'chatter' but he was also unhappy with their 'mangled grammar and illiterate pronunciation'.

The letters of Archdale and Beale generated a response from Richie Benaud of Coogee. While he admitted that it was preferable in television to talk 'as briefly as possible', he argued on 10 January that it was necessary to add all relevant facts, comments and opinions to the picture on the screen 'for the benefit of *all classes of viewers*':

> Those viewers range through those who have played cricket well, moderately or badly, housewives peering at the screen through a mist of washing-up, children wanting to be educated in the game, those who through some physical handicap or employment have been unable to get to the ground, and some who have never before seen a cricket match on television.

This foreshadowed the full-scale Establishment–WSC debate of 1977–79. As captain of the 1934 English women's team, Betty Archdale had a deep knowledge of the game, consequently she found many comments superfluous and even patronizing. Richie Benaud was more realistic and pragmatic and recognized the need to strike a balance between cricket's varied followers.

Another more obvious and more publicized strain in the cricket world was the growing player disenchantment with payments. With the limited crowd growth in the 1950s and 1960s player returns from the game had declined in real terms since the 1930s. At the height of the Depression a Test player was paid £30 ($60) per Test, which was about nine weeks' pay for a worker on the basic wage. This meant that a player who appeared in the entire series was paid the equivalent of almost a year's basic wage salary. In the 1950s and the 1960s Test payments failed to keep pace with the cost of living increases: by 1954 players received only £60 ($120) per Test which represented approximately five weeks' salary under the basic wage award. And payments in the late 1950s and 1960s fell even further behind wage increases. On the other hand players' overseas allowances more than doubled from the 1930s to the 1950s (£600 in 1938; £1,200 in 1953 and about the same in 1956). During that period, however, the basic wage increased by about 450%. Players were encouraged to participate in cricket for the love of the game, which most accepted, but few could fail to observe the big money that was now being earnt by other sportsmen such as tennis players and golfers.

Television transformed the player payment debate. Players were now no longer watched by a crowd of 20,000 or even 40,000 but their efforts were studied by hundreds of thousands and even millions in peak periods. As media stars they felt entitled to just remuneration.

Crowd size became the central issue in the debate emerging within the cricket world. The increased scope of public interest sparked discussion about the purpose and presentation of the game, the adequacy of facilities, and the relevance of a traditional programme formula. Cricket commentators also had to decide whether to cater more to an established audience or whether to woo, consolidate and possibly even add to, cricket's newer and less initiated followers.

The 'Ugly Australian' at Cricket

Cricket administrators must have rubbed their hands with glee at the return of the crowds in the 1970s and at cricket's more youthful, dynamic, contemporary, and even up-market, image in this era. They were somewhat less pleased, and less prepared for, the behaviour of some patrons at the ground. In many respects cricket crowds returned to the bad old days of the larrikin era: pitch invasions became a regular occurrence, violence against umpires and players became commonplace, spectators were arrested in greater numbers, brawls and mêlées in the Outer broke out frequently, and more and more police were ushered in. Players too began again to question decisions and to debate rules with umpires; and 'sledging' (organized and persistent baiting of players) emerged as an institution at this time. The reputation of the Australian crowd as a good-natured, fair-minded and knowledgeable assembly began to nosedive and the Hills of the country became synonymous with cheap jingoism, boorishness, partisan barracking, intimidation, vulgar abuse and, to many, ugly ockerism.

While discussing the crowd unrest of the 1970s, and for that matter of the 1980s, two issues must be borne in mind because they have been regularly raised in the media. The first centres on the question of whether or not the behaviour of the contemporary cricket crowd is worse than that of earlier times. Was the behaviour of the 1970s a return to the unrest which characterized pre-1914 crowds and is violence in popular culture a cyclical occurrence? Is the ocker or the yobbo at cricket simply a larrikin, even the grandson of a larrikin, in a new guise? And what elements of his behaviour constitute a revival of the larrikin mode and what elements are new?

The second issue relates to the cause, and possible solution of crowd unrest. The most popular explanation, which undoubtedly contains much truth, is that cricket crowd unrest is merely a reflection of a larger social malaise, a decline in social standards and accepted conventions. Significantly, the re-emergence of hooliganism in the late 1960s co-incided with the high point of

"I'd have thought they'd use some underarm in this heat!"

Ockers and yobbos have not been treated kindly by the press. To the purists, also, the high profile of ockers symbolizes the decline of the cricket crowd.

the anti-Vietnam War movement and the emergence of the more conservative but nonetheless anti-Establishment ockerism in the 1970s. If this theory is the sole explanation of crowd unrest, cricket crowds will not behave well again until some new social consensus emerges.

While this explanation is plausible in some respects, it is also likely that the crowd disorder problem has been made much worse by an official inability to analyse and cope with the problem, to devise appropriate techniques of crowd management. From the time John Snow was manhandled by a drunken spectator in February 1971, officials had due warning of the extent of the problem but it is debatable how much real progress has been made in the decade from this event to the time of the Alderman incident in December 1982. Crowd management is not an easy task because it cannot be achieved simply by short-term measures alone, such as a greater police presence; it also requires better organization and planning and longer-term solutions, notably better facilities for spectators. This in turn requires considerable financial outlay and a more professional presentation of the game.

The tone of the decade was established during the volatile, and sometimes violent, 1970–71 series. The worst incidents occurred at Melbourne and Sydney. On the first day of the Sixth Test at the MCG there was a stampede of some 2,000 spectators (out of a crowd of 42,372) on to the ground at 5.22 p.m. to congratulate Ian Chappell on his century. Players were angered by the invasion, none more so than Chappell who was 'severely pummelled' by over-enthusiastic fans. At the end of the day a visibly shaken

Chappell was quoted by the *Age* of 22 January 1971 to have declared: 'I was petrified I would fall and be trampled under all those feet... It is ridiculous this sort of thing should go on. If it hadn't been for a couple of strong spectators who tried to protect me, I'm sure I would have fallen.' During the break in play Cowdrey also had his cap pilfered, one stump was stolen, a small section of the Test wicket was damaged by footmarks and Snow clashed heatedly with several teenage boys. The invasion occurred despite several requests from MCC Secretary, Ian Johnson, for patrons not to go on to the oval during play.

Reviewing the incident in the *Age* on 22 January Bill O'Reilly maintained that beer had helped to make the crowd 'really nasty'. On the same day Percy Beames expressed concern that Brian Luckhurst was jeered and barracked for slow scoring which had resulted from an injured finger. Beames was one person who retained some faith in the Australian spectator because he believed that had the 'real reason' been known Luckhurst would not have been abused. However, as the decade progressed it became quite rare for any journalist to defend the Australian barracker.

Frank Tyson described the slow-scoring last day of the Test in the *Age* of 26 January as 'wet entertainment' and suggested that the crowd of 25,639 absorbed in the region of 50,000 cans of beer — a rate of 250 cans per run! Just how Tyson worked out his crowd-can figure is a mystery — no doubt it was an inspired guess — but undoubtedly he was correct to point to the significance of the spectator–can ratio. During the 1970s cans became more and more numerous at all sporting events at the SCG; in fact one spectator was 'buried' under a mountain of cans at a Rugby League Grand Final in the later 1970s (it could easily have been at a cricket match). He was not discovered until the next morning when a fork-lift vehicle was about to move in on the hill of cans when an arm was noticed protruding. The spectator, when finally revived, was found to have suffered no ill effects from his night on the Hill.

Unfortunately the cricket statistician lacks reliable and regular data on the number of cans and eskies taken to cricken matches. Indicative of a new era of cricket crowds, however, he does have a new set of figures for international matches: the number of ejections from the ground, the number arrested, the reasons for the arrests and the number injured from cans.

The Chappell stampede was the worst of the series but there were a number of other invasions mainly to congratulate batsmen who reached their century. In his book, *Umpire's Story*, published in 1972, former Test umpire, Lou Rowan stated that he didn't believe that the problem had been faced up to by administrators.[2] And indeed it took officials a long time to come to terms with crowd invasions. Possibly because they were pleased to see so many children at cricket, they took the easy option of turning a blind eye to invasions of the field at major milestones. Perhaps some took the view that crowd invasions were now a fact of life, so it was better to allow one or two per day when there was genuine cause for celebration in the hope that this would satisfy the juvenile followers and prevent regular stoppages. To some extent this policy worked at the Shield level because invasions were small and interruptions to play were brief, but Test cricket posed a greater problem.

Some administrators preferred the tougher option of threatening intruders with arrest, but in most cases threats were not followed up with action because most officials shied away from arresting children. With the adoption of an unambiguous hard line at Sydney and Melbourne in the 1980s — spectators who jump over the fence during play are arrested — along with greater surveillance of the crowd and more effective police presence, the problem of crowd invasions has been greatly diminished.

The 'ugly' Australian crowd came of age and became a media reality when the worst incident of the series took place in the Seventh Test at Sydney. In the previous Test there, the Fourth, the crowd had expressed its dissatisfaction with slow scoring and had barracked John Edrich by banging empty beer cans together, which, according to the *Sun Herald* of 10 January, caused the Hill to 'glint spectacularly in the sunshine'. Edrich was so concerned by the flashes during the 'beer-can banging polka' that he

Ian Chappell (obscured) and umpire caught in the 1971 MCG stampede. Note the youthful spectator joyously holding Chappell's cap aloft.

appealed to umpire Brooks to do something. Unfortunately Brooks could do nothing to stop such a protest. Edrich was rather more successful when he again complained of light being reflected into his eyes in the Seventh Test. The guilty party this time was an individual, who sat near the Randwick sightscreen and who tormented Edrich by reflecting the sun off his lunch tin. He was arrested.

The John Snow incident took place during the same match on Saturday 13 February before a crowd of just under 30,000. By the time the last session began the Hill was in an ugly mood: there had been many eruptions of can throwing during the day and a 'wild all-in-brawl' just 15 minutes before tea. When the brawl erupted the police moved in quickly but they too were peppered with cans.

Terry Jenner was felled by a Snow bumper and sustained a deep gash to the back of his head. After he was assisted from the field and a heated exchange took place between umpire Rowan, Illingworth and Snow, the bowler 'defiantly snatched his cap' at the end of the over and headed towards his fielding position under the Paddington Hill. When he reached there he was grabbed by the shirt by an inebriated spectator who tried to drag him over the fence. *Age* writer, Peter McFarline, who was sitting just a few metres from the incident, wrote on 15 February that the incident made him feel 'ashamed to be an Australian' and that he was disgusted by the Hill spectators. McFarline suggested that, whatever the rights and wrongs of Illingworth's decision to take his team off the field, the crowd was not justified in hurling cans and bottles at Snow 'as he called on them to fight him'. Eight people were arrested during the near-riot which followed although there is no record that Snow's assailant was one of them.

The *Sun-Herald* quoted several authorities who maintained that it was the 'worst display of hooliganism' at an Australian cricket match and the 'worst ever seen' at the SCG. However, such a comment can only be accepted if one adds the phrase 'in living memory' for unquestionably the 1879 happening — a full-scale riot which lasted a considerable time and constituted a much greater threat to player safety — was very much worse. Many too would contend that while the 'deafening din' of 1971 was comparable with the uproar which occurred when Oldfield was felled by Larwood at Adelaide in 1933, there was a much greater threat of crowd invasion at Adelaide. Many of those present there feared an imminent mass invasion of the pitch whereas no one has written of this possibility in 1971.

There were fewer incidents during the less well patronized series against Pakistan (1972–73) and New Zealand (1973–74) but even so New Zealand captain, Bevan Congdon, expressed mild surprise at the behaviour of the Sydney crowd which he thought was very partisan. The *Sydney Morning Herald* of 29 January 1974 agreed with Congdon and quoted a source which suggested that this was not the case ten years ago when the local crowd was 'fairly noisy but basically good-humoured and, as home crowds go, not exceptionally partisan'. There had been, it contended, three marked changes since then. First, was the invasion of the playing area by small (and not-so-small) boys when a batsman scored a century. Although roundly denounced by all the experts, nobody seemed able to stop it. The SCG Trust made 'minatory loud-speaker announcements' threatening prosecution 'but these had no effect.' Next was the wide popularity of the beer can and portable cooler (esky) which had added to the crowd's irascibility particularly in the late afternoon. Because of its lightweight character, the esky made it possible to lug a large consignment of beer from the parking lot to the Hill. It had been a lot more difficult to cart substantial quantities of liquor into the ground before this. Keith Dunstan recalled a 'most beautiful act of devotion' when four characters 'sweated, heaved and carried in a vast, old ice chest full of beer' at the Gabba in 1958 and commented, 'They don't make stalwarts like that any more.'[3] The third change was the fact that cricket was again enjoying 'something of a vogue' among younger people. The *Herald* believed that 'not only are they ill-informed about the basics (let alone the finer points) of the game, but that they are less interested in watching what is happening than in playing the role of spectators — as if they were actors and actresses'.

With more young people attending cricket there was a greater dimension of hero-worship which brought out the ugly side of some cricket crowds. For example, during the 1974 Test against Pakistan at the SCG, one spectator pointed out in a letter to the *Sydney Morning Herald* of 28 January that Australian batsmen, and Redpath in particular, were consistently barracked 'for lagging superfluous on the stage', thus delaying the entry of local hero, Doug Walters. The booing of fieldsmen who cut off potential Walters' boundaries near the fences was another manifestation of the Walters cult. When Greg Chappell was preferred to Walters as a change bowler in the Test against New Zealand the crowd set up a sustained chant of 'Walters, Walters'. When the captain finally called Walters to the bowling crease it was as though 'a principal matador was being heralded into the arena'.

Philip Derriman, in his history of the SCG, has analysed some of the ingredients of the Doug Walters cult which reached its peak in the mid-1970s with the unveiling of the 'Doug Walters Stand' tarpaulin banner. Derriman argues that Walters' appeal was a 'mystery' because Walters never played to the crowd and never 'by the slightest gesture or expression, encouraged the people on the Hill to cheer him'. In fact, he had behaved as if the crowd 'did not exist at all'. Former Australian captain, Bob Simpson, believed that people on the Hill liked Walters because they could identify with him: he smokes, drinks beer out of a can, 'doesn't take himself or his cricket too seriously', supposedly he doesn't practise too hard and 'never puts on airs'. His run up to the wicket was 'quintessentially modest, though mysteriously effective'. Another element of the Walters tradition was that he struck 'a sympathetic chord with spectators because of his fallibility', at least, on some occasions.[4]

In the public mind Walters was an archetypal 'ocker'. Consciously or unconsciously Walters conformed to this image, as demonstrated by an incident recounted in his autobiography, *The Doug Walters Story*.[5] During the 1969–70 tour of South Africa Walters and room-mate, Brian Taber, had enjoyed a surprise breakfast of six bottles of beer prior to the match against Western Province. As they were about to leave for the ground the bar opened on the first floor and Taber went straight in and ordered two beers. Walters wrote, 'I was trying to rush him to the ground, but I couldn't leave him to drink on his own, could I?' Walters and Taber finally arrived at the ground just five minutes before the match — they were supposed to be there one hour before — and he went out and made his only century in South Africa.

Such a story is in the best ocker tradition as it confirms the fundamental belief that life and cricket can be improved with a few beers.

Sydney has lost its monopoly on partisan behaviour since it became the norm at most grounds in the 1970s. Sometimes it was directed against visiting international sides but more often it was aimed at players and teams from other States. Terry Jenner was shocked to be booed at the Gabba in 1976 when he was playing for Australia. Admittedly Jenner helped to rile the crowd. On one occasion, he admitted, with refreshing honesty, that he made finger signs to the Gabba crowd and on another, having marked his fielding position at mid-off, he was rebuked by a member of the crowd. Jenner's reaction was to dig further and provoke an even bigger reaction. Jenner even ran foul of some sections of his home crowd and he felt the hostility of Members in particular. On one occasion Jenner almost hit a Member with a bat when remarks were passed as he returned from the oval. (The Member was later suspended.)

Along with an increase in partisan comments, local players had to contend with a greater number of parochial comments. Keith Stackpole recalled an incident when Australia lost two very early wickets (both Victorians) against England at the WACA in 1970. A Victorian friend of his went to the bar where the crowd was far from gloomy. 'Why are you so happy with such a sorry score line,' he enquired? The reply came: 'Australia's not two for 20 [Lawry and Stackpole had been dismissed by the score of eight and by 20 Ian Chappell had been out also], the Vics are two for 20.'

Homosexual comments were a new ingredient in cricket barracking in the 1970s and 1980s. It became commonplace, according to Trevor Laughlin, for some West Australian spectators to call Victorians 'poofters'. He remembered one incident when he made use of a box when fielding close-up for a possible bat-pad catch off Jim Higgs. When he moved out to the boundary at the end of the over he removed his box and deposited it in his back pocket. As he reached his position a spectator yelled: 'Always knew you were a poofter, Laughlin, with your balls in your back pocket.'

Comments from the Outers of the country mirrored a vulgarized and conservative response to the gay rights movement and with a wider range of sexist, chauvinist and racist remarks, the Hills provided views on a number of other reform movements, such as rights for women and blacks.

Changing spectator standards were linked with altered player behaviour on the field. It is difficult to determine which was cause and which was effect but there is no question that greater player aggression, antics and disputes in play encouraged more volatile spectator behaviour. Ross Duncan believed that the practice of 'sledging' began during the 1971–72 season. A form of sledging had existed previously but it is better described as 'gamesmanship'. For instance, teams decided not to talk to Norman O'Neill at the beginning of his innings knowing that this would not help him to establish himself: O'Neill was a nervous starter who would talk with anyone and everyone as a means of relaxing himself. However, the practice of baiting opposition players was a 'new' development, though there were some precedents for this in the tactics employed by W. G. Grace in the late Victorian era. Sledging differed from Grace's 'sharp practice' (such as trying to put off a fieldsman who was about to take a catch) in that it was practised on a more regular basis and by more than one individual (sometimes by a whole team), and because it unearthed new levels of abuse.

The changes in standards both inside and outside the boundary fence occurred at about the same time and reflected widespread community debate and questioning of many time-honoured conventions of public behaviour. There was also much discussion about the purpose and morality of playing cricket. Winning assumed larger and larger importance and almost any tactic was condoned to achieve success.

The two dramatic and exciting series in the mid-1970s brought a new dimension to crowd behaviour: whereas crowd demonstrations and incidents had surfaced previously in just one or two Tests in a series, they now became the norm at almost every Test. In fact newspaper reports of Test cricket were spiced with almost daily revelations of crowd behaviour. Prior to the 1974–75 series, for example, the placid and conservative Adelaide crowd had established a reputation for its dignified observance of play. However, during this Test, crowd behaviour became such a problem that administrators decided to prohibit spectators from bringing alcohol into the ground. Since the 1975–76 series, Adelaide patrons have only been able to secure liquor from outlets at the ground where beer was sold in plastic cups rather than cans.

There were a number of advantages in this reform. It certainly cut down on crowd violence and injury since a war of plastic cups was less likely to result in injuries and to provoke retaliation. Presumably, too, a crowd drinks less under such circumstances as it is more difficult to fight one's way up to the bar and there is also a good prospect that a certain amount of beer will also be spilt before it can be consumed. A loaded esky by one's side is much more convenient. WACA officials had taken action on this front in December 1974 when 'beer cans, bottles and the like' were banned from the ground. For the Test the drinking area at the ground was extended so that spectators could buy drinks at the bars and drink them in the Outer area immediately in front of the new grandstand. The centre of the wet area in the Outer, the bar underneath the commentary box, was a focal point for the raucous elements.

It is surprising then that plastic cups, or 'loose liquor' sales as they are called, were not introduced at some other grounds, notably Sydney, until a decade later, for the 1983–84 season. The issue had been raised regularly by spectators and by the police who became so fed up with the problem that they came out in favour of a complete ban of alcohol during the 1982–83 season. For a while change was resisted largely because of the revenue involved. Cans were still sold at Sydney in preference to plastic cups because they could be dispensed to the public at a faster rate. There was also the problem that the pipes which conveyed draught beer from below the scoreboard to the bar had been taken out around 1980 and the cost of replacement was considerable.

The enthusiasm of the Adelaide crowd of 1974–75 was replicated at Perth where the younger patrons initiated a deafening accompaniment to the game by rhythmically banging on the tin advertisements which hung from the fence. So along with the tribal roars and chants, cricket now had its tribal drum-beats to spur on the local warriors.

The worst incidents of the 1974–75 series were reserved for Sydney and Melbourne. Sydney had its usual spate of can incidents. A first-day Saturday crowd of 52,164 was spoken to by umpire Brooks during the afternoon session after cans were thrown on to the ground. When the players left the field at tea some spectators turned on the scoreboard which was pelted with cans: the shutters were hastily put down but not before the board was damaged.[6]

The next day Tony Greig was temporarily rattled by the crowd. After returning an orange into the crowd he was pelted with rubbish and cans. Captain Edrich was forced to place Greig elsewhere in the field. On most occasions Greig had an excellent rapport with Australian crowds, as he did with those in many other countries, such as India, since he was always prepared to play along with them. In fact he often went out of his way to entertain them.

On the fourth day some hundreds of spectators staged an impromptu football game when rain halted play, and continued despite repeated official requests to clear the oval. Officials, it

Policemen close in on an impromptu football match at the SCG in the Fourth Test 1974–75 when rain stopped play. None of the performers seemed unduly concerned by the approach of the law.

seems, were quite at a loss to deal with the situation. In his match comments in the *Sydney Morning Herald* of 7 January 1975, Bill O'Reilly took Sydney's 'hill-billies' to task and commented that 'most of the people around the ground were thoroughly ashamed of them'.

The *Sydney Morning Herald* of 10 January 1975 thundered that urgent consideration should be given to banning beer cans from the ground though it weakened its case when it accepted the reluctance of the Trust to initiate such a reform because of the 'feeling that crowds would be greatly reduced if beer cans and beer bottles were banned'. Some crowd unrest, however, must be put down to poor facilities. Spectators with a reserved seat, which provides an adequate view of the game and reasonable access to food and toilet facilities are less likely to indulge in anti-social behaviour. A seat also provides a spectator with his or her own defined territory whereas an open undefined area, such as the Hill, has fewer physical constraints and provides greater opportunity for individuals to join to compete for territory. Proper facilities also encourage the more conservative spectator and even the family to join the Outer crowd. This, in turn, sets up buffer zones in the Outers which provide brakes on the behaviour of the more unruly. Perhaps, too, grass and earth, unlike concrete, bring out some of the more basic elements of

Alternative umpires about to be escorted off the MCG during the 1974–75 series. Note the extra arm and pair of legs.

behaviour. Melbourne, unlike Sydney, has no reported instances of defecation and sexual intercourse taking place in the Outer at a cricket match.

During the 1974–75 series Melbourne was not immune from 'ugly' incidents. On the first day of the Third Test Melbourne authorities underestimated the size of the crowd of 77,167 — they anticipated 50–60,000 — and there were long queues at catering booths and many complaints. During the day there were five separate incidents of spectator intrusion on the ground and on each occasion 'the crowd roared lustily'. The *Age* of 27 December 1974 reported that a young man at one time ran towards John Edrich 'with his fists clenched' and Greg Chappell moved towards him fearing an attack. The man swerved away at the last moment and was taken away by police. There had also been several vicious brawls which had resulted in one man being taken away in a stretcher.

A more light-hearted event took place on the second day of the Test. After a 20-minute stoppage due to bad light two 'umpires' appeared at the gate dressed appropriately in regulation white and black. After proceeding about 40 metres on to the ground they paused to inspect the sky and one of them raised his hat to reveal 'glasses, goatee beard and extremely un-umpiring locks'. The crowd roared with amusement. The two 'umpires' were escorted off the oval but were then allowed to resume their seats.

The pattern of the crowd behaviour was repeated in the next season during the West Indies tour of Australia. When a near-record crowd of 85,661 turned up for the first day of the Third Test at the MCG, Paul Heinrichs of the *Age* celebrated the event with a feature article on 27 December 1975 entitled 'What a GAS (Great Australian Slob) day'. It was, he began, a 'Ripper Day at the MCG' starting from the early morning when he could see it was to be 'Great Drinking Weather'. And it wasn't hard to pick him (the slob) at the ground: 'He wore loose shorts, a coloured T-shirt (usually with something written on it) and thongs. Invariably, he was 18–25.' He would have objected to the term 'slob' preferring to be called an 'ocker', or even a 'yobbo', since Paul Hogan had developed a positive, humorous and popular image for the ocker. He was in some senses a modern-day 'larrikin' except that drinking was rather less important to the former larrikins. In some of the bays of the Southern Stand

Batsman John Edrich does not allow a scuffle between umpire Brooks and a spectator to interfere with his concentration at the MCG during the 1974–75 series.

A section of the 85,661 crowd at the MCG, 26 December 1975, to see Australia play the West Indies.

islands of cans formed about 2.5 metres in diameter which were surrounded by pools of spilled beer and foam. By 4 p.m. some spectators had even given up watching the game to barrack the 'spunkies' (women in denim shorts).

There were the usual can fights, carousing and arrests. At the end of one day the crowd scoreboard read: ten charged with incidents during the day; 14 charged with incidents after the cricket, including nine who were drunk and disorderly, and another ten likely to be summonsed after incidents during the day.

On 30 December the *Age* declared that the 'ugly Australian lives' and regretted the 'destructive antics of the selfish minority of body-line boozers among the spectators'. The *Age* supported the possible extension of dry areas at the ground but noted that there was a need to better police the existing areas. The introduction of dry areas was the Melbourne response to the alcohol problem; patrons in these areas were confined to the wings of the ground in less favourable watching positions. The

A streaker at Perth, January 1976. When this picture was published in the *West Australian*, the genitals of the streaker were blacked out.

issue had to be confronted by administrators, added the *Age*, because if the 'ascendancy of the drunken spectators continued' it would drive away 'the ordinary family spectator'.

Crowd behaviour at Melbourne had not improved by the Sixth Test when the *Age* noted on 2 February 1976 that 'spectators influenced by heat and alcohol clashed violently with police'. The *Age* believed that serious consideration would have to be given to the banning of alcohol.

Amongst those arrested in the Third Test at the MCG were three streakers. Streaking was another new dimension in crowd behaviour and enjoyed a vogue in the mid-1970s. While players had a chuckle when streaking first emerged, such as when, as Ian Chappell put it, that 'well-built lad romped across Lords' during the Second Test in 1975, they quickly became bored and irritated by a host of imitators who appeared at many Australian grounds during the following season. When streakers intruded on to the ground just before tea on the first day during the January 1976 Test the Australians were deprived of a vital extra over of bowling at Clive Lloyd just because of the selfish vanity of a streaker.

Streaking continued for a season or two but then the custom

vanished almost overnight, as quickly as it had surfaced. Kersi Meher-Homji believed that Pakistani, Sadiq Mohammad, helped to kill the practice at Sydney when he took action against a streaker when he chased him: 'Taken aback the latter [the streaker] fell face down (ouch!) and returned to his hill-mates in utter shame. Suddenly, the "daring" act looked ridiculous and went out of fashion.'[7]

It is likely that exhibitionists have always come to cricket and made their presence felt in some way or another. Television has, however, provided them with a greater incentive and coverage. As Bill O'Reilly put it in the *Sydney Morning Herald* on 7 January 1975, 'The play-acting goes on tiresomely in the late afternoons when the telecast goes to screen.' This was a perceptive comment indicating another era of television influence on the game. While it would be impossible to determine the exact extent to which television altered spectator behaviour at the ground, there is no doubt that it inspired publicity-seeking behaviour whether it took the form of the outrageous streaker, a clever banner or an original costume or routine. The reward was national television exposure as more and more cameras prowled the crowd looking for newsworthy happenings to fill in the many gaps and slow periods of play. In order to provide a continuity of visual action television needed the crowd even more than radio since the latter medium had many alternative 'fillers' such as anecdotes from the past. Television commentators have the more difficult task of always remaining in touch with the visual present.

From the mid 1970s Australian crowds have not only had the opportunity to watch themselves on television and to copy customs from other grounds, such as the MCG banners, they have also been able to observe crowd behaviour in England. It is probable that the orgy of flag-waving in the 1982–83 Australian season was partly inspired by English flag-waving in the 1981 season which in turn is a likely borrowing from English soccer. As a result contemporary cricket crowds are behaving more and more like football crowds and many of the unique national traditions of cricket-watching are diminishing.

Perhaps Sydney authorities learnt something from the troubles at the MCG: when 53,001 turned up for the first day of the Fourth Test in January 1976 and were packed in like sardines there was a force of 200 policemen in readiness at the ground. During the day there were very few incidents but even so 20 were arrested — a revealing figure considering that authorities regarded it as a 'good day'. No doubt they were even more pleased by the behaviour on the second day, Sunday, for 'only seven arrests' were recorded.

Ground Improvements at the Gabba

The revival of cricket in the 1970s ushered in a new era of improved facilities and stand construction beginning with the erection of the Test stand at the WACA in 1970, followed by the

Bradman Stand at the SCG in 1974, and a complete face-lift for the Gabba, which included a number of new stands and complexes. This too was finished in 1974.

Of all the ground developments the Gabba was by far the largest and most significant. It involved an outlay of $3.3 million from 1971–74 which was spent on improvements to the wicket and a number of new stands — the Sir Leslie Wilson Stand, the Clem Jones Stand, the J. S. Hutcheon Stand and a new Members' Stand. The Sir Leslie Wilson Stand provided first-class seating for 3,400 and boasted an excellent bar and kiosk facilities, along with indoor wickets, squash courts and a sauna room. It was, according to Keith Dunstan in the *Sydney Morning Herald* of 4 September 1982, 'A cantilevered thing in colours of such charm that it looks like a trendy bathroom.' The Clem Jones Stand replaced the dilapidated old stands of the Outer and provided substantial covered seating for ordinary patrons. Other renovations included the Arthur Didbin Complex which was also opened in 1974. It contained a new Members' Dining Area, Trust and Executive viewing rooms, Umpires' and Players' Rooms and the new J. S. Hutcheon Stand. Another new building complex was the Sir Gordon Chalk Building which catered both for cricket and greyhound patrons. Along with seating facilities, and dining arrangements for 250, were totalizator outlets with bookmakers situated conveniently in front of the Members' Bar. Indicative of a new concern for the welfare of the spectator and in an attempt to woo women to the Gabba the decision was taken to extend child-care facilities for greyhound patrons at the ground.

The changes were dramatic and transformed the Gabba from the ugly duckling of Australian cricket grounds to one of the most modern, complete with almost every spectator comfort. The capacity of the ground had been reduced from over 60,000 to around 22,000 with the result that almost all Gabba cricket patrons can now count on a seat, a good view and reasonable access to ground facilities. Before this change the Gabba had a capacity of 61,200 with seating for only one-third of the crowd.

There were a number of reasons for the Gabba face-lift. First, many of the existing stands were in disrepair: the old Members' Stand was 'dangerous' and the Outer stands were dilapadated.

A second reason was that the Rugby League had long left the Gabba — it went in the mid-1950s — for its own home ground at Lang Park. With its departure there was no longer any need for a large capacity ground for it was the football Tests alone which had necessitated a 60,000-plus capacity. Cricket had only once passed the 30,000 mark, when 30,598 attended the Saturday of the December 1936 Test. With the departure of the established winter tenant from the Gabba — a trend which was repeated at the WACA, the Adelaide Oval, and to some extent at the MCG — officials were confronted with the additional problem of how to make up the football revenue loss and how to make the Gabba pay.

The primary reason for change, however, was the vision,

Technology, in this case telecommunications, helped to expand interest in the game. Cricket had a special phone number, for up-to-the-minute recorded results, long before any other sport.

energy and power of Alderman Clem Jones who in the crucial years of renovation, 1971–74, virtually ran Queensland cricket. At one time the Brisbane Lord Mayor held the following positions in Queensland cricket: Chairman of the BCG Trust, Member of the QCA Executive, Queensland delegate on the Board of Control and President of the Gabba Greyhound Racing Club. He also helped out for a time as QCA Secretary and was Curator at the Gabba itself for a few seasons. Such a wide power base enabled Jones to create a new order at the Gabba.

Jones was a controversial figure in Queensland cricket. He

made many enemies and became, as he himself admitted, 'one of the most disliked people in Brisbane'. Many believed that he acted in an unprofessional manner when he took on the task of preparing wickets at the Gabba in addition to running the city and Queensland cricket. Wicket-preparation, it was contended, should be left to a specialist curator. Others criticized the wickets produced by Jones as sub-standard.

Still others were unhappy with the links between cricket and the greyhound industry even though they resulted in an enormous financial boost to cricket which provided the basis for the rebuilding programme at the Gabba. In order to provide a track of sufficient length for greyhound racing the oval was rebuilt into a pear-shape — unique in the world. To minimize the anomaly of the 'pear' a roped boundary removes the narrowest section from the playing area during cricket matches so that it is oval shaped.

There were also a number of teething problems in relation to the operation of the greyhound track. When the Gabba was filled during a Test match the crowd was permitted to sit on the turf of the dog track. This caused no end of worry for greyhound officials because 'next day the grass was a sea of beer can ring-pulls' which did terrible things to the dogs' feet. It was necessary to use a metal detector to get rid of them all.[8]

It was a supreme irony that just about the time when renovations were completed and just before the new stands and complexes were opened, the cricket empire of Clem Jones began to crumble. He was soundly beaten at the annual meeting of the QCA for the prestigious position of Queensland delegate (one of two) to the Australian Cricket Board of Control. Even so he was not yet finished as a curator for some time and prepared the 1974 (and 1975) Test wicket which marked the emergence of the Lillee–Thomson pace duo. His name too remained on one of the new stands along with his co-architect of Gabba reconstruction, Treasurer, Sir Gordon Chalk.[9]

While many came to criticize Jones for his divisive personality there is no doubting the legacy he left Queenland cricket. Jones anticipated, rather sooner than most administrators in the country, the need to establish smaller, better-appointed stadiums which offered spectator comfort and good facilities. Although he was accused of being unprofessional (in taking on the role of curator), he was pointing cricket administrators towards a more professional presentation of the game. Cricket now had to compete with other sports and with television, it needed superior facilities and attractions to woo people to the ground. This in turn necessitated a degree of compromise and even accommodation with other tenants, such as the greyhound industry, so that necessary improvements could be funded adequately.

In the past decade Queensland has had fewer crowd incidents than the other four Test centres. The vastly improved conditions at the Gabba have made this possible.

CHAPTER SIX

World Series Cricket And Beyond

Bottoms On Seats

World Series Cricket (WSC), which became known to the world on 9 May 1977, is one of the most striking examples of a revolutionary movement emerging in a sport. Like any good revolution it was hatched in secret because it represented a concerted attempt to overthrow a sporting establishment. WSC introduced a host of promotional innovations — night cricket, the white ball, coloured clothing, hot-house pitches, better television photography, improved sound effects, interviews with outgoing batsmen, glossy new magazines, the song 'Come on, Aussie, come on', wider advertising, promotional gimmicks such as give-away bats, t-shirts, hats, WSC logos and general razzamatazz.

Behind these changes was a different philosophy of the game: the long-oppressed proletarians (players) should be better rewarded for their labour and the game should be promoted as entertainment along more capitalist (American) lines rather than the long-established, amateur-inspired, English bureaucratic tradition. Television provided the rationale behind the change. If the traditional game of cricket could be better geared to this medium it could benefit not only from a wider audience but also from bigger sponsorship. The revolution also attempted to woo new groups to cricket, notably younger children and teenagers, blue collar workers, and women. In the process, however, it alienated many of the traditional middle-class supporters of cricket who preferred the dignified and hallowed traditions of Test cricket.

The nature of the revolution was somewhat hidden from the public because it was made out of an alliance between key international players and a media magnate, Kerry Packer. No one doubted that the players had genuine grievances and were entitled to a greater slice of an expanding cake. However, many expressed doubts about Packer's motives suggesting that his main interests were counter-revolutionary (selfish) in that they were designed to promote himself and Channel 9 and did not arise out of any genuine interest in the development of the game. In an attempt to establish whether Packer had the real interests of cricket at heart, time and time again he was asked if he

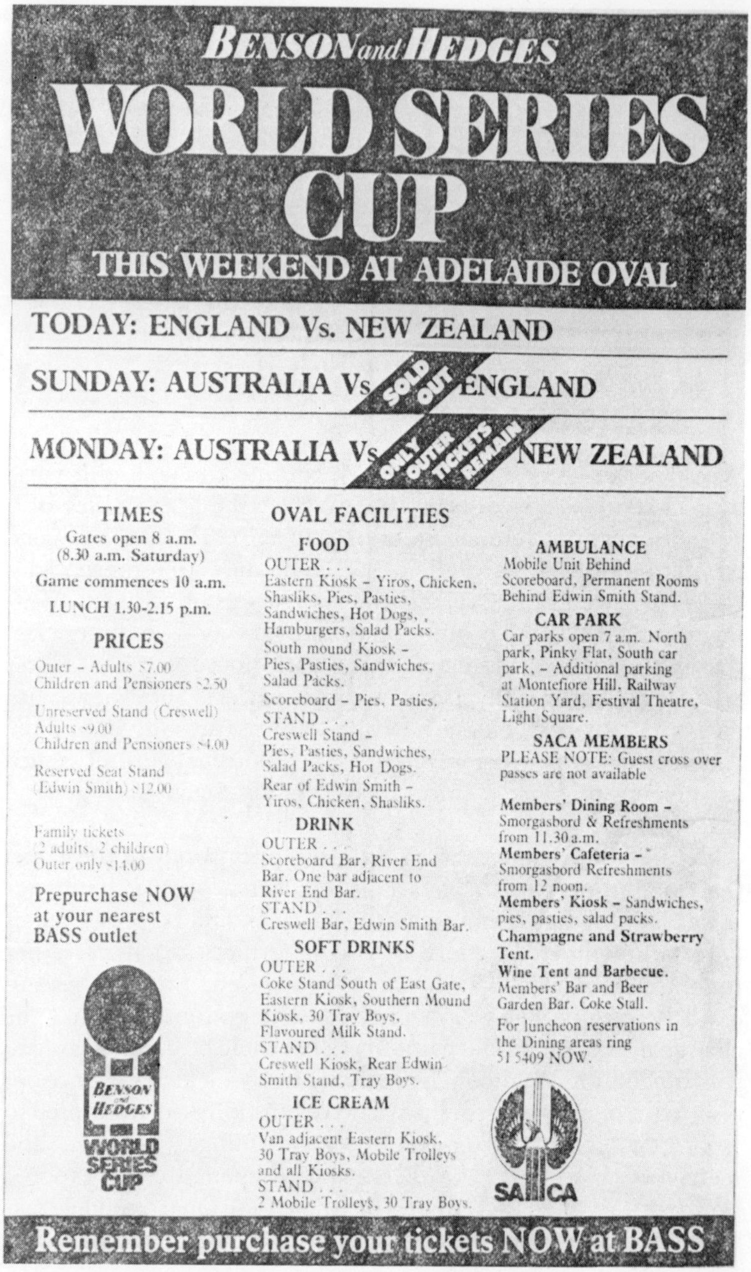

Catering for the Adelaide crowd, 28–30 January, 1983. Members have many alternatives including the Dining Room, the Champagne and Strawberry, and the Wine Tents.

intended to plough WSC profits back into the game to promote coaching and junior cricket and to improve the lot of cricketers below the top level. No doubt some of the issues in what became a long and hot public debate were obscured because Packer became a convenient symbol (an ogre with a 'meat-mangler smile' as one journalist put it) for the opponents of change in the same way that Jack Kramer had been singled out and vilified by all those who didn't like open tennis in the 1950s.

From May 1977 the battle was on for players, grounds and, above all, for spectators — the ultimate arbiters of who would control cricket. WSC, with the long purse strings of Packer, was successful in attracting most of the best players in the world: the cream of the Australian, West Indian and Pakistani sides, and some of the leading South African, English and New Zealand players. Only the Indian team remained totally loyal to Establishment cricket. One of the major assets of the 'revolutionaries' was the Channel 9 network which televised 306 hours of cricket in 1977-78, considerably more than the ABC figure of 234 hours and more than three times the 170 hours televised in the six-Test 1974–75 series. Following the tradition of American television, sport came more and more to dominate of the local airwaves in the late 1970s. During the summer of 1977–78 cricket dominated the ABC and the Nine Network while another station provided extensive coverage of tennis. Channel 9, Sydney, helped to promote televised sport by improving the technical quality of cricket broadcasts, a fact which almost everyone had to acknowledge: even the severest Packer critic, the pro-Establishment *World of Cricket* of June 1977, had to agree that 'his network's technical excellence overshadowed the ABC's traditional and, by comparison, dull coverage'. This excellence was achieved by doubling the barrage of cameras, from four to eight so that proceedings could be filmed from both ends of the wicket — a camera was always behind the bowler — and by a vast technical support system which included among many innovations the use of zoom lenses to capture the expression on the face of the batsman (and then the bowler) immediately after a delivery. Zoom lenses enabled WSC to heighten the entertainment value of cricket by injecting the cult of the personality into the commentary and this in turn made players more aware of their role as media entertainers.

On the debit side WSC was handicapped by its failure to gain access to any major cricket ground in 1977–78 and it had to be content with matches staged at two football grounds (in Melbourne and Adelaide), an agricultural showground (in Sydney) and a trotting park (in Perth). Matches were only possible at several of these venues because groundsman John Maley performed the miracle of creating hot-house pitches. During the 1977–78 season no WSC match was played in Brisbane.

Establishment cricket, on the other hand, started with the major disadvantage of a dearth of experienced Test players; many dubbed the 1977–78 Test team as the third-string Australian team — which it virtually was. However, Establishment cricket started the 1977–78 season with rather more assets than WSC. It had, first of all, the weight of tradition behind it: a monopoly on established venues, on the institution of Test cricket, and on legitimacy in the eyes of the majority of the public. It also had the unqualified support of the ABC, the traditional broadcaster of cricket, which virtually ignored WSC in its initial season. And finally it had something which without question was its greatest asset — the enthusiastic and vocal support of the

Renovations carried out at the Gabba in the early 1970s have enabled the Outer crowd to now watch in comfort. Note that some of this crowd is seated inside the fence on the Greyhound track.

majority of cricket followers. Letter columns of major newspapers and cricket magazines were full of angry complaints about WSC, such as the following which was quoted in *World of Cricket*, June 1977:

> After the fluctuations, tensions and excitement of the recent Centenary Test in Melbourne, why change the nature of the game? The wide appeal of true international Tests can never be replaced by this contrived contest, where everyone will be playing for money rather than for his country.

Behind this anger was a fear that WSC would alter the game so that Test cricket would never be the same again. The same writer continued:

> I foresee that to make the circus more attractive to the Esky-toting crowds they wish to attract, and advertisement-consuming TV viewers at home, the circus proprietors will gradually change the rules (and perhaps the tools) to make the spectacular quicker and more exciting by their standards.

Who was to say where WSC would stop? Perhaps cricket would transform itself into a variant of baseball. The Establishment case was further strengthened by the vigorous support of the majority of the country's journalists and newspapers. The popular Press — which might be expected to support a more popular brand of cricket — was among the most vehement critics of WSC.

WSC was quickly labelled as 'selfish' and 'adventurist' in that it was designed to scoop off match profits for a privileged few, the 'mercenaries', while the rest of the cricket world suffered. They popularized the belief that WSC was a 'circus' which put on 'exhibition' games; by implication the matches were not serious, but were artificially contrived to produce a close and exciting result. Consequently, there was the very real prospect that at least some of the games were 'fixed'. Thus a long-standing Australian suspicion of professional sport was reinforced. Many papers, too, discriminated against WSC either by ignoring it altogether or by providing it with meagre coverage. The leading Australian cricket annual, *Cricketer*, provided extensive space to the 1977–78 Test series, Shield cricket and the Gillette Cup but consigned WSC to the category of 'Other Cricket, 1977–78' where it was sandwiched in among many other entries and was given only six pages out of 178. To counter this lack of coverage WSC launched its own stable of cricket magazines which were heavily promoted on television.

Despite a great deal of publicity WSC made an inauspicious start in its battle for the spectator. The first day of the much-publicized Super Test series (the term implying that the game would be superior to a Test series) drew a disappointing 2,847 fans to the almost 80,000-capacity VFL Park in Melbourne. English journalist John Thicknesse described the crowd as being 'scattered round like confetti in a graveyard'. This crowd was especially disappointing considering that the teams were made up from the core of the two best sides in the world, Australia and the West Indies. There was very little atmosphere at the game. Brian Mossop stated in the *Sydney Morning Herald* of 3 December 1977 that there was 'a sense of futility, a feeling that no matter what happened in the middle it was of no importance'.

In retrospect the First Super Test was played at the wrong time, at the wrong place and spectators were charged the wrong price. While it was no fault of WSC officials that the match was staged at the outer Melbourne suburb of Glen Waverley — they were denied access to the MCG — it was decidedly risky to stage an international match in Melbourne so early in the season because invariably the best cricket crowds there did not turn up until the Christmas–New Year period. There was also a steep rise in charges: the $6 entry fee represented a 100 per cent increase on the Centenary Test played just nine months before. (The entry fee was later reduced to $4.) Given the populist overtones of WSC — the organizers claimed they were taking cricket to the masses — the initial entry fee was both excessive and unwise.

The rival Establishment series started just one hour later at Brisbane (which meant that viewers could easily compare the alternatives) and drew 6,015 — more than twice the WSC figure.

This was a respectable first-day Brisbane figure when compared with the first-day attendance at the last Test against India there in 1968 — 4,641. The result was an encouraging sign to the Australian Cricket Board that the Australian public would continue to vote for Test cricket even though the Australian side was very much under-manned.

WSC officials were a little more hopeful when 7,520 turned up on the first day, Friday, of the Second Super Test at the Sydney Showground. Many of this crowd noted the *Sydney Morning Herald* of 17 December 1977 'sat around the roped boundary in gaily coloured chairs' which gave the ground the 'atmosphere of an English county oval'. However, the Saturday crowd of 6,700 was well below expectations. WSC officials must also have been disappointed by the West Indian pace battery's first-day over rate of just ten per hour which seemed to cast some doubts on the contention that WSC would provide brighter cricket.

Despite various setbacks, Sydney was the only venue where there was some public acceptance of the Super Test concept: 23,762 attended the three-day Second Super Test and 36,424 (including a Saturday crowd of 18,000) turned up for the Fourth Super Test, making a two-Test total of 60,168. Sydney fans for once outnumbered their more conservative Melbourne counterparts: two Super Tests there attracted only 35,171. The response in Adelaide and Perth was even more disappointing. Faced with indifference in Adelaide, where one Super Test drew only 15,613, WSC officials scrapped Adelaide as the venue for the International Cup Finals, set down for 3–5 February. Perth was no better: 13,562 spectators provided a gate of about $42,000 which was far short of the match expenditure of $65,000 which consisted of air fares and accommodation for the WSC party of 140, ground rental and an advertising bill of $14,000.

Meanwhile Establishment Test cricket, bolstered by the return of experienced campaigner, Bob Simpson, and benefitting from a closely fought series, fared rather better. The five-Test series drew 256,954 spectators (an average of 51,391 per Test), a much higher figure than the 124,532 who went to six Super Tests (an average of 20,755 per match). The Establishment figures also compared favourably with the last Indian tour against a full-strength Australian side (captained in two Tests by Simpson) when an average of 30,434 attended each of four Tests. The result of the series must have given the cricket Establishment much encouragement. It seemed to indicate that the public was attracted more to a 'real' Test series, even if the home side lacked well-known, experienced players. It also seemed to suggest that the Establishment was winning, and would win, the battle for the Test spectator.

The Super Test front was but one theatre of the cricket war: WSC also took the battle to the virtually unoccupied territories of one-day and country cricket — the Gillette Cup was its only rival as there was no one-day fixture between India and Australia in 1977–78, although India did play a one-day match against

Tasmania. The absence of one-day international cricket from the Australian calendar provided another example of official conservatism, especially since one-day cricket had been introduced in England in 1963 and had proved successful in bringing back the crowds to the county grounds. The potential Australian audience for this game was amply demonstrated on 5 January 1971 when some 46,006 turned up at the MCG at a hastily organised international in place of the scheduled 31 December–5 January Australia vs England Test match which had been abandoned after three days of rain. The very popular Prudential World Cup in 1975 had further indicated the spectator drawing-power of international one-day cricket.

WSC was rather more successful in initiating one-day cricket than in promoting Super Tests. A significant turning-point in its campaign was the introduction of night cricket at VFL Park on 14 December 1977 which received an enthusiastic reception from the crowd of 6,300. Two facts are worth noting about this crowd. It built up as the game progressed, presumably as office workers got away from their jobs and unlike previous WSC crowds this was a very 'vocal' assembly which seemed to have more in common with a noisy football crowd than traditional cricket spectators.

The match proved a harbinger of a brighter future for WSC which was realized when three back-to-back night matches, 23–25 January 1978, attracted a total of 52,831 to VFL Park, with 24,636 attending the Australia vs West Indies clash. Kerry Packer, who had remained tight-lipped after the opening day of the First Super Test, now declared the result to be 'fantastic' and beyond expectations: he had hoped for just one crowd to reach 18,000. John Cornell, WSC principal, elaborated on the significance of this record one-day crowd in the *Age* of 25 January 1978: 'The crowds have shown they will accept professional cricket. They have watched it on television, they have seen it is fair dinkum, they know they are the best players in the world, and now they are coming to see them.' The Press could no longer afford to denigrate WSC and the *Age* headed its story of 26 January: 'Who's Smiling Now!'

Two weeks earlier one-day cricket had drawn well in Perth with a total attendance of 26,713 at three games. However, cricket writer Henry Blofeld, claimed that it was an open secret that at least half the crowd were given complimentary tickets — so it is advisable to retain a healthy scepticism about WSC figures.[1] The day-time final of the International Cup at the Sydney Showground attracted 20,443. And even Adelaide produced one good one-day crowd of 7,166 when the West Indies played the World on 28 December 1977.

When the largest crowd of the WSC season turned up at VFL Park there was one (very familiar) 'blot' on the night's proceedings — a lack of crowd control. According to Stephen Phillips, who wrote in the *Age* of 25 January:

> Twice during the Australian innings large sections of the crowd jumped the fence and invaded the ground and both times the results could have been ugly.
>
> Greg Chappell was bowled by Joel Garner on the last ball before dinner but was then forced to fight his way through hundreds of children to get to the dressing rooms.
>
> Chappell, badly bruised on his right arm after being struck by spectators on Monday night, was again injured.
>
> As he ran through the crowd, brandishing his bat in front of him, a youngster punched him in the small of the back.
>
> The Australian vice-captain turned and tried to catch him but the culprit managed to escape.

By encouraging children and young people to attend cricket and by generating an atmosphere of excitement, WSC undoubtedly added to cricket's existing problem of unruly crowds.

The presence of a number of South Africans in the World XI led to a few scattered and isolated anti-apartheid protests. While the presence of a South African Rugby team had generated widespread public protest and attempted disruption of games in the early 1970s, the appearance of individual South Africans did not attract much political interest even though it had significant implications for individual South African sportsmen. Four women interrupted the Fourth Super Test at Sydney for several minutes when they invaded the pitch waving anti-apartheid banners; their target was batsman, Barry Richards. Earlier a Canberra match had been interrupted when two men and three women carried their placards on to the field in protest against another two South Africans, Eddie Barlow and Mike Proctor, who were members of the World team. On the whole, however, political comments and banners have been rare at Australian cricket although there have always been a few exceptions such as a 'no dams' banner which appeared at the 1983 Sydney Test.

The success of night cricket in particular and one-day cricket in general provided a much-needed fillip for WSC whose strategy was ultimately geared to the potentially enormous home audience. A reasonably large and enthusiastic crowd, such as the 24,636 at VFL Park, was necessary to generate a match atmosphere which would stimulate viewer interest and gain support from advertisers who had held back uncertain of the rating potential of alternative cricket. When the crowd finally arrived at WSC cricket it became a very important ingredient of the telecast because cricket, unlike football, has so many pauses in play that photographers have considerable 'loose' time which can be spent prowling around the ground looking for action. Crowd action, and the crowd interaction with players (exchanges, banter, autograph signing, banners with messages to players) all became grist to the WSC commentary mill as they represented another means of squeezing more hype and excitement out of the contest. Bigger and more reactive crowds at the ground undoubtedly won over more viewers — at least those who needed some convincing about the quality of the product offered —

which in turn generated more advertising.

It is rather more difficult to assess the success of the Country Cup where international cricketers trundled around the four eastern States, reaching as far north as Rockhampton and as far south as East Devonport. It is harder to accurately judge the validity of country crowd figures (were they accurate statistics or inspired guesses or promotional wish fulfilments?) than those of city crowds where journalists had some yardsticks of comparison to check the figures given out by WSC. However, even possibly inflated figures, such as the 6,500 who turned up at East Devonport to see Australia vs the World on 12 February 1978, seem to suggest that many country patrons responded very enthusiastically to the rare opportunity of seeing top-class cricket. This was an impressive figure because the population of Devonport was only 25,000 although there were another 75,000 in its rural hinterland, which included a number of smaller towns such as Burnie, Wynyard and Ulverstone. The crowd figure also indicated that there was a country market for international cricket which has hardly been tapped.

Summing up the achievements of WSC in its first year, *Cricket Close-up*, the annual of the *Cricketer* magazine, stated that the total attendance of 354,933 at all levels of cricket (Super Tests, the International and Country Cups) was 'well below expectations'. In a balanced assessment it suggested that WSC was 'far from a great success but not a failure. In other words, a qualified success.' On balance Establishment cricket appeared more successful than WSC, because it proved superior to WSC in the one area of competition, Test cricket. However, the success of the one-day competition did provide WSC with some hope for the future.

In deciding who was the winner of the television war the same magazine was appropriately circumspect since both parties had some grounds on which to claim success. In terms of Test cricket more viewers had remained loyal to the ABC and traditional cricket and preferred a technically inferior coverage of a 'real' Test to a better-presented Super Test. However, when it came to one-day cricket there was quite naturally a much greater television audience for the International Cup than the rival Gillette Cup. It is difficult, however, to say anything beyond this because cricket is played outside the ratings period and consequently any figures put forward by interested television parties must be treated with caution. Ratings are still largely a matter of guesswork when it comes to measuring the following of a sport even if it is played in the ratings period because the statistics do not incorporate variables such as the potential size of the audience (a Saturday audience is larger, for instance, than a Sunday one).

Tony Cozier, West Indian and WSC commentator, provided a frank and realistic assessment of WSC's position at the end of the first season in the *Sun-Herald* of 5 February 1978. On the positive side WSC had realized many of its aims: player salaries had been increased, cricket had been promoted aggressively, there was night cricket, the white ball, and above all, television coverage which would never be the same again following the ingenious direction and camera-work that captured 'every stroke, every wicket, every catch and every emotional reaction with such precision'. Despite this WSC had suffered some disappointments not the least of which had been the lack of public response to competitions in which the world's best players were involved. Cozier believed that the decision to stage the Super Tests in opposition to the ACB Tests against India was a blunder because traditions established over a century 'do not die easily'. Another problem faced by WSC was that it was seen too much as 'Packer cricket': it appeared that many people didn't like the idea of one man controlling the game 'purely because he happened to be wealthy'. Cozier suggested that Packer should take a lower profile and that WSC should be run more by a Committee of Management. Finally he warned that WSC would face its sternest test in the following season with the stiffer competition of an Ashes series.

Cozier's fears proved to be unfounded because the following season was a 'triumph' for Kerry Packer. By contrast Establishment cricket, and the ACB in particular, was brought virtually to its knees during 1978–79. The Establishment position was greatly weakened by the retirement of Bob Simpson, who had held an inexperienced and youthful side together, and the absence of key bowler, Jeff Thomson. Interest in the series quickly dwindled after the Fourth Test when it was clear that the two sides were mismatched. Overall Test crowds were down by 50 per cent on the last English tour while the Test average of 53,731 per match for the eight Tests (which included two against Pakistan) was only just larger than the number for the Indian series in 1977.

Plummeting Shield attendances were an ever greater problem for the Board: the season total of 134,153 was the lowest since 1914–15 and the Board could not take any consolation from the comparison because only six games were played in 1914–15 compared with 25 in 1978–79. The average match attendance in 1914–15 (12,407) was more than twice the 1978–79 figure of 5,366.

Looked at in terms of average daily and match attendances 1978–79 was unquestionably the worst-attended Shield season ever. The main cause of decline was quite obvious: too much cricket at the major centres. There was only a moderate decrease in Western Australia (2,432 per day) and Tasmania (1,693) where the Shield had limited competition from international cricket, but in New South Wales and Victoria the spate of international cricket matches virtually killed all interest in the Shield. Sydney, for instance, had an average of just 827 persons per day. The Melbourne figure of 1,733 per day was more respectable but Melbourne too was heading towards a daily three-figure average.

For Kerry Packer there was no greater triumph in this season than 28 November 1978 when the lights were turned on for the first time at the SCG. He had hoped for a crowd of about 20,000 but by 7.20 p.m. 44,374 had passed through the turnstiles at which point the organizers decided that they could not guarantee a view for any more spectators, and stopped charging with the result that many more came in free, and the crowd swelled to more than 50,000 plus. No one knows precisely how many people saw this historic match. Tony Adams, writing for *World of Cricket*, captured some of the excitement of the occasion:

> The moment that the 50,000-plus crowd was waiting for had come: somewhere a master switch was flicked and the six gargantuan towers splashed the ground with white light — and a new era in Sydney sport was born.
>
> The gloom was instantly transformed into brilliant brightness which was, if anything, clearer than daylight...
>
> The buzz of excitement never left the game throughout the Australians' innings as the players stood out like white porcelain statues on the light green field.
>
> And when Ian Davis hit the winning run, the sky lit up with a barrage of fireworks as thousands of children invaded the pitch.
>
> The crowd loved it; Kerry Packer, television entrepreneur, was happy, and it was obvious from the press next day that the arrival of night cricket had swept Sydney off its feet and it was here to stay, at least for the moment.[2]

The final note of caution about the future of night cricket was unnecessary for from this time on it became as much an integral part of a Sydney summer as the annual expansion of the city's cockroach population. Adams added that he had seen many great Rugby League games and memorable cricket Tests at the SCG 'but nothing will ever match my first visit to the famous arena after dark'. Even Bill O'Reilly, no admirer of WSC, admitted in the *Sydney Morning Herald* of 29 November that night cricket was an 'incredible performance' and that the enthusiastic crowd had taken on the appearance of a 'football final afternoon'. Kerry Packer, he added, had won this first Sydney round of the 1978–79 season by the proverbial mile.

However, not everyone was impressed with developments at the SCG. English scribe John Woodcock stated that the addition of the light towers to the historic SCG amounted to 'Mona Lisa smoking a pipe' and a local architect complained to the *Sydney Morning Herald* of 29 November that the lights were an 'environmental disaster' because they cause an incredible glare for almost a kilometre from the ground.

Not surprisingly there was the usual quota of fights on the Hill, arrests (13 spectators) and incidents such as the pelting with beer cans of two young boys who carried an Australian flag around the ground. A mother of three claimed that she was forced to take her children to the Bradman Stand to escape the 'animal behaviour' of the Hill. The catering arrangements were far from adequate and many spectators had to wait for two hours to get cold pies and hot-dogs. The next morning the Hill was a 'giant rubbish tip': 80 workers were needed to clean up the mess.

During the 1978–79 season attendances at the one-day International Cup almost trebled from 136,954 in 1977–78 to 360,912. In the process WSC made significant inroads in Melbourne, initially one of the most anti-WSC cities. There were now regular crowds at VFL Park in the vicinity of 20,000. WSC also gained access to the Gabba, in addition to the SCG, where a reconstituted Trust, more sympathetic to the populist appeal of WSC, allowed WSC access to the ground. There was a good response at the Gabba including an enthusiastic 31 December crowd of 18,000. Attendances at the Tests still favoured the Establishment but even here WSC had some grounds for optimism as the spectator gap between Tests and Super Tests was narrowing. While the official Tests witnessed very little crowd growth, the average Super Test figure jumped from 20,755 to 31,372. All in all WSC almost doubled its crowds in its second year of operation:

	1977–78		**1978–79**	
Super Tests	124,532	(6 Tests)	156,859	(5 Tests)
International Cup	136,954	(15 games)	360,912	(21 games)
Country Matches (Country Cup, 1977; Cavaliers, 1978)	60,983	(30 days)	58,575	(31 days)
TOTAL	322,469		576,346	

While Packer must have been heartened by the spectator swing towards WSC cricket, he must also have been aware of the implications of the deteriorating situation in Establishment cricket, which spelt trouble for cricket as a whole. With eight Establishment Tests, five Super Tests, 17 WSC one-day internationals and four finals, and another three Establishment one-day games, together with a host of country international games, cricket was in danger of over-exposure. There were many signs that the public had had a surfeit of cricket and were becoming bored with the amount of cricket served up on television. In some respects cricket had returned to the scenario of 1888 when rival claimants for the mantle of authority in the cricket world had diminished the mystique, and consequently, the spectator drawing-power of the game.

By May 1979 both sides needed a break. It was obvious to the Establishment that a continuation of the conflict could only further erode their power and spectator support. WSC appeared to be winning the war for the control of cricket, but there was still the very real prospect that if the battle for control persisted they might not only bring the Establishment to its knees, but also cricket itself. Eventually Kerry Packer opted for a compromise: he achieved some of his specific objectives, such as the Channel 9 rights for the one-day games, but he did not continue to challenge the Board's right to overall control of the game.

The SCG's monumental 'hangover' after the first WSC night match there.

The truce brought a rapid and remarkable end to much of the acrimony which had ruined friendships and just about torn the cricket world apart. In the aftermath of the 'revolution' there was a great sense of relief on all sides that cricket had not been divided permanently and that the two styles could co-exist. The truce also suggests that perhaps Packer had in mind something less than 'total revolution' but that the commercialist and populist forces he unleashed, and the purist backlash which this generated, might even still bring about a major split in the cricket world.

New Fans

While WSC might have enticed away a few of the traditional supporters of cricket, it is clear that new fans constituted the great majority of its following. This resulted from a concerted attempt to market cricket as entertainment and to woo hitherto under-represented groups in the cricket crowd — younger children, teenagers, women and blue collar workers. PBL Marketing conducted research at WSC matches and analysed the composition of the crowds. It assumed, correctly, that up to 1977 the typical supporter of cricket was an Anglo-Saxon male, who had an inside knowledge of the structure and rituals of the game since he had been brought up on cricket and probably had played it for a considerable time at school and beyond.

One-day cricket, the main thrust of WSC, was a simpler and faster-moving brand of cricket ideally calculated to appeal to those who did not know much about, and possibly felt overawed, by the intricacies of Test cricket. One-day games usually followed a basic pattern which was easy to understand: there was an initial period of slow batting and consolidation; a middle period of gradual acceleration; and then a final flurry of about ten overs of aggression and excitement. One-day cricket was a convenient introduction for some who wished to enter the imposing and daunting world of cricket.

There were a number of strategies developed to market cricket more widely and expand its social base. Channel 9 commentators did not assume that their audience was familiar with the game. The basics of cricket were explained with a plethora of maps (for field placings) and animated diagrams (to explain the difference between a leg break and a googly or what a yorker is). Channel 9 commentators were also more Australian in accent and more excitable — more like football commentators — than their well-modulated and less passionate ABC counterparts.

The results of these strategies were impressive. Research indicated that there was, for instance, a significant increase in the number of children (under 14) attending cricket. Although it is difficult to ascertain what was the major attraction for this group, there is no doubt the many prizes and free tickets WSC offered were partly responsible for the dramatic increase. From season 1979–80 to 1980–81 the percentage of Members at the Benson and Hedges World Cup dropped from 21.87 to 19.25 per cent, while the percentage of children rose from 29.62 to 34 per cent. At some of the one-day internationals in 1978–79 children constituted almost half, and at one game more than half, the crowd. It is likely then that a majority of a typical one-day assembly was youthful. WSC also accelerated a trend in Test cricket which had emerged from about 1970. At the WACA, for instance, the proportion of children in the Test outer crowd had increased from 25 per cent in 1970, to 29 per cent in 1974, and to 32 per cent in 1978.

A 1979 survey undertaken at the predominantly multi-cultural and working-class St Mary's (Cathedral) Christian Brothers High School in Sydney hinted at another area of WSC achievement. St Mary's was typical of less affluent Catholic schools which have tended to concentrate on Rugby League with cricket a rather distant second. English master, Tony Luff, asked more than 434 boys to rate the sports which they most liked to watch. WSC cricket was nominated by some 18 per cent of students, and ranked a close second to Rugby League, nominated by 21 per cent, as the most popular sport. Establishment cricket finished well down the list with only a 4 per cent preferred rating. The study implied (though it didn't demonstrate) that cricket was moving away from an exclusive 'Anglo' base to appeal to some of the sons of immigrants.[3]

Cricket's English cultural roots, its class bias and perhaps the lack of an official multicultural programme have hampered the game's appeal to other communities. Whereas many Greek-, Italian- and Yugoslav-Australians had reached the top in Australian Rules by the 1970s — and the Australian Rugby League team has been captained by a Greek-Australian (George Peponis) and a Yugoslav-Australian (Max Krilich) in recent times — cricket could only claim one 'ethnic' Test cricketer in recent decades, Len Durtanovich. Significantly, he is rather better known as Len Pascoe, he anglicized his name early in his cricket career. The composition of the 1982 Australian Under-19 XI indicated that there is no reason why cricket support should be circumscribed by its Anglo-Saxon past or that the sons of immigrants, who move through the Australian school system, are almost as likely to play cricket and local football as soccer: this team included Mike Veletta (Italian-Australian background) and Bronko Djura (Croatian-Australian background).

Women at Cricket

WSC, undoubtedly too, added many women to the cricket crowd. Jill Mullens, writing in the *Sun-Herald* on 28 January 1983 argued that many women, particularly housewives, were 'turned on by go-go [one-day] cricket'. She noted that while there was scarcely a woman to be seen at Test matches, except in the Members' areas, at the one-day WSC games the situation is the reverse: 'From long-on to deep fine leg the oval is ringed with women of all ages, shapes and sizes.' Mullens suggested three reasons for this development. First, it was likely that countless housewives found cricket a homeviewing substitute for the 'soapies'. Cricket also provided real-life heroes. As Mullens put it 'Women not only love heroes, we actually *need* them.' An even more basic reason for getting hooked on cricket, she argued, was the 'overt sexuality' of the game:

> The rubbing of the ball on the trousers, the speculation in vaseline soaked jock-straps, the close fitting gear, the similarity of cricketers' padding to a knight's armour, the continual hitching of protectors (not evidenced much in the English team. Is there a message here?) all constitute pretty heady stuff to the female watcher.

The promoters of WSC were well aware that sex could be used to sell cricket like anything else. Sexually explicit advertisements were commonplace and fitted in with WSC's strategy to promote player personality cults and to encourage more flamboyant behaviour on the field, such as war whoops, victory dances and embraces. Some t-shirt advertising cashed in on the Playboy image by using such popular slogans as 'Big boys play at night'.

Kath Smith, Australian vice-captain, takes block in 1934. Women's Test matches drew sizeable crowds in the 1930s and 1940s but have dwindled since then.

WSC's television coverage not only captured the sweat of the stars, their grunts and groans, and sometimes even their oaths, but it laid bare much of their personal life, their moments of anguish and jubilation, and their reactions to success and failure off the field. For the fan who wished to delve deeper into the personality of the top cricketers the PBL magazine *Australian Cricket* included a 'star spot' which provided a host of personal details. WSC's television coverage also paid a great deal of attention to the women — invariably young and physically attractive — in the crowd. Perhaps such camera work was designed to suggest the glamour of the game or maybe it was intended to titillate male viewers. Perhaps it was just to give the commentators a chance to talk about something other than the game.

There was, however, a great irony in this situation. WSC did introduce many more women to cricket and it expanded their access to the game, but at the same time it heightened and added to certain long-established chauvinist traditions in cricket. For while appealing to women, WSC also rode the crest of the wave of a burgeoning ocker 'nationalism' which found vigorous expression in the cricket Hills around the country — perhaps more so there than anywhere else — and which was deeply conservative in its attitude to women. It is also revealing that while some women were excited by a much less restrained presentation of cricket, and even came to view cricket stars as sex symbols, some men came to cricket to escape from their wives and partners.

Feminist, Lois Bryson, has developed this point further. After attending a Test match at the SCG in the early 1980s she wrote:

> Sitting on 'the hill' I was struck forcibly and almost painfully by the ritual quality of the occasion: a sense of a gigantic, centrally orchestrated ritual, involving players and spectators. Clapping was on cue, individuals would stand at apparently appropriate moments and make smart comments which were responded to by mass incantations in a continuous and post-scripted stream. Nothing perhaps I should have been surprised at, but what did surprise me was that this was an entirely male rite. Even as spectators, and there was a fair scattering of them, females had no real role except to be the object of whistles and cat-calls as they moved about the ground, 'objects' within the male ceremony. I felt unnerved by the experience and tried to understand why, since I've always known sport is sexist, a male preserve. What this experience did bring home was that this was not just men acting out their superior position within the sporting institution of society — a preserve I had been able to see as not of key importance — but a ritualistic celebration of male dominance and superiority in general.[4]

No one can dispute her contention that there is some measure of sexism in almost all Australian sport, as in almost any Australian institution, and that some sporting crowds constitute an expression of male solidarity, the tone of which many would consider objectionable. However, such an argument ignores the possible degrees of sexism in a sport or a crowd. Tennis has a much higher female following than cricket. In fact, in a 1983 Australia-wide McNair Anderson Poll, tennis was nominated by 41 per cent of women as their favourite sport. It is not hard to appreciate why: it is not only a game in which women are prominent but it is also a sport which has less sexual stereotyping than some of the team sports. On the other hand, it could be argued that the presentation and context of cricket is less sexist than Rugby League which comes at the top of the chauvinist ratings. Macquarie University demographer, Geoff Pollard, found in 1977 that while 21 per cent of Sydney men nominated League as their favourite sport, a meagre 3.5 per cent of women opted for League compared with 25 per cent who preferred tennis.

Cricket's chauvinist standing and rating as a family sport is rather more difficult to categorize. However, the 1983 McNair

Anderson Poll did suggest that while cricket was rather more popular with the men — 46 per cent of men participated in or followed cricket — there was a substantial female following for the game: 29 per cent nominated cricket as a sport which they participated in or followed. This is a very high figure because it is not much lower than the 41 per cent who nominated tennis as their favourite sport in the same survey.[5]

Perhaps a more intriguing question, one which would rather more tax the mind of number-conscious administrators, is whether a degree of sexism augments or diminishes the potential audience for a sport. Would Rugby League gain more followers (women and family groups) if it toned down its macho image? But would it, in the process, lose much of its traditional clientele which preferred a rough-and-tumble no-holds-barred sport? WSC officials clearly believed that no harm, and possibly some advantage, could result from what was seen as a humorous, mildly chauvinistic ockerism in the late 1970s. They could also point to results on the board: never before had cricket attracted so many women (and families for that matter) to all sections of the cricket ground, and particularly to the Outer sections.

Cricket Ockerism

By the 1980s, some officials began to worry about the context and image of cricket and the effect of deteriorating crowd behaviour in some of the Hills of the country on the potential appeal of the game to women and family groups. There was considerable evidence that cricket ockerism was degenerating from a mildly amusing, relatively harmless, chauvinistic though mindless form of behaviour to something more strident and jingoistic, at times ugly and violent, that was spawning what the majority considered gross forms of exhibitionism, such as defecation which occurred on a number of occasions on the Sydney Hill. There is also no question that comments from the Outer became

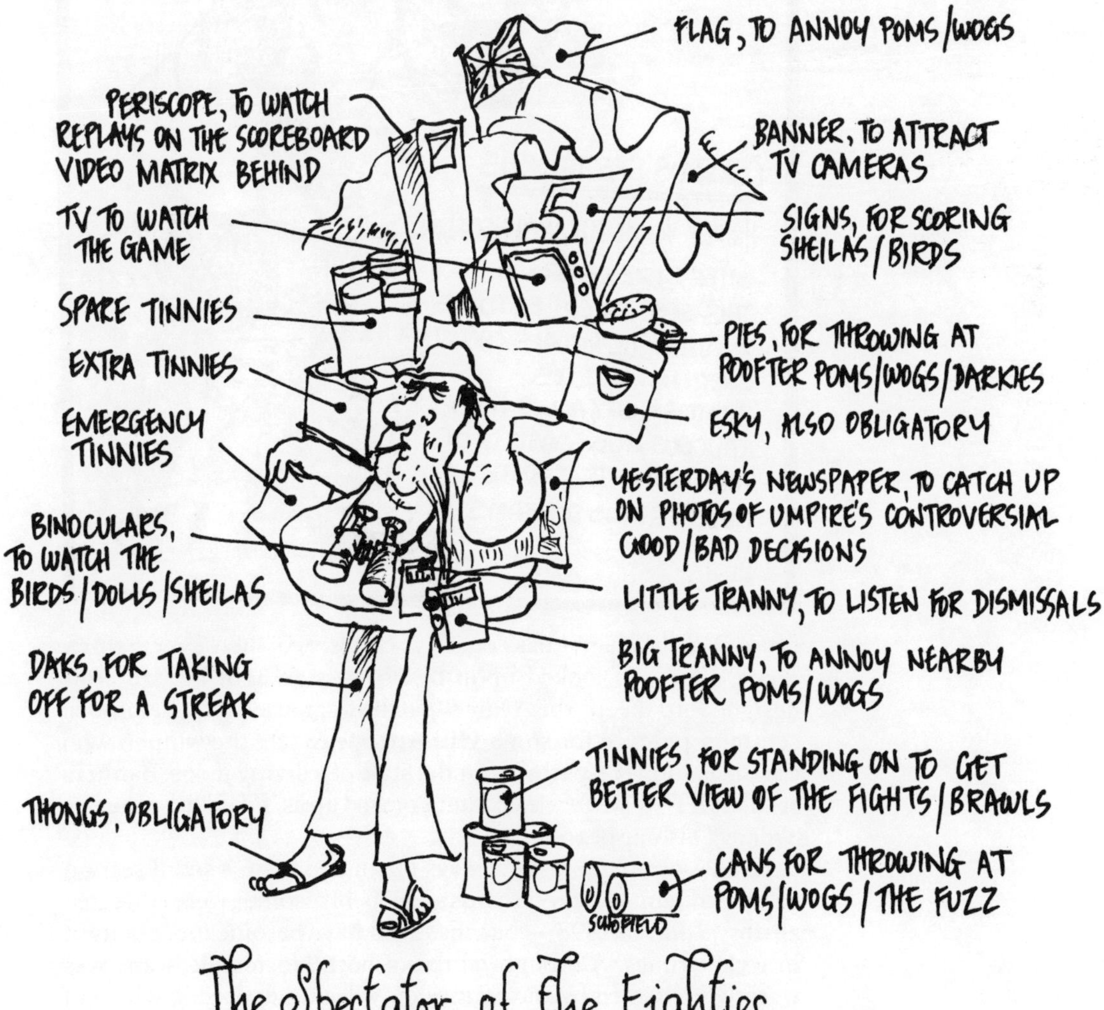

The Spectator of the Eighties

more openly chauvinist, racist and obscene than ever before. Some of it was looked upon by officials as light-headed stuff designed to keep the Outer patrons 'amused'. It became a common practice for some Hill patrons to rate the women who paraded along the pathway in the style of a diving judge. Banners such as 'ET's sister' (which later showed up as 'ET's half-sister' at Sydney) also appeared.

Racist comments have always emanated from a small section of Australian cricket crowds — possibly some were directed against Ranji in 1898 — but these too have become more blatant in recent times. Although Jamaican-born Norman Cowans was warmly acclaimed by the Sydney crowd as an underdog who had been treated unfairly (underbowled) by his captain, Bob Willis, he was subjected to many unthinking remarks from the Sydney

"IT'S JOHNSON, SKIPPER—BEEN DOWN AT FINE LEG ALL AFTERNOON!"

Hill such as, 'Why don't you get out of your own shadow, Norman?' Australian cricketers have not suffered from racist remarks mainly because Australia has never had an Aboriginal Test cricketer, and very few Aboriginal Shield players. This indicates something about cricket's class base which does not apply to boxing, Australian Rules football and Rugby League in which there are many Aboriginal players. However, ethnic slurs against some local players are more common.

In recent years officials at Adelaide have taken some action to halt the declining standard of public comment at cricket. On the third day of the 1982 Test police, presumably acting in concert with officials, confiscated a number of signs from the Hill. Some of the banner makers could not understand why the signs were confiscated by police because they thought it was all 'good fun' and 'entertaining' to the Hill crowd.

A more far-reaching and positive move to alter cricket's image was the introduction of a family ticket at the Adelaide Oval in the early 1980s. The ticket enabled two adults and two children to attend a game at a saving of about 25 per cent. The concept of a family ticket, however, is still new at international cricket and it is yet to have a significant impact on Adelaide crowds. Even so, family tickets represented about 4 per cent of ticket sales at one-day internationals and a little over 2 per cent at Test and Shield matches at Adelaide in 1982–83.

Officials at other grounds, and notably Sydney, have yet to tackle this question. At Sydney children who wish to sit in the best public stands, the Brewongle and the Bradman, are charged the full adult rate. And given that few family groups would choose to venture into the cheapest areas of the ground, they are left with the moderate but somewhat antiquated, and far more expensive, comfort of the Sheridan Stand.

Violence: An Old Problem

During the 1980s cricket crowd violence assumed larger proportions and the relationships between police and spectators deteriorated to a lower point than ever before. In certain respects there had been worse incidents in earlier times, for example the 1879 Harris incident which stands out clearly as the worst-ever cricket riot. Even though Terry Alderman suffered a more serious injury than Lord Harris, the 1982 incident or riot was brief, confined to a few, law and order was quickly re-established on the field; and the threat of a larger popular explosion was less real in 1982 than in 1879. The crowd invasions of the field in the early 1970s were much more frequent and involved many more people than the early 1980s. In 1982–83 the invasion at Perth was the only significant crowd intrusion on the field in the entire season. In fact this problem had been virtually solved at Melbourne and Sydney by 1982 with better techniques of crowd control. However, in no previous season had there been so many incidents of crowd violence and at so many grounds; and there seems little doubt that the number of ejections, arrests, and crowd injuries sustained reached record proportions.

Symptomatic of the extent of the problem was that violence erupted not only in the established trouble-spots of Sydney and Melbourne but also occurred at the previously quiet Hobart, Perth and Adelaide grounds. The weekend before the Alderman incident there were ugly scenes between police and spectators at Hobart during McDonald's Cup matches. On a very hot Saturday, 6 November 1982, when the ground was almost enveloped by smoke from bushfires burning around Hobart, police arrested 24 people on the Hill. Among them was a truck driver who resisted violently and in the process punched one officer, kicked another and bit a third on the leg. The policeman who was kicked collapsed and died two days later whereupon the charge against the assailant was changed from obstruction and assault to manslaughter. Months later the charge of manslaughter was dropped; some medical evidence suggesting a disruption in the chain of causation may have been found which disassociated the officer's death from the kick on the leg alone. The Secretary of the Tasmanian Cricket Association (TCA), Kevin Connor, believed that the violence was 'drink-induced' and there was plenty of evidence to support that contention: it had taken about a dozen people more than 30 hours to clean up the mess (made by a crowd of just 7,296) and two bulk waste-disposal trucks to take it away.

The TCA took immediate action and patrons were not permitted to take liquor into the ground at subsequent Hobart matches in that season. Prior to this there had been very few recorded crowd incidents in Tasmania. Tasmania has the most English-style grounds in the country, at Launceston and Hobart, and a National Trust-classified English-style small scoreboard at Hobart. Prior to 1982 its Shield crowds seemed to have reacted more along restrained English lines although its one-day crowds, particularly when Tasmania won the Gillette Cup in 1979, were much more exuberant.

The much-publicized Alderman incident, and the most celebrated injury in Australian cricket history, occurred on Saturday, 13 November 1982 at the WACA. When England reached 400 some dozen spectators, including one who was waving a Union Jack, ran on to the ground, presumably to congratulate the Englishmen. One of the invaders, 19-year-old Gary Donnison, an Englishman settled in Perth, delivered what Alderman later referred to as a thump on the back of his head as he ran past; he was then hotly pursued by Alderman and brought down in what appeared to television viewers as a regulation Rugby tackle. Unfortunately Alderman sustained a serious injury to his shoulder which kept he out of the rest of the season, ruled him out of the World Cup and deprived him of substantial cricket

Jeff's comment on the Alderman incident.

earnings. As Alderman lay on the ground clutching his arm Lillee grabbed one tattoed young man and Border rushed over to lend a hand. Chappell then led his team off the field as police moved in to break up scuffles in the crowd which continued throughout the afternoon. The 'English' contingent was eventually ejected from the ground or arrested. The match resumed after a break of some 20 minutes and after numerous replays of the violence from every possible angle.

Post mortems of the 'Test riot', as one paper dubbed it, continued for weeks. There were two main schools of thought. Initially a popular theory was that Australia had inherited an 'English' problem and that the violence could be put down to 'visiting hooligans'. It was not until later that it was established that the chief assailant was not a transient Englishman, but an Englishman who had lived in Perth for some time.

It did not take long for an alternative explanation to surface. Former English Test batsman, Tom Graveney was quoted in the *Sydney Morning Herald* of 15 November 1982 that a decline in player behaviour over recent years had encouraged 'loutish behaviour' but, more specifically, pointed the finger at Channel 9's advertisements 'which showed people in England poking fun at Australia' which might have influenced feelings at Perth. The view was endorsed by no less than the British Sports' Minister, Neil MacFarlane, who suggested that the advertisements may have encouraged a 'combative atmosphere' leading to violence.

Others directed their criticism not specifically at Channel 9 advertisements but at commercialism, and its offspring, one-day cricket, and the legacy of WSC in general. Celebrated commentator, John Arlott, argued that hooliganism in Perth was a 'predictable consequence of one-day cricket'. Later in the season *Wisden* Editor, John Woodcock, filed a stinging critique of the 11 January SCG one-day crowd which was printed in the *Sydney Morning Herald* of 13 January:

> England was drowned in a sea of jingoism in yesterday's World Series Cup...
>
> Of the many day-night matches I have seen in Sydney, this, more than all the others, had about it the lust and passion of the bull ring ...
>
> By 8.30 any resemblance between what was happening and any normal game of cricket was coincidental... The sounds of fury, the beating of the boards, and the booing of English batsmen were orgiastic.
>
> This was not so much sport as jingoism. But there it was... The scenes of mass hysteria as Australia surged to victory were, to me at any rate, discordant and unattractive.

Several comments can be made on this debate. It is clear that some journalists and followers of cricket were still far from reconciled to the more overt commercialist side of cricket which had emerged in 1977 and seemed to hanker after a dual order in world cricket: an amateur-Test-purist league and a more professional-commercial-populist alternative which Bill O'Reilly suggested could be called 'kickit' (a phrase coined after the Lillee–Miandad incident), 'snickit' or 'cashit'. Many argued that there was a very real danger that the new fans would dominate the game and discourage the traditional supporter. From the time of the truce, 1979, a surge in one-day numbers and a decline in Test crowds seemed to support this contention and to suggest that the future of Test cricket was in doubt. The 1982–83 Ashes series reversed the slide in Test attendances but, even so, some wondered whether this was a long-term trend or merely a temporary reprieve for Test cricket. Others asked whether it was worth having new fans at cricket if it led to so much violence and hooliganism.

To blame Channel 9 for cricket violence was a convenient and all too simple explanation propagated by those who were hostile to the commercial presentation of the game and who denigrated one-day cricket. There is no question that Channel 9 may have added to a violent atmosphere, but it is unlikely that it caused or created, in any significant sense, the combative climate which spawned an event such as the Alderman incident. There has been considerable debate recently about whether television can alter behaviour — change voting behaviour for instance — and can cause violence. Most authorities now reject technologically-determinist perspectives and suggest that the effects of the medium has often been exaggerated.

As far as cricket is concerned it is very unlikely that television advertising could make an individual violent or even more inclined to violence unless he or she was so inclined anyway. Television did not cause the violence of 1982–83, it merely reflected violence in Australian society; there were more basic socio-economic reasons for crowd unrest. During 1982–83 there was a mood of jingoism which swept through the country and was manifest at many sporting assemblies: it was much in evidence at the Commonwealth Games where it was encouraged (not caused) by the ABC. Along with the jingoism there was increasing lawlessness, anarchy and crime which undoubtedly reflected the harsh economic times, soaring unemployment, widening social rifts and lack of social consensus.

The Spread of Violence

Cricket authorities at other grounds braced themselves for the worst after Perth. The NSWCA met to consider whether the SCG should have a barbed-wire fence. This proposition had been considered two years previously after can-throwing and various other incidents at the one-day internationals. A new wire fence was installed in 1982 and although there was provision for a barbed-wire extension to be fitted to the oval fence none has been erected yet at a cricket match. (It was used at the 1983 Rugby League Grand Final.) It appears unlikely that barbed wire will ever separate players from spectators because of the possibility of

After the game at Hobart.

injury if players run over the rope into the wire. There is still, however, the probability of some other barrier being erected in future if current methods of crowd management fail.

When the next Test began at Adelaide there was a larger-than-usual police contingent ready to deal with any crowd trouble. Up to this time Adelaide had had a reputation as one of the best-behaved crowds in the country but on the Saturday of the Test even this crowd turned nasty when a policeman was kicked in the head with a steel-capped boot and sustained concussion. This was the beginning of a series of incidents which led to 14 arrests and 80 ejections. Among those arrested was South Australian Shield player Tony Handrickan. After he was charged with using offensive language, resisting arrest and refusing to give his name and address to police and fined $205 he was dropped from the State side. On the following day 11 arrests were made and 46 people were thrown out.

A spokesman for SACA and the police linked the violence with liquor and expressed concern at the amount of liquor smuggled into the ground. Undoubtedly restrictions on drinking within the ground had helped to reduce drunkenness and incidents in the past, however it is difficult to establish the importance of smuggled liquor. On a hot Saturday and an even hotter Sunday the bars around the ground did a roaring trade. Many of the Outer patrons blamed — as they always tend to do — the heavy hand of the police for the incidents. However, after what happened in Perth, police were in no mood to tolerate even minor disorder and acted deliberately and decisively.

Adelaide had never seen an incident like this. There has been a long tradition of jeering at the police but never of actually 'putting the boot in'. Many were able to blame the English for what happened in Perth but the message from Adelaide seemed to be that Australia was developing its own cricket hooligans. The pattern established at the Test was repeated to some extent at the three one-day matches of late January: 44 people appeared before magistrates charged with offences which included among other things resisting arrest and returning to a public place after being removed by police.

While Hobart, Perth and Adelaide provided the most ugly incidents of the 1982–83 season, there is little doubt that the Sydney Hill became the undisputed violence capital of Australia: there were more arrests, more injuries, more running battles with police and more examples of outrageous behaviour which built up a formidable and progressively odious reputation. The pattern of crowd behaviour was established on the rain-affected first day of the Fifth Test. Although the *Sydney Morning Herald* of 3 January 1983 described the crowd as 'unusually well behaved' — the journalist rightly expected that worse could be expected later — the Police Band was pelted with fruit when it wheeled too close to the Hill and the score at the end of the day was four charged with serious affront and another eight detained.

The figures escalated when the one-day series began. The first day–night encounter on 11 January resulted in a reported 100 arrests and one man was charged with assaulting not one but three officers — one policewoman and two policemen. After another match on 19 January 60 intoxicated spectators were detained at the Darlinghurst and Central police stations from four to eight hours. Another 43 were arrested and 42 were detained owing to intoxication at the first Final match played on 9 February.

No doubt the length of playing time, the influence of a hot sun and the less continuous action of a cricket match provide spectators with more opportunities for getting drunk and organizing crowd diversions which may or may not lead to violence. However, problems of crowd control do not begin and end with the drunken spectator. It was on 9 February that a 15-year-old youth fell to his death when he attempted to jump from one section of the Manufacturers' Pavilion to another building in the adjacent Showground. There was little the police could do to prevent this accident because the boy was not in the Cricket Ground when he fell. There were another 40 children on the roof at the time. Members of the Cliff Rescue Squad are now located on the roof of the Ladies' Stand during major matches.

During the 1982–83 season Executive Chief-Superintendent Ray Williams, who had a long association with the SCG, introduced measures which substantially reduced the problem of crowd violence. The measures included a greater surveillance of smuggled liquor at the gate; a reduced crowd to about 40,000; the use of a rope two metres inside the pickets to enable the police to circle the ground inside the fence, and operation of a new combat unit, the Tactical Response Group, on the Hill.

The establishment of a Command Post also contributed to more co-ordinated crowd management. Hidden from the public at the top of the Brewongle Stand, this nerve centre of control includes officers armed with binoculars, sound equipment and a plan of the ground which is divided up into a grid system so that if trouble surfaces in one area the Command Post can simply inform its force: 'move to G6', or some other number. This is an important development because policemen on the Hill itself can't see very far beyond their immediate environment when the Hill is crowded. Another problem for policemen on the Hill is that there are no defined paths of access up and down the Hill which makes it difficult to patrol. The NSWCA is giving serious consideration to a proposal to construct two tiers of well-marked steps running up the Hill which would be patrolled by police and which would also provide spectators with greater access to the amenities.

Another solution advocated by the police for the problem of crowd violence was either a total ban on alcohol at the SCG or the introduction of plastic tumblers. The SCG finally made some changes in the 1983–84 season after the police insisted that there be a variation in the liquor licence for bars 4 and 5 (under the Scoreboard and the Sheridan Stand) so that no cans could be sold. The Trust then agreed to install new pipes so that draught beer could be sold to the Outer patrons and in the 1983–84 season plastic tumblers replaced the ubiquitous can. The construction of a new Outer stand should also add to facilities because spectators will have more access to food and liquor outlets. Whether or not this will solve the problem of violence on the Hill — it will undoubtedly reduce it — is another matter.

While SCG authorities struggled to get on top of the violence-on-the-Hill problem, other crowd measures designed to prevent interruptions to the game were very successful. Prior to the Test match spectators were warned by police that anyone who ran on to the ground would be arrested, regardless of age. The warning was repeated numerous times over the loud-speaker at the ground. Police and ground officials patrolled the two metres between the rope and the fence. Some people, such as ABC commentator Jim Maxwell, thought this made the ground unattractive but it was surely preferable to barbed wire.

During the Test there was only one ground invader: on the last day, when the crowd was sparse and the Test was slumbering to a draw, a boy jumped the fence to field a ball but quickly retreated. Mid-way through a one-day international there were two or three solo intrusions on to the ground, but an announcement, reminding spectators of the penalty for jumping the fence, quickly put a stop to this.

Successful crowd control at the SCG has resulted from good management procedures. With positive and decisive action, particularly in the regulation of liquor sales and the provision of adequate facilities, there seems little doubt that violence on the Hill can be reduced if not eliminated. Ultimately the Hill can be retained. Otherwise, the days of this historic Sydney landmark might well be numbered.

Crowd management techniques were so effective at the MCG during the 1982–83 season that there were no reported incidents of crowd violence, despite the much larger crowds. NSWCA Secretary, Bob Radford, believes that there were several reasons for Melbourne's better record. First, the ground and the facilities make it much easier to control a crowd. Next, there has been a greater continuity in police operations at the MCG: for about 15 years the ground was under the control of recently retired Sergeant Brian Wakins, who had the business of crowd control down to a fine art. Sydney, by comparison, has had a fairly rapid turnover of top police personnel associated with the SCG and until recently there has also been some reluctance to adopt a tough stance in regard to spectator violence.

Sydney's New Stands

For better or worse cricket watching is becoming more geared to technology in general and television in particular and is being marketed along more professional and commercial lines. *World of Cricket*, for instance, advised its readers in December 1978 that cricket promoters had now entered the computer age and as a result 'cricket lovers will no longer need to queue' in one or another capital city. They could buy their tickets at the nearest shopping centre through Computicket, and after its demise, through Mitchells Bass Agencies. More often than not those who purchased a ticket through a computer-based agency were provided with a particular numbered seat in the style of theatre or concert bookings.

A major step to enhance cricket-watching traditions (at least for some) at Sydney was taken with the construction of a new Brewongle Stand which was opened in June 1980 at a cost of $8.7 million. According to SCG historian, Philip Derriman, it provided 'a standard of comfort not previously known in Australia': the 'most striking innovation' being the row of 24 private 'boxes' each consisting of a small air-conditioned lounge and balcony with bar and television facilities and capable of accommodating 20 people. The new stand, in the opinion of *Wisden Cricket Monthly* editor David Frith, is 'a beauty' and it even seems to blend well with its National Trust-classified neighbours, the Sheridan Stand to the south and the Ladies' Stand to the north.

The public, too, responded enthusiastically to the new stand which suggests that its erection met a long-felt need for better facilities. Many people have been willing to pay higher prices providing that they can be guaranteed a seat removed from the troubles of the Hill which also has a degree of comfort, a good view and cover overhead. It cost twice as much for a daily ticket in the Brewongle Stand ($15) as on the Hill ($7) but as the season progressed it was common to find that the Brewongle Stand was sold out whereas there was plenty of room on the Hill.

The 24 boxes in the Brewongle Stand have become the best-patronized areas of the ground. There is always a good crowd there even for a McDonald's Cup match where attendance is sparse to moderate in other parts of the ground. It is easy to understand why. The guests of the corporate sector enjoy convivial surroundings and the cricket provides a convenient backdrop for business and social discussion or perhaps business provides a convenient excuse for watching cricket in air-conditioned comfort.

Such has been the success of the Brewongle Stand that a similar stand, the Hills Stand, with a seating capacity of 4,500, will be constructed by 1984. The stand, which will span the area from the old Paddington Hill to where the Bob Stand, now moved to North Sydney Oval, and the Amenities Stand were, will consist of bucket seats and another 21 private boxes on the top level with air-conditioned interiors and outside balconies. It is expected that the new stand would increase the capacity of the ground to 54,000.

The new stands will have a marked impact on the SCG cricket crowds. First of all, they have replaced a significant area of very ordinary, moderately priced accommodation with superior, even luxury, higher priced seating. In the process they have whittled away the size of the Hill, and the standing–seating area. Over the years the main southern Hill has become smaller and smaller with the encroachment of the Amenities Stand (now to be swallowed up), small, covered, standing concrete areas at the top of the Hill and now the lights and the new video matrix scoreboard have consumed many square metres of grass. By 1983–84 the Paddington Hill was extinct and replaced by a sea of bucket seats and a small covered area.

One danger is that in future few will be able to afford to attend live cricket and economic necessity will force the ordinary spectator to follow the game on television. It is also revealing that cricket crowds are again becoming more segregated as they were in the late nineteenth century, though the divisions now are not based so much on sex and status group as on money and influence.

Along with the new stand Sydney had a $4.2 million giant video screen in November 1983. Located on the southern end of the Hill, between the old scoreboard and the Sheridan Stand, it did not cost the public or the Trust a cent because the screen was financed by Mitsubishi Electric who will recoup their investment and benefit from advertising sponsorship. (Sydney, unlike Melbourne, plans to retain its old scoreboard, which still has the name-plate rolls of many former greats — Bradman, Trumper, Kippax — in dusty cupboards.) When a similar screen operated for the first time in a Test match in Melbourne in December 1982 it proved a popular innovation. Some even suggested that the cheers for replays were even louder than those for the original event which would have confirmed the worst fears of the purist Cardus. But the majority of to-day's fans are not purists and appreciate the additional information and entertainment to cover the major intervals and the minor ones, the drinks break, and to give them something to occupy their mind while yet another fast bowler returns once again to his mark.

Today's cricket spectators are very much more geared to watching cricket with the assistance of technology, so it was not surprising that the tradition of clever banners, which began in Melbourne and has now spread to other grounds, has become very much television related since the clever message will always get good media exposure. Cricket spectators now use banners to send messages to family and friends and to publicize obscure towns, such as Buckleboo and Yackandandah while other signs advertise events in a town's history such as the January 1983 Adelaide sign, 'Broken Hill Centenary Stand'. Many of the signs refer to television commentators, most notably Channel 9's Lawry, Tyson, Stackpole and Benaud. Lawry's nose was the subject of one January 1983 MCG banner: a two-metre square white banner was declared to be 'Bill Lawry's hanky'. Even the television scorers, who are spoken to but rarely appear in the coverage, have become minor celebrities. One of them featured in a January 1983 Sydney banner: 'Henry Blofeld asks whether Irving Rosenwater has ever scored with Wendy Wimbush.' There was also some mild criticism of the precise and pithy and much less ocker (when compared with Lawry) commentary of Richie Benaud: one Adelaide sign advised Channel 9 to 'replace Benaud with Hawkeye' (Neil Hawke) while another Sydney sign declared, unflatteringly, 'Benaud — elephant man'.

There are far fewer ABC-related banners around the ground: presumably the ABC does less to promote commentary personalities and to provide itself with free advertisements by zeroing in on banners. It could do more if it was so inclined: Nuggett 'gold, gold, gold' Norman May can be just as excitable as Bill Lawry. The only attempt to compete with Channel 9 was a campaign to cash in on the legendary Alan McGilvray.

After World Series Cricket

While there was a meeting of the minds of the Establishment and WSC authorities in May 1979, it has taken the best part of four seasons to work out a formula that will appeal to the diverse interests of the old and new fans of cricket. Many of the traditional followers of the game found it difficult to come to terms with the mixed menu of cricket served up in the first post-WSC season. It appeared to many as a jumble of Test and one-day games in which two short Test series were intertwined. Gilbert Mant, who had covered the Bodyline tour, struck a popular chord in the *Sydney Morning Herald* of 20 March 1980 when he wrote a letter to the paper expressing his 'bitter disillusionment with post-Packer cricket' and stating that he intended to resign his membership of the SCG which he had held for 25 years. Other cricket followers, however, found the post-WSC programme exciting because it was rather more geared to one-day than Test cricket. Central to the former, for instance, was the notion of a three-way contest. This in turn meant that the tried and trusted formula of one five- or six-Test series — which if both sides were well matched built up to a climax in the last Tests — was scrapped in favour of two short and mixed Test series against the two visiting teams. Not surprisingly there was a decline in public support of Test cricket, so much so that many wondered about the future viability of Test cricket. One-day cricket, on the other hand, prospered and appeared more and more to be carrying Test and Shield cricket. It seemed that many of the new fans continued to patronize cricket, and even brought others along, whereas a significant number of the traditionalists virtually dropped out. This process may have been speeded up by the ABC's loss of cricket television rights in 1979–80 and 1980–81 which meant that the traditionalists had no choice but to watch the game on commercial television.

Wiser planning decisions made prior to the 1982–83 season recognized the separate interests of the new and the old fans and the differing demands of Test and one-day cricket. It was decided to divide the season into separate compartments: to restore the proven formula of a five-Test series against one country which would be followed by a three-way one-day series. The move was an outstanding success. The Ashes Test series was the best patronized since the mid-1970s and indicated that Test cricket still had wide appeal if presented in the right context. Another bonus for officials was that the euphoria generated by an old-fashioned Australia–England series carried over into the one-day contests. For example, the best attended one-day match at Sydney was the first game there on 11 January 1983, just four days after the Test. The gates were closed early in the afternoon with 42,030 inside and another 10,000 outside.

Another positive sign for some cricket followers was that the ABC had re-established itself by 1982–83 as a disseminator of television cricket and was able to provide some alternative

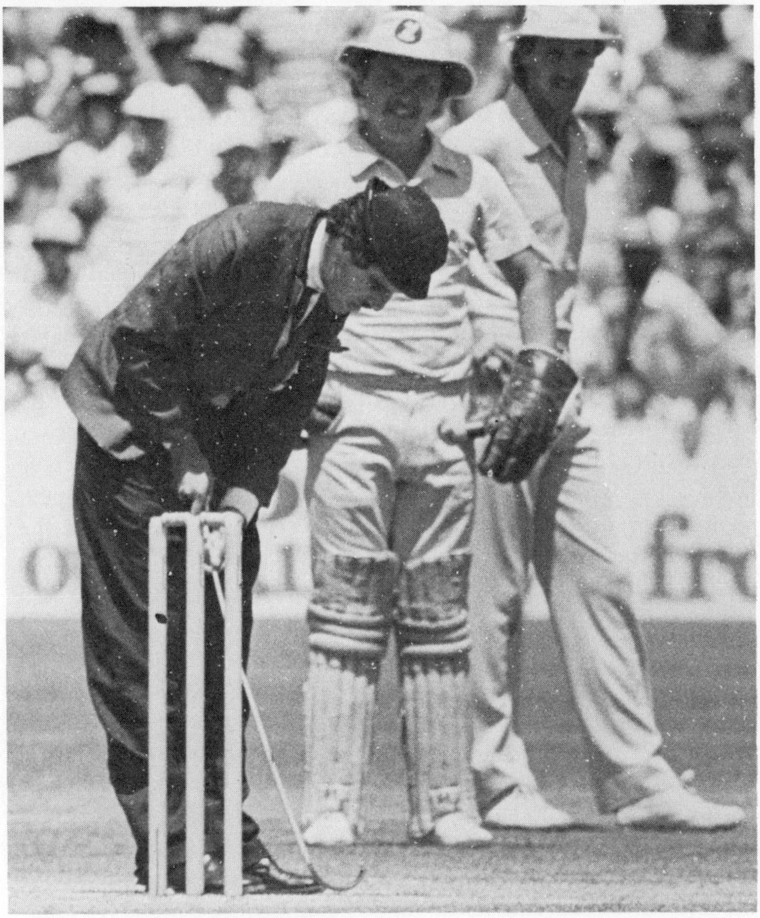

A contemporary character, Franco Dominic Princi, alias Charlie Chaplin, at the wicket at Adelaide on 29 January 1983.

commentary to Channel 9, at least for one session per day so far as the Tests were concerned. (Channel 9 retained the exclusive rights for one-day cricket in Australia.)[7]

While officials have rediscovered a successful formula for the promotion of Test cricket, there is still room for improvement in the scheduling of the one-day series. In almost every other sport the largest crowds turn up for the finals series rather than the lead-up matches but the reverse has occurred in the one-day series on most occasions. The most likely explanation is that there are too many lead-up games so that by the time the finals come round the public interest has begun to wane. The United States World Series of baseball provides an alternative and successful formula which might be considered: after a short lead-up series — four teams play three games each to decide the final contenders — there is a best-of-seven series to decide the winner.

At the end of the 1982–83 season officials had good reason to look with confidence to the future of cricket as a major spectator sport. Cricket is more than holding its own despite an apparent spectator decline in some team sports, notably Rugby League, during the past few decades primarily because of greater competition from more individualistic sports such as tennis, golf, surfing, motor car and bike racing. In fact a 1983 McNair Anderson Poll nominated cricket as the most popular sport in the country: 38 per cent of Australians participate in or follow cricket, followed by tennis (37 per cent); Australian Rules (35 per cent); swimming and surfing (26 per cent) and Rugby League (19 per cent).

Perhaps cricket's greatest asset is that by the 1920s and 1930s it had established and consolidated a national base: it was identified with Australian nationalism, it was followed in all States, it appealed to all classes, and particularly after the introduction of radio and television, it could count on sizeable female support. Cricket has suffered from some periods of decline but more often than not this has been due to bad planning or poor presentation of the game or simply a dull series or two.

A history of Australian cricket crowds suggests that there have been many cycles in Australian popular culture which repeat themselves: the larrikin of the 1870s seems to turn up as the ocker in the 1970s; invasions of the pitch became fashionable again in the 1970s; and crowd comments made in one generation are recycled, or perhaps even reincarnated, in the next. There also seems a cyclical pattern in official programme planning and reactions to crowds. The over-exposure of cricket in 1888 was repeated in 1978; official soul-searching about the possible deleterious effect of radio on crowds was forgotten by the 1960s when officials again worried themselves — unnecessarily it seems because radio suggested a lesson which was not learnt — over the impact of television. Even remarks by some of cricket scribes fall into this pattern. The fears expressed by Cardus about the impact of the transistor on the game were echoed by Tatz, some three decades later, who focused on the slow-motion replay.

There can be no doubt, however, that technology, commercialism and professionalism have altered for ever the once English-amateur-inspired game; its shape has changed, the way people watch it has altered, as have the very idea and meaning of cricket. It would not have survived without significant adaptation to the values and mores of contemporary society. Perhaps the most significant change that has overtaken cricket is that it is no longer Australia's national game because no one game or activity can any longer capture the imagination of such a pluralistic society.

Increasingly since 1945 many have questioned both the entertainment value and the worth of organised sport in general and of team sports in particular and have shown a preference for alternative leisure. To ensure cricket's survival officials will have to stir themselves to even more activity, to promote the game aggressively, to initiate change, and to persuade the largest possible number of people of its attractiveness.

It is unlikely that Australian cricket will ever see another Yabba. Clever comments from the Outer are much less common today and even the perennial "Ave a go, yer mug!' has fallen from

The record crowd at the WACA, 20 December 1981 (Australia vs West Indies). Note the crowd inside the boundary alongside the rope.

favour. Our cricket crowds have become more imitative in their behaviour of other crowds, notably football, and of crowds overseas. Television has been the great leveller in that it has made crowds more cosmopolitan in outlook. With the ever-expanding time allocated to television sport Australia is now producing more 'dead-set Norms' than original barrackers. To many of the older followers of cricket this adds up to a decline in our crowds. While this is true in some respects, it ignores the fact that many more people now have access to a game and, for better or worse, cricket has become a more democratic game. Such a process has led to some dilution of the hitherto elitist traditions of barracking and commentary and even writing about and reporting on the game.

While there is now a greater sameness in cricket crowds around the world, the mass of humanity which collects at one or another Australian ground still continues to express a form of Australian popular culture whether it be a primitive form of nationalism, or jingoism, or the partly manufactured cult of ockerism. To be lost in the cricket crowd still helps many Australians, just as much as it did their ancestors, to cope with recessions, to escape from some of the harsh realities of their lives and to enjoy one of the few long-established traditions of this country.

Notes

Chapter One

1. There are no precise figures available for the minimum wage in the nineteenth century but from the 1860s an unskilled labourer earnt from 5/- to 7/- per day. The basic wage in the 1930s rose from £3/1/1 to £3/13/-.
2. Keith A. P. Sandiford, 'English Cricket Crowds During the Victorian Age', *Journal of Sport History,* vol. 9, no. 3, Winter 1982, p. 12.
3. Philip Derriman, *The Grand Old Ground: A History of the Sydney Cricket Ground,* Cassell, Sydney, 1981, p. 6.
4. Keith Dunstan, *The Paddock That Grew: The Story of the Melbourne Cricket Club,* Cassell, Melbourne, 1974, p. 17.
5. K. Dunstan, *op cit.,* p. 22.
6. P. Derriman, *op cit.,* p. 17.
7. P. Derriman, *op cit.,* pp. 6–7, 95–6; K. Dunstan, *op cit.,* p. 55.
8. Susan I. Millbank, 'South Australian Cricket Association, Cricket and South Australia: 1871–1914', unpub. B.A. hons thesis, Flinders University, 1981, ch 4.
9. J. W. C. Cumes, *Their Chastity was not too Rigid: Leisure Times in Early Australia,* Longman, Melbourne, 1979, pp. 139, 140, 142; Ronald Cardwell, 'The Birth of International Cricket in Australia', *World of Cricket Monthly,* no. 6, June 1977, pp. 6–8.
10. W. F. Mandle, 'Cricket and Australian Nationalism in the Nineteenth Century', *Journal of the Royal Australian Historical Society,* 59, pt 4, December 1973, p. 227; K. S. Inglis, 'Imperial Cricket: Test Matches between Australia and England 1877–1900', in Richard Cashman and Michael McKernan (eds), *Sport in History: The Making of Modern Sporting History,* University of Queensland Press, Brisbane, 1977, pp. 164–5.
11. Quoted in K. S. Inglis, *op cit.,* pp. 163, 204.
12. W. F. Mandle, 'Games People Played: Cricket and Football in England and Victoria in the Late Nineteenth Century', *Historical Studies,* 15, no. 60, April 1973, p. 526; K. S. Inglis, *op cit.,* p. 166.
13. *Sydney Morning Herald,* 9 March 1871.
14. *Sydney Morning Herald,* 23 January 1874.
15. *Sydney Morning Herald,* 7 February 1863; *Argus,* 7 February 1863.
16. *Sydney Morning Herald,* 23 February 1861; *Australasian,* 15 February 1879.
17. W. F. Mandle, 'Cricket and Australian Nationalism . . .', p. 240.
18. W. G. Grace, *"W. G." Cricketing Reminiscences and Personal Recollections,* James Howden, London, 1899, pp. 68–9; *Argus,* 15

December 1873; *Australasian,* 20 December 1873, pp. 10, 17, 24, 31, 1874.
19. W. G. Grace, *op cit.,* p. 84.
20. K. S. Inglis, *op cit.,* p. 168.
21. Benny Green (ed), *Wisden Anthology 1864-1900,* Queen Anne Press, London, 1979, pp. 819–23.
22. P. Derriman, *op cit.,* p. 64.
23. J. W. C. Cumes, *op cit.,* p. 142.
24. B. Green, *op cit.,* p. 823.
25. Jack Pollard, *Bumpers, Brickbats and Boseys,* Murray, Sydney, n.d., pp. 97, 124–32.
26. K. S. Inglis, *op cit.,* pp. 159–60.

Chapter Two

1. *Australasian,* 28 December 1867, noted: 'We [the Victorians] arrived at the [Melbourne] wharf, bringing news of our own defeat' after the first intercolonial match at Sydney.
2. Prince Ranjitsinhji, *With Stoddart's Team in Australia,* James Bowden, London, 1898, p. 66.
3. K. Sandiford, *op cit.,* pp. 8–9, 14.
4. Chris Cunneen, 'Elevating and Recording the People's Pastimes: Sydney Sporting Journalism 1886–1939', in Richard Cashman and Michael McKernan (eds), *Sport: Money, Morality and the Media,* New South Wales University Press, Sydney, 1981, pp. 162–76.
5. Albert E. Knight, *The Complete Cricketer,* Methuen, London, 1906, p. 276; Maxwell L. Howell, 'Will the Real Victor Trumper Please Stand Up?', unpub. paper.
6. Barry Andrews, *'Tugging Four Bits off the Deck at the WACA': Australian Sport and Australian English,* in Cashman and McKernan, *Sport,* p. 142.
7. P. Derriman, *op cit.,* p. 95.
8. George Giffen, *With Bat and Ball,* Ward, Loch & Co., London, 1898, p. 25.
9. David Frith, *'My dear victorious Stod:' a biography of A. E. Stoddart,* privately published by the author, New Malden, 1970, p. 107.
10. John Berry Hobbs, *My Cricket Memories,* Heinemann, London, 1924, pp. 76–7.
11. J. B. Hobbs, *op cit.,* pp. 79–80.
12. A. E. Knight, *op cit.,* pp. 275–6; A. A. Lilley, *Twenty-Four Years of Cricket,* Mills & Boon, London, 1912, p. 89.
13. H. V. Hordern, *Googlies: Coals from a Test Cricketer's Fireplace,* Angus & Robertson, Sydney, 1932, p. 162.
14. P. F. Warner, *How we recovered the Ashes,* Chapman & Hall, London, 1904, pp. 125–6; P. Derriman, *op cit.,* p. 96.
15. D. K. Darling, *Test tussles on and off the Field,* privately published by the author, Hobart, 1970, pp. 35–6; Frank Laver, *The Australian Cricketer on Tour,* George Bell, London, 1905, p. 169.
16. Wray Vamplew, 'Sports Crowd Disorder in Britain, 1870–1914: Causes and Controls', *Journal of Sport History,* vol. 7, no. 1, Spring 1980, pp. 5–20; 'Ungentlemanly Conduct: The Control of Soccer Crowd Behaviour in England, 1888–1914', in T. C. Smout (ed), *The Search for Wealth and Stability,* Macmillan, London, 1979, pp. 139–54; K. Sandiford, *op cit.,* pp. 18–19.
17. E. H. D. Sewell, 'Has Public Interest in First Class Cricket

Declined?', *Badminton Magazine,* 37, 1913, p. 193, quoted in W. Vamplew, 'Sports Crowd Disorder', p. 15.
18. K. Sandiford, *op cit.,* p. 16; T. Mason, *Association Football and English Society 1863-1915,* Harvester, Sussex, 1980, pp. 138-74.

Chapter Three

1. K. Dunstan, 'The Changing Face of the 'Gabba', *Queensland Centenary Programme,* pp. 29-30.
2. *Australian Cricket,* January 1970, pp. 42-4.
3. Harold Larwood with Kevin Perkins, *The Larwood Story,* W. H. Allen, London, 1965, pp. 63-6.
4. H. Larwood, *op cit.,* p. 66.
5. R. W. E. Wilmot, *Defending the Ashes 1932-1933,* Robertson & Mullens, Melbourne, 1933, p. 87.
6. C. G. Macartney, *My Cricketing Days,* Heinemann, London, 1930, pp. 236-8.
7. J. H. Fingleton, *Cricket Crisis,* Cassell, London, 1946, pp. 87-8.
8. Keith Miller, *Cricket Crossfire,* Oldbourne, London, 1956, p. 80.
9. For material on Yabba see: Ray Robinson, *From the Boundary,* Collins, London, 1950, pp. 122-4; *Australian Dictionary of Biography,* vol. 8, p. 629; J. Pollard, *op cit.,* pp. 92-3; *Sydney Morning Herald,* 26 February 1955, 12 and 14 May 1956, 25 June 1961.
10. *Sydney Morning Herald,* 16 December 1982.
11. Ken Inglis, 'Sport and the Australian Broadcasting Commission, 1932-1945', unpub. paper, p. 2.
12. *Sydney Morning Herald,* 4 January 1933, quoted in Martin Sharp, 'Professionalism and Commercialism in Australian Cricket during the 1930s: the origins of the Cricket Revolution', unpub. B.A. hons thesis, University of New South Wales, 1981, pp. 8-9.
13. Jack Pollard, Australian Cricket: The Game and the Players, Hodder & Stoughton, Sydney, 1982, p. 156; *Sydney Morning Herald,* 9 May 1933.
14. R. W. E. Wilmot, *op cit.,* pp. 84-91.
15. Quoted in *Australian Cricket,* 30 December 1933, pp. 246-7.
16. K. Inglis, 'Sport and the ABC', pp. 10-12.
17. Ken Piesse (ed), *The Great Australian Book of Cricket Stories,* Currey O'Neil, Melbourne, 1982, pp. 266, 269.

Chapter Four

1. QCA Minutes, 1950s.
2. There was a change in the mood of crowds from era to era. Crowds in the 1900s, and again in the 1970s and 1980s, expressed a vigorous nationalism at cricket, which was not nearly so evident in the 1950s and 1960s. Australian players were then placed in an invidious no-win situation because it assumed that they should win against the emerging cricket nations and anything less than a decisive victory could attract criticism and abuse.
3. Quoted in *Cathedral End,* vol. 3, no. 4, Winter 1983.
4. Officials in New South Wales, Victoria and South Australia had been more reluctant to accept change and it was not introduced into the Shield until 1968-69 (SCG and MCG) and 1969-70 (Adelaide Oval). Sydney had Sunday Test play in 1969 but it did not come to Adelaide until 1972 and Melbourne in 1973. The experiment was

even abandoned for a period in Sydney: the majority of Shield matches at the SCG from 1971–76 were scheduled for three weekdays and a Saturday. Since that time, Sunday has become a regular playing day at all grounds.

5. *Cricketer,* December 1976, pp. 22–3.
6. Professor Colin Tatz argued in the *Sydney Morning Herald* of 7 January 1983 that the slow-motion replay had become the bane of modern cricket because it had taken much of the excitement and uncertainty out of the game by offering viewers the opportunity to revel, not in the 'actual and real' but in the 'second-hand'.
7. David Frith is engaged on a study of how cricketers cope with life after a brief career as a sporting star. The transition from a media personality to an ordinary citizen is not an easy one. Frith has found, not surprisingly, that top cricketers have a comparatively high rate of alcoholism, divorce and suicide.
8. *Sydney Morning Herald,* 16 February 1963; 17, 18, 21 and 28 January 1967; K. Dunstan, *op cit.,* p. 207.

Chapter Five

1. Colin Tatz quoted in *Sydney Morning Herald,* 7 January 1983.
2. Lou Rowan, *Umpire's Story,* Jack Pollard, Adelaide, 1972.
3. *Sydney Morning Herald,* 4 September 1982.
4. P. Derriman, *op cit.,* p. 103.
5. Doug Walters, *The Doug Walters Story as told to Ken Laws,* Rigby, Adelaide, 1981, p. 84.
6. The six scoreboard attendants sometimes got their own back on the Hill crowd. During the 1970s, on some occasions, the attendants would leave some sections of the board open, during a Hill attack, so as to stockpile ammunition. Then they would batten down the board and wait for some time before letting fly on an unsuspecting enemy.
7. *Sadiq Mohammad Souvenir,* 1981–2.
8. *Sydney Morning Herald,* 4 September 1982.
9. There are in fact many more stands in Australia dedicated to officials and politicians as against players: the only Test cricketers so honoured are George Giffen at Adelaide and Bradman and Noble at Sydney. There are some consolation prizes such as the Victor Richardson Gates at Adelaide, the Don Tallon and Wally Grout bars at Brisbane and the Bill O'Reilly Bar at Sydney.

Chapter Six

1. Henry Blofeld, *The Packer Affair,* Collins, London, 1978, p. 172.
2. *World of Cricket,* January 1979, p. 21.
3. Tony Luff, 'The Role of Sport in the Catholic Education System', unpub. paper.
4. Lois Bryson, 'Sport *is* Sexism', unpub. paper.
5. *Daily Telegraph* and *Sunday Telegraph,* 9–14 May 1982; Geoff Pollard and G. Ramakrishna, 'Report on a Survey of Attitude to Sport Interest in Sport', unpub. paper, Macquarie University, 1976.
6. P. Derriman, *op cit.,* p. 112.
7. It was ironic that Channel 9, which had fought so long and at such cost for the exclusive rights to television cricket had been willing to shed some parts of its monopoly so quickly. The change dated from the 1981 tour of England when Channel 9 dropped out of the

England–Australia Test series and left the television field to the ABC. It was even more surprising that Channel 7 was able to secure the rights for the 1983 Prudential Cup. Presumably domestic one-day cricket is more attractive to Channel 9 because it represents a cheap means of providing Australian-content programmes.